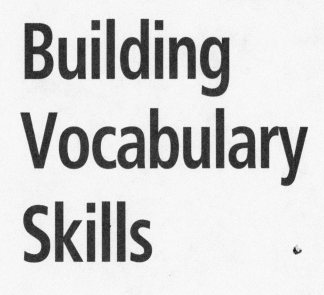

Building Vocabulary Skills

Fourth Edition

Building Vocabulary Skills

Fourth Edition

Sherrie L. Nist
Professor Emerita, University of Georgia

TP

Townsend Press Reading Series
Groundwork for College Reading with Phonics
Groundwork for College Reading
Ten Steps to Building College Reading Skills
Ten Steps to Improving College Reading Skills
Ten Steps to Advancing College Reading Skills
Ten Steps to Advanced Reading

Townsend Press Vocabulary Series
Vocabulary Basics
Groundwork for a Better Vocabulary
Building Vocabulary Skills
Building Vocabulary Skills, Short Version
Improving Vocabulary Skills
Improving Vocabulary Skills, Short Version
Advancing Vocabulary Skills
Advancing Vocabulary Skills, Short Version
Advanced Word Power

Supplements Available for Most Books
Instructor's Edition
Instructor's Manual and Test Bank
Online Exercises
PowerPoint Presentations
Blackboard Cartridges

ISBN-13 (Student Edition): 978-1-59194-188-0
ISBN-10 (Student Edition): 1-59194-188-1
ISBN-13 (Instructor's Edition): 978-1-59194-192-7
ISBN-10 (Instructor's Edition): 1-59194-192-X

Send book orders and requests for desk copies or supplements to:
Townsend Press Book Center
439 Kelley Drive
West Berlin, New Jersey 08091

For even faster service, contact us in any of the following ways:
By telephone: 1-800-772-6410
By fax: 1-800-225-8894
By e-mail: cs@townsendpress.com
Through our website: www.townsendpress.com

Contents

NOTE: Twenty-six of the chapters present ten words apiece. The other four chapters each cover ten word parts and are so marked. For ease of reference, the title of the selection that closes each chapter is included.

Unit Four

Unit Five

Appendixes

Preface: To the Instructor

The problem is all too familiar: *students just don't know enough words.* Reading, writing, and content teachers agree that many students' vocabularies are inadequate for course demands. Weak vocabularies limit students' understanding of what they read and the clarity and depth of what they write.

The purpose of *Building Vocabulary Skills* and the other books in the Townsend Press vocabulary series is to provide a solid, workable answer to the vocabulary problem. In the course of 30 chapters, *Building Vocabulary Skills* teaches 260 important words and 40 common word parts. Here are the book's distinctive features:

1 **An intensive words-in-context approach.** Studies show that students learn words best by reading them repeatedly in different contexts, not through rote memorization. The book gives students an intensive in-context experience by presenting each word in **six** different contexts. Each chapter takes students through a productive sequence of steps:

- Students infer the meaning of each word by considering two sentences in which it appears and then choosing from multiple-choice options.
- On the basis of their inferences, students identify each word's meaning in a matching test. They are then in a solid position to deepen their knowledge of a word.
- Finally, they strengthen their understanding of a word by using it three times: in two sentence-length practices and in a passage practice.

Each encounter with a word brings it closer to becoming part of the student's permanent word bank.

2 **Abundant practice.** Along with extensive practice in each chapter, there are a crossword puzzle and a set of unit tests at the end of every six-chapter unit. The puzzle and tests reinforce students' knowledge of the words in each chapter. In addition, most chapters reuse several words from earlier chapters (such repeated words are marked with small circles), allowing for more reinforcement. Last, there are supplementary tests in the *Instructor's Manual and Test Bank* and the online exercises that accompany the book. All this practice means that students learn in the surest possible way: by working closely and repeatedly with each word.

3 **Controlled feedback.** The opening activity in each chapter gives students three multiple-choice options to help them decide on the meaning of a given word. The multiple-choice options also help students complete the matching test that is the second activity of each chapter. A limited answer key at the back of the book then provides answers for the third activity in the chapter. All these features enable students to take an active role in their own learning.

4 **Focus on essential words.** A good deal of time and research went into selecting the words and word parts in each book in the TP vocabulary series. Word frequency lists were consulted, along with lists in a wide range of vocabulary books. In addition, the authors and editors each prepared their own lists. A computer was used to help in the consolidation of the many word lists. A long process of group discussion then led to final decisions about the words and word parts that would be most helpful for students on each reading level.

5 **Appealing content.** Dull practice materials work against learning. On the other hand, meaningful, lively, and at times even funny sentences and passages can spark students' attention and thus enhance their grasp of the material. For this reason, a great deal of effort was put into creating sentences and passages with both widespread appeal and solid context support. We have tried throughout to make the practice materials truly enjoyable for teachers and students alike. Look, for example, at the selection on page 11 that closes the first chapter of this book.

6 Clear format. The book has been designed so that its very format contributes to the learning process. Each chapter consists of two two-page spreads. In the first two-page spread (the first such spread is on pages 8–9), students can easily refer to all ten words in context while working on the matching test, which provides a clear meaning for each word. In the second two-page spread, students can refer to a box that shows all ten words while they work through the fill-in activities on these pages.

7 Supplementary materials.

a A convenient *Instructor's Edition* is available at no charge to instructors using the book. It is identical to the student book except that it contains answers to all of the activities and tests.

b A combined *Instructor's Manual and Test Bank* is also offered at no charge to instructors who have adopted the book. This supplement contains a general vocabulary placement test as well as a pretest and a posttest for the book and for each of the five units in the text. It also includes teaching guidelines, suggested syllabi, an answer key, and an additional mastery test for each chapter as well as an additional mastery test for each unit.

c *PowerPoint presentations and Blackboard cartridges* are available for the book and may be downloaded from the "Supplements" area for instructors at www.townsendpress.com.

d *Online exercises,* available at the Online Learning Center area of www.townsendpress.com, also accompany the book. These exercises consist of two additional tests for each vocabulary chapter in the book. In addition, they include—at the instructor's option—some of the practice material in the book itself. The program includes a number of user- and instructor-friendly features: brief explanations of answers, a sound option, frequent mention of the user's first name, a running score at the bottom of the screen, a record-keeping file, and actual pronunciation of each word.

　　Probably in no other area of reading instruction is the computer more useful than in reinforcing vocabulary. These online exercises take full advantage of the computer's unique capabilities and motivational appeal. Here's how the program works:

● Students are tested on the ten words in a chapter, with each word in a sentence context different from any in the book itself.

● After students answer each question, they receive immediate feedback: The program states that the answer is right or wrong and why, frequently using the student's first name and providing a running score.

● When they complete each test, students receive their scores. If they repeat the test, they then receive a new score, labeled "R" on the scores report, with a number following the "R" indicating how many times they have taken the same test. What is so valuable about this, of course, is that the program gives students immediate additional practice with the words they need to review.

● In addition, the online exercise program offers a second, more challenging "Word Definitions" test in which students must identify the meanings of the chapter words without the benefit of context. This test is a final check that students have really learned the words. And, again, there is the option of a retest, with its own score.

● Finally, if the instructor so chooses, the online program will provide the student with two of the exercises in the book—Sentence Check 2 and the Final Check. Students can take these exercises online and receive immediate feedback and the option of a retest.

　　Once students complete these exercises, their knowledge of each word in the chapter will have been carefully reinforced. And this reinforcement will be the more effective for having occurred in an electronic medium that especially engages today's students.

To obtain a copy of either the *Instructor's Edition* or the *Instructor's Manual and Test Bank*, instructors may contact Customer Service at 1-800-772-6420 or at cs@townsendpress.com.

8 **Realistic pricing.** As with the previous editions, the goal has been to offer the highest possible quality at the lowest possible price. While *Building Vocabulary Skills* is comprehensive enough to serve as a primary text, its modest price also makes it an inexpensive supplement.

9 **One in a sequence of books.** The most fundamental book in the Townsend Press vocabulary series is *Vocabulary Basics*. It is followed by *Groundwork for a Better Vocabulary* (a slightly more advanced basic text) and then by the three main books in the series: *Building Vocabulary Skills* (also a basic text), *Improving Vocabulary Skills* (an intermediate text), and *Advancing Vocabulary Skills* (a more advanced text). The most advanced book in the Townsend Press vocabulary series is *Advanced Word Power*. There are also short versions of the *Building, Improving,* and *Advancing* books. Suggested grade levels for the books are included in the *Instructor's Manual.* Together, the books can help create a vocabulary foundation that will make any student a better reader, writer, and thinker.

Notes on the Fourth Edition

A number of changes have been made in the fourth edition of *Building Vocabulary Skills:*

- **A full-color design.** Color has been carefully used throughout, not as window dressing but to add clarity and readability to the different parts of each chapter and the different sections of the book.

- **Thirty new graphics.** To engage today's visual learners, a full-color illustration has been added to the Final Check passage in each chapter.

- **Additional multicultural names and repeated words.** To broaden both the appeal and the effectiveness of the practice materials, ethnic names have been used more frequently, and even more vocabulary words have been repeated in the Final Checks.

- **Revised and updated practice items.** As always, a number of practice items throughout the book have been revised or updated to ensure that each item works as clearly and effectively with students as possible.

Acknowledgments

I am grateful for the enthusiastic comments provided by users of the Townsend Press vocabulary books over the life of the first three editions. I appreciate as well the work done on earlier editions by Eliza Comodromos, Beth Johnson, John Langan, and, in particular, Carole Mohr. I would also like to thank Kathryn Bernstein, Denton Cairnes, and Rick Moore for design, editing, and proofreading assistance with the fourth edition. And I owe special thanks to two TP editors who brought their exceptional talents to this revision. Barbara Solot is responsible for a four-color text design that is as clear as it is inviting. The result of her artistry is a strikingly attractive book that both students and teachers will enjoy. Janet Goldstein, in addition to providing significant design and content input, has lent her extraordinary editing and proofreading skills to this project. Under her guidance, the vocabulary series has been in the best possible hands.

Sherrie L. Nist

Introduction

Why Vocabulary Development Counts

You have probably often heard it said, "Building vocabulary is important." Maybe you've politely nodded in agreement and then forgotten the matter. But it would be fair for you to ask, "*Why* is vocabulary development important? Provide some evidence." Here are four compelling kinds of evidence.

1 Common sense tells you what many research studies have shown as well: vocabulary is a basic part of reading comprehension. Simply put, if you don't know enough words, you are going to have trouble understanding what you read. An occasional word may not stop you, but if there are too many words you don't know, comprehension will suffer. The content of textbooks is often challenge enough; you don't want to work as well on understanding the words that express that content.

2 Vocabulary is a major part of almost every standardized test, including reading achievement tests, college entrance exams, and armed forces and vocational placement tests. Test developers know that vocabulary is a key measure of both one's learning and one's ability to learn. It is for this reason that they include a separate vocabulary section as well as a reading comprehension section. The more words you know, then, the better you are likely to do on such important tests.

3 Studies have indicated that students with strong vocabularies are more successful in school. And one widely known study found that a good vocabulary, more than any other factor, was common to people enjoying successful careers in life. Words are in fact the tools not just of better reading, but of better writing, speaking, listening, and thinking as well. The more words you have at your command, the more effective your communication can be, and the more influence you can have on the people around you.

4 In today's world, a good vocabulary counts more than ever. Far fewer people work on farms or in factories. Far more are in jobs that provide services or process information. More than ever, words are the tools of our trade: words we use in reading, writing, listening, and speaking. Furthermore, experts say that workers of tomorrow will be called on to change jobs and learn new skills at an ever-increasing pace. The keys to survival and success will be the abilities to communicate skillfully and learn quickly. A solid vocabulary is essential for both of these skills.

Clearly, the evidence is overwhelming that building vocabulary is crucial. The question then becomes, "What is the best way of going about it?"

Words in Context: The Key to Vocabulary Development

Memorizing lists of words is a traditional method of vocabulary development. However, you are likely to forget such memorized lists quickly. Studies show that to master a word (or a word part), you must see and use it in various contexts. By working actively and repeatedly with a word, you greatly increase the chance of really learning it.

The following activity will make clear how this book is organized and how it uses a words-in-context approach. Answer the questions or fill in the missing words in the spaces provided.

Inside Front Cover and Contents

Turn to the inside front cover.

- The inside front cover provides a _____ that will help you pronounce all the vocabulary words in the book.

Now turn to the table of contents on pages v–vi.

- How many chapters are in the book? _____

- Most chapters present vocabulary words. How many chapters present word parts? _____

- Four sections follow the last chapter. The first of these sections provides a limited answer key, the second gives helpful information on using _____, the third contains _____, and the fourth is an index of the 260 words and 40 word parts in the book.

Vocabulary Chapters

Turn to Chapter 1 on pages 8–11. This chapter, like all the others, consists of five parts:

- The *first part* of the chapter, on pages 8–9, is titled _____.

The left-hand column lists the ten words. Under each **boldfaced** word is its _____ (in parentheses). For example, the pronunciation of *acknowledge* is _____. For a guide to pronunciation, see the inside front cover as well as "Dictionary Use" on page 181.

Below the pronunciation guide for each word is its part of speech. The part of speech shown for *acknowledge* is _____. The vocabulary words in this book are mostly nouns, adjectives, and verbs. **Nouns** are words used to name something—a person, place, thing, or idea. Familiar nouns include *boyfriend, city, hat,* and *truth.* **Adjectives** are words that describe nouns, as in the following word pairs: *former* boyfriend, *large* city, *red* hat, *whole* truth. All of the **verbs** in this book express an action of some sort. They tell what someone or something is doing. Common verbs include *sing, separate, support,* and *imagine.*

To the right of each word are two sentences that will help you understand its meaning. In each sentence, the **context**—the words surrounding the boldfaced word—provides clues you can use to figure out the definition. There are four common types of context clues: examples, synonyms, antonyms, and the general sense of the sentence. Each is briefly described below.

1 Examples

A sentence may include examples that reveal what an unfamiliar word means. For instance, take a look at the following sentence from Chapter 1 for the word *drastic*:

The company's new president took **drastic** steps, closing two factories and laying off three hundred employees.

The sentence provides two examples of steps that are drastic: the closing of two factories and the laying off of three hundred employees. To figure out what *drastic* means in this sentence, think about these examples. What kinds of steps are being described? Look at the choices below, and in the answer space provided, write the letter of the one you think is correct.

____ *Drastic* means   A. unimportant.   B. extreme.   C. easy.

The steps being described in the sentence are rather severe, or extreme. So if you wrote *B*, you chose the correct answer.

2 Synonyms

Synonyms are words that mean the same or almost the same as another word. For example, the words *joyful, happy*, and *delighted* are synonyms—they all mean about the same thing. Synonyms serve as context clues by providing the meaning of an unknown word that is nearby. The sentence below from Chapter 1 provides a synonym clue for *appropriate*.

Although it is **appropriate** for a man to take his hat off in church, in a synagogue it is proper for a man to cover his head.

Instead of using *appropriate* twice, the author used a synonym in the second part of the sentence. Find that synonym, and then choose the letter of the correct answer from the choices below.

____ *Appropriate* means   A. illegal.   B. fun.   C. proper.

In the sentence from Chapter 1, *proper* is used as a synonym for *appropriate*. Both words refer to something that is considered correct. Therefore, the correct answer is *C*.

3 Antonyms

Antonyms are words with opposite meanings. For example, *help* and *harm* are antonyms, as are *work* and *rest*. Antonyms serve as context clues by providing the opposite meaning of an unknown word. For instance, the sentence below from Chapter 1 provides an antonym clue for the word *comply*.

If someone with an iron pipe demands your wallet, it is safer to **comply** than to resist.

To make a point, the author used an antonym of *comply*. Find the antonym, and then choose the letter below of the meaning of *comply*.

____ *Comply* means   A. to argue.   B. to do as asked.   C. to hear.

The sentence includes two reactions to being asked for your wallet: to comply and to resist. Since *comply* is probably the opposite of *resist*, we can conclude that *comply* means "to do as asked."

4 General Sense of the Sentence

Even when there is no example, synonym, or antonym clue in a sentence, most of the time you can still figure out the meaning of an unfamiliar word. For example, look at the sentence from Chapter 1 for the word *acknowledge*.

Even after most of the votes had been counted, Senator Rice refused to **acknowledge** that he had lost.

After studying the context carefully, you should be able to choose the meaning of *acknowledge* from the three options presented. Write the letter of your choice.

____ *Acknowledge* means   A. to deny.   B. to admit.   C. to remember.

From the general sense of the sentence above, we can guess that the senator refused "to admit" that he had lost. Thus answer *B* is correct.

By looking closely at the pair of sentences provided for each word, as well as the answer choices, you should be able to decide on the meaning of a word. As you figure out each meaning, you are working actively with the word. You are creating the groundwork you need to understand and to remember the word. *Getting involved with the word and developing a feel for it, based upon its use in context, is the key to word mastery.*

It is with good reason, then, that the directions at the top of page 8 tell you to use the context to figure out each word's _____. Doing so deepens your sense of the word and prepares you for the next activity.

● The *second part* of the chapter, on page 9, is titled _____.

According to research, it is not enough to see a word in context. At a certain point, it is helpful as well to see the meaning of a word. The matching test provides that meaning, but it also makes you look for and think about that meaning. In other words, it continues the active learning that is your surest route to learning and remembering a word.

Note the caution that follows the test. Do not proceed any further until you are sure that you know the correct meaning of each word as used in context.

Keep in mind that a word may have more than one meaning. In fact, some words have quite a few meanings. (If you doubt it, try looking up in a dictionary, for example, the word *make* or *draw*.) In this book, you will focus on one common meaning for each vocabulary word. However, many of the words have additional meanings. For example, in Chapter 1, you will learn that *avert* means "to prevent," as in the sentence "Stop signs avert accidents." If you then look up *avert* in the dictionary, you will discover that it has another meaning—"to turn away," as in "The suspect averted her head to avoid being recognized." After you learn one common meaning of a word, you will find yourself gradually learning its other meanings in the course of your school and personal reading.

● The *third part* of the chapter, on page 10, is titled _____

Here are ten sentences that give you an opportunity to apply your understanding of the ten words. After inserting the words, check your answers in the limited answer key at the back of the book. Be sure to use the answer key as a learning tool only. Doing so will help you to master the words and to prepare for the last two activities and the unit tests, for which answers are not provided.

● The *fourth and fifth parts* of the chapter, on pages 10–11, are titled _____ and _____.

Each practice tests you on all ten words, giving you two more chances to deepen your mastery. In the fifth part, you have the context of an entire passage in which you can practice applying the words.

At the bottom of the last page of this chapter is a box where you can enter your score for the final two checks. These scores should also be entered into the vocabulary performance chart located on the inside back cover of the book. To get your score, count the number of items that you answered correctly in each section. Then add a zero. For example, if you got seven answers right in Sentence Check 2, you would write "70" on the first line in the score box.

Word Parts Chapters

Word parts are the building blocks of many English words. Learning word parts can help you spell and pronounce words, unlock the meanings of unfamiliar words, and remember new words.

This book covers forty word parts—prefixes, suffixes, and roots. **Prefixes** are word parts that are put at the beginning of words. When written separately, a prefix is followed by a hyphen to show that something follows it. For example, the prefix *pre* is written like this: *pre-*. One common meaning of *pre-* is "before," as in the words *prefix* and *preview*.

Suffixes are word parts that are added to the end of words. To show that something always comes before a suffix, a hyphen is placed at the beginning. For instance, the suffix *ful* is written like this: *-ful*. A common meaning of *-ful* is "full of," as in the words *beautiful* and *forceful*.

Finally, **roots** are word parts that carry the basic meaning of a word. Roots cannot be used alone. To make a complete word, a root must be combined with at least one other word part. Roots are written without hyphens. One common root is *vis*, which means "see," as in the words *visible* and *vision*.

Each of the four chapters on word parts follows the same sequence as the chapters on vocabulary. Keep the following guidelines in mind as well. To find the meaning of a word part, you should do two things.

1 First decide on the meaning of each **boldfaced** word in "Ten Word Parts in Context." If you don't know a meaning, use context clues to find it. For example, consider the two sentences and the answer options for the word part *ex-* in Chapter 6. Write the letter of your choice.

> "Inhale as you lower your head," called out the exercise instructor, "and **exhale** as you do the sit-up."
>
> My uncle isn't a very good businessman. He once tried to **export** rice to China and perfume to France.
>
> ___ The word part *ex-* means   A. before.   B. out.   C. not.

You can conclude that *exhale* means the opposite of *inhale* ("to breathe in"); therefore, *exhale* means "to breathe out." You can also determine that *export* means "to send goods out of a country to sell them."

2 Then decide on the meaning that the two boldfaced words have in common. This will also be the meaning of the word part they share. In the case of the two sentences above, both words include the idea of something going out. Thus *ex-* must mean _____.

You now know, in a nutshell, how to proceed with the words in each chapter. Make sure that you do each page very carefully. *Remember that as you work through the activities, you are learning the words.*

How many times in all will you use each word? If you look, you'll see that each chapter gives you the opportunity to work with each word six times. Each "impression" adds to the likelihood that the word will become part of your active vocabulary. You will have further opportunities to use the word in the crossword puzzle and tests that end each unit and in the online exercises available at www.townsendpress.com.

In addition, many of the words are repeated in context in later chapters of the book. Such repeated words are marked with a small circle (°). For example, which words from Chapter 1 are repeated in the Final Check on page 15 of Chapter 2?

_____   _____

Analogies

This book also offers practice in word analogies, yet another way to deepen your understanding of words. An **analogy** is a similarity between two things that are otherwise different. Doing an analogy question is a two-step process. First you have to figure out the relationship in a pair of words. Those words are written like this:

LEAF : TREE

What is the relationship between the two words above? The answer can be stated like this: A leaf is a part of a tree.

Next, you must look for a similar relationship in a second pair of words. Here is how a complete analogy question looks:

LEAF : TREE ::

  A. pond : river   C. page : book
  B. foot : shoe   D. beach : sky

And here is how the question can be read:

___ LEAF is to TREE as

   A. *pond* is to *river.*   C. *page* is to *book.*
   B. *foot* is to *shoe.*   D. *beach* is to *sky.*

To answer the question, you have to decide which of the four choices has a relationship similar to the first one. Check your answer by seeing if it fits in the same wording as you used to show the relationship between *leaf* and *tree:* A ___ is part of a ___. Which answer do you choose?

The correct answer is *C.* Just as a leaf is part of a tree, a page is part of a book. On the other hand, a pond is not part of a river, nor is a foot part of a shoe, nor is a beach part of the sky.

We can state the complete analogy this way: *Leaf* is to *tree* as *page* is to *book.*

Here's another analogy question to try. Begin by figuring out the relationship between the first two words.

___ COWARD : HERO ::

   A. soldier : military   C. actor : famous
   B. infant : baby   D. boss : worker

Coward and *hero* are opposite types of people. So you need to look at the other four pairs to see which has a similar relationship. When you think you have found the answer, check to see that the two words you chose can be compared in the same way as *coward* and *hero:* ___ and ___ are opposite types of people.

In this case, the correct answer is *D*; *boss* and *worker* are opposite kinds of people. (In other words, *coward* is to *hero* as *boss* is to *worker.*)

By now you can see that there are basically two steps to doing analogy items:

1 Find out the relationship of the first two words.

2 Find the answer that expresses the same type of relationship as the first two words have.

Now try one more analogy question on your own. Write the letter of the answer you choose in the space provided.

___ SWING : BAT ::

   A. drive : car   C. catch : bat
   B. run : broom   D. fly : butterfly

If you chose answer *A,* you were right. *Swing* is what we do with a *bat,* and *drive* is what we do with a *car.*

Here are some other relationships often found in analogies:

- **Synonyms:** freedom : liberty (*freedom* and *liberty* mean the same thing)
- **Item to category:** baseball : sport (baseball is one kind of sport)
- **Item to description:** school bus : yellow (*yellow* is a word that describes a school bus)
- **Producer to product:** singer: song (a singer is the person who produces a song)
- **Time sequence:** January : March (January occurs two months before March)

A Final Thought

The facts are in. A strong vocabulary is a source of power. Words can make you a better reader, writer, speaker, thinker, and learner. They can dramatically increase your chances of success in school and in your job.

But words will not come automatically. They must be learned in a program of regular study. If you commit yourself to learning words, and you work actively and honestly with the chapters in this book, you will not only enrich your vocabulary—you will enrich your life as well.

Unit One

Chapter 1

acknowledge	candid
alternative	compel
anecdote	comply
appropriate	concise
avert	drastic

Chapter 2

dialog	illuminate
erratic	isolate
extensive	refuge
forfeit	reminisce
fortify	urban

Chapter 3

delete	menace
impartial	morale
integrity	naive
legitimate	overt
lenient	undermine

Chapter 4

agenda	prospects
antidote	radical
apathy	reinforce
bland	relevant
propaganda	ruthless

Chapter 5

endorse	illusion
erode	impact
gruesome	imply
hypocrite	novice
idealistic	obstacle

Chapter 6

auto-	re-
ex-	super-
-ful	un-
multi-	uni-
pre-	vis, vid

acknowledge	candid
alternative	compel
anecdote	comply
appropriate	concise
avert	drastic

Ten Words in Context

In the space provided, write the letter of the meaning closest to that of each **boldfaced** word. Use the context of the sentences to help you figure out each word's meaning.

1 acknowledge
(ăk-nŏl′ĭj)
-verb

- Stubborn people often find it difficult to **acknowledge** their errors. They hate to admit they were wrong.
- Even after most of the votes had been counted, Senator Rice refused to **acknowledge** that he had lost.

___ *Acknowledge* means   A. to deny.   B. to admit.   C. to remember.

2 alternative
(ôl-tûr′nə-tĭv)
-noun

- The teacher stated the **alternatives** to Tim—either retake the test or get a D for the course.
- When her dog began to suffer from cancer, Wanda felt she had no **alternative**. He would have to be put to sleep.

___ *Alternative* means   A. a choice.   B. a command.   C. an assignment.

3 anecdote
(ăn′ĭk-dōt′)
-noun

- Dad told the children an **anecdote** about getting his tie caught in a file cabinet at work just as the boss walked in.
- I once heard an **anecdote** about a stagehand's revenge on a bossy actor. The stagehand put wheels on a table used in the play, so when the actor leaped onto the table during the most dramatic scene, he rolled off the stage.

___ *Anecdote* means   A. an error.   B. a short, interesting story.   C. an article.

4 appropriate
(ə-prō′prē-ĭt)
-adjective

- Chuck has little sense of what is socially **appropriate**. For example, he wore jeans and running shoes to his sister's wedding.
- Although it is **appropriate** for a man to take his hat off in church, in a synagogue it is proper for a man to cover his head.

___ *Appropriate* means   A. illegal.   B. fun.   C. proper.

5 avert
(ə-vûrt′)
-verb

- Renata **averted** an unpleasant meeting with her ex-boyfriend by leaving the store before he saw her.
- To **avert** an accident, Larry turned the steering wheel sharply to the right—and ran into a stop sign.

___ *Avert* means   A. to begin.   B. to prevent.   C. to report.

6 candid
(kăn′dĭd)
-adjective

- I'll give you my **candid** opinion, but you may not like what you hear.
- My heart always sinks when Robbie invites me to his house for dinner. He's a wonderful person, but to be **candid**, he's a terrible cook.

___ *Candid* means   A. honest.   B. friendly.   C. careful.

7 compel
(kəm-pĕl′)
-verb

   ● My history teacher would often **compel** us to do useless work, such as memorizing the date each state entered the union.

   ● If the law did not **compel** people to pay taxes, no one would pay them.

__ *Compel* means   A. to help.   B. to forbid.   C. to force.

8 comply
(kəm-plī′)
-verb

   ● If someone with an iron pipe demands your wallet, it is safer to **comply** than to resist.

   ● "My wife is so used to being the boss at work," Martin said, "that she is annoyed when I don't **comply** with her every request at home."

__ *Comply* means   A. to argue.   B. to do as asked.   C. to hear.

9 concise
(kŏn-sīs′)
-adjective

   ● Because of limited space, most newspaper articles must be **concise**.

   ● Unlike many politicians, our mayor is **concise**—his speeches are short and to the point.

__ *Concise* means   A. wordy.   B. correct.   C. clear and brief.

10 drastic
(drăs′tĭk)
-adjective

   ● The company's new president took **drastic** steps, closing two factories and laying off three hundred employees.

   ● The most common punishment in schools is detention. If that does not work, then schools resort to something more **drastic**.

__ *Drastic* means   A. unimportant.   B. extreme.   C. easy.

Matching Words with Definitions

Following are definitions of the ten words. Clearly write or print each word next to its definition. The sentences above and on the previous page will help you decide on the meaning of each word.

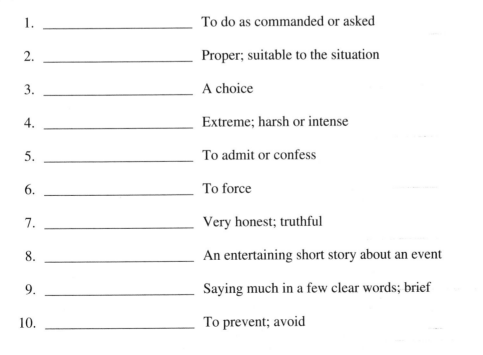

1. _____ To do as commanded or asked

2. _____ Proper; suitable to the situation

3. _____ A choice

4. _____ Extreme; harsh or intense

5. _____ To admit or confess

6. _____ To force

7. _____ Very honest; truthful

8. _____ An entertaining short story about an event

9. _____ Saying much in a few clear words; brief

10. _____ To prevent; avoid

CAUTION: Do not go any further until you are sure the above answers are correct. Then you can use the definitions to help you in the following practices. Your goal is eventually to know the words well enough so that you don't need to check the definitions at all.

Sentence Check 1

Using the answer line provided, complete each item below with the correct word from the box. Use each word once.

A. **acknowledge**	B. **alternative**	C. **anecdote**	D. **appropriate**	E. **avert**
F. **candid**	G. **compel**	H. **comply**	I. **concise**	J. **drastic**

_____ 1. Because Frank seems so ___, everyone believes him even when he tells a lie.

_____ 2. The drummer told interesting ___s about famous rock singers he had played with.

_____ 3. People often take ___ steps in anger and later regret their extreme actions.

_____ 4. When he saw no way to ___ the plane crash, the pilot parachuted to safety.

_____ 5. In a traditional wedding, the person performing the ceremony is often wordy, while the bride and groom are very ___, saying just "I do."

_____ 6. Any player who does not ___ with the rules will be dropped from the team.

_____ 7. A couple of older boys tried to ___ some first-graders to hand over their lunch money.

_____ 8. To earn money for college, Lonnie felt he had to either join the army or get a job. He didn't like either ___.

_____ 9. When the real murderer confessed, the police had to ___ that the wrong man had been jailed.

_____ 10. In most American schools, it is not ___ for students to call their teachers by their first names.

NOTE: Now check your answers to these items by turning to page 177. Going over the answers carefully will help you prepare for the next two practices, for which answers are not given.

Sentence Check 2

Using the answer lines provided, complete each item below with **two** words from the box. Use each word once.

_____
_____ 1–2. "I ___ that you have a perfect right to do whatever you like with your hair," said the teenage girl's mother. "But, to be ___, I don't find green curls attractive."

_____
_____ 3–4. In colonial America, it was thought ___ for a wife to ___ with all her husband's commands.

_____
_____ 5–6. "The poor economic situation leaves me no ___," said the company president. "It ___s me to lay off some of our workers."

_____   7–8. Our business instructor told an ___ about a company that ___(e)d failure by
_____   giving each worker a small share of the profits.

_____   9–10. The sale sign was huge but ___. It said only, "___ Price Cuts."
_____

Final Check: _Taking Exams_

Here is a final opportunity for you to strengthen your knowledge of the ten words. First read the following selection carefully. Then fill in each blank with a word from the box at the top of the previous page. (Context clues will help you figure out which word goes in which blank.) Use each word once.

There are four test-taking methods to consider when faced with exams. The first is to impress your teachers with very clever answers. For example, you might respond to any question beginning with the word "Why" with a simple, (1)_____ reply: "Why not?" This is not recommended, however, unless you know that your instructor has a remarkable sense of humor. A second method is to avoid answering the questions at all. You might try writing something like, "Should teachers (2)_____ students to take tests? Doesn't this go against our great American tradition of freedom? Besides, anyone who wants answers to these questions can find the information on the Internet." This method should not be used unless you are in (3)_____ need, as it involves a great deal of risk.

It is (4)_____ only if you have shown yourself to be very brilliant throughout the course and you are the teacher's pet. Otherwise, you can expect your teacher to fail you. A third way of dealing with a test is to be (5)_____ and admit helplessness. According to one (6)_____, a student openly (7)_____(e)d ignorance by writing, "Only God knows the answer to this question." Unfortunately, the instructor's response was, "God gets an A. You get an F." The fact is, none of these three methods works very well. If you truly want to (8)_____ failure, you have no (9)_____—you must (10)_____ with school rules. The fourth method is the only sure-fire one for dealing with exams: _study hard and learn the material._

| Scores | Sentence Check 2 _____% | Final Check _____% |

dialog	illuminate
erratic	isolate
extensive	refuge
forfeit	reminisce
fortify	urban

Ten Words in Context

In the space provided, write the letter of the meaning closest to that of each **boldfaced** word. Use the context of the sentences to help you figure out each word's meaning.

1 dialog
(dī′ə-lŏg′)
-noun

● The movie was shown with English subtitles because all its **dialog** was in French.
● At the PTA meeting last night, a **dialog** between parents and the faculty helped to clear up some differences between them.

___ *Dialog* means   A. a title.   B. talk.   C. an action.

2 erratic
(ĭ-răt′ĭk)
-adjective

● Children's eating habits are **erratic**. One day they'll barely eat, and the next day they'll eat enough for three.
● The driver ahead of me was **erratic**—he kept changing his speed and his lane.

___ *Erratic* means   A. noisy.   B. healthy.   C. irregular.

3 extensive
(ĕk-stĕn′sĭv)
-adjective

● Selena did **extensive** research for her paper—it took her several weeks.
● To save the wounded police officer, doctors performed **extensive** surgery that lasted for hours.

___ *Extensive* means   A. done quickly.   B. risky.   C. large in amount.

4 forfeit
(fôr′fĭt)
-verb

● The basketball players were upset when the team bus broke down and they had to **forfeit** an important game.
● If Phil gets into one more accident, he will **forfeit** the right to drive his parents' car.

___ *Forfeit* means   A. to give up.   B. to win.   C. to ignore.

5 fortify
(fôr′tə-fī′)
-verb

● The night before running a marathon, Elsa **fortifies** herself by eating a large plate of pasta.
● The builders plan to **fortify** the old tower with steel beams.

___ *Fortify* means   A. to relax.   B. to strengthen.   C. to prove.

6 illuminate
(ĭ-lōō′mə-nāt′)
-verb

● Before electricity, streets were **illuminated** by gaslight.
● On Halloween, we use a flashlight to **illuminate** our way when we go trick-or-treating after dinner.

___ *Illuminate* means   A. to lose.   B. to clean.   C. to light.

7 isolate
(ī′sə-lāt′)
-verb

● I thought I would enjoy **isolating** myself at the vacation cabin, but I soon felt lonely.

● Freddy was such a troublemaker that the teacher put his desk in a far corner to **isolate** him from the other students.

___ *Isolate* means   A. to protect.   B. to separate.   C. to recognize.

8 refuge
(rĕf′yo͞oj)
-noun

● A motorcycle offers no **refuge** in bad weather. If you have to ride in the rain, you'll get soaked.

● My boyfriend and I first met when we took **refuge** in the same doorway during a sudden rain.

___ *Refuge* means   A. a shelter.   B. transportation.   C. a reason.

9 reminisce
(rĕm′ə-nĭs′)
-verb

● On their wedding anniversary, Lenny and Jean like to **reminisce** about their first date.

● My father showed me his trophy and **reminisced** about his years as a star basketball player.

___ *Reminisce* means   A. to remember.   B. to forget.   C. to ask.

10 urban
(ûr′bən)
-adjective

● Skyscrapers make for tightly packed **urban** populations. For example, some 16,000 people work in the Sears Tower in Chicago.

● Gladys likes **urban** living because she grew up in the city, but Emilio, who grew up on a farm, prefers country life.

___ *Urban* means   A. country.   B. city.   C. national.

Matching Words with Definitions

Following are definitions of the ten words. Clearly write or print each word next to its definition. The sentences above and on the previous page will help you decide on the meaning of each word.

1. _____ To light up

2. _____ To lose through some fault; to be forced to give up by way of penalty

3. _____ Shelter; protection

4. _____ Of or in a city

5. _____ A conversation; the conversation between characters in a story, novel, or play

6. _____ To separate from others

7. _____ Large in space or amount

8. _____ To strengthen

9. _____ To remember and talk about the past

10. _____ Not consistent

CAUTION: Do not go any further until you are sure the above answers are correct. Then you can use the definitions to help you in the following practices. Your goal is eventually to know the words well enough so that you don't need to check the definitions at all.

Sentence Check 1

Using the answer line provided, complete each item below with the correct word from the box. Use each word once.

A. **dialog**	B. **erratic**	C. **extensive**	D. **forfeit**	E. **fortify**
F. **illuminate**	G. **isolate**	H. **refuge**	I. **reminisce**	J. **urban**

_____ 1. The skater's ___ performances showed that she was too inconsistent to hire for the ice show.

_____ 2. In London during World War II, bomb shelters provided ___ from air attacks.

_____ 3. Vitamins and minerals ___ the body against disease.

_____ 4. Politicians who are caught taking bribes ___ their good names.

_____ 5. Criminals are put in prison to ___ them from the rest of society.

_____ 6. The night before graduation, my friends and I ___(e)d about our four years together.

_____ 7. The pioneers used candles to ___ book pages at night.

_____ 8. The author's ___ was always sharp and bare: "You love me?" "Uh-huh." "Good."

_____ 9. Before his parents visit him, Denzel gives his apartment a(n) ___ cleaning; he dusts or scrubs every surface.

_____ 10. There's a big difference between a(n) ___ sky and a country sky. In the country, there are no bright lights to block the starlight.

NOTE: Now check your answers to these items by turning to page 177. Going over the answers carefully will help you prepare for the next two practices, for which answers are not given.

Sentence Check 2

Using the answer lines provided, complete each item below with **two** words from the box. Use each word once.

_____
_____ 1–2. The loud celebrating on the Fourth of July is so ___ in my neighborhood that the only place I find ___ from the noise is my basement.

_____
_____ 3–4. Curt ___(e)d for hours, revealing that his life had been very ___. At some points in his life, he was very busy, married, and well off. At other times, he lived alone and was out of work.

_____
_____ 5–6. Because criminals work in darkness, one way to reduce ___ crime would be to ___ streets and playgrounds with brighter lights.

_____   7–8. To keep the opposing army from trying to ___ his weaker force from the rest
_____   of the unit, the general decided to ___ his defenses.

_____   9–10. In a ___ with the boss, several employees learned that they would ___ their
_____   bonuses if they kept coming to work late.

Final Check: _Nate the Woodsman_

Here is a final opportunity for you to strengthen your knowledge of the ten words. First read the following selection carefully. Then fill in each blank with a word from the box at the top of the previous page. (Context clues will help you figure out which word goes in which blank.) Use each word once.

Nate had spent most of his seventy years in the woods. As a young man, he had the alternative° of working in the city with his brother. But he decided that (1)_____ life was not for him. He preferred to (2)_____ himself from others and find (3)_____ in nature, far from the crowds and noise of the city. He was more than willing to (4)_____ such advantages as flush toilets and computers for the joy of watching a sunrise (5)_____ the frozen pines.

Because Nate had lived alone for so long, his behavior was (6)_____. For example, one minute he'd be very quiet, and the next he'd (7)_____ at length about his youth. His knowledge of nature was (8)_____, and so I learned much from him through the years.

I will tell you an anecdote° that shows how wise he was about the woods. One evening Nate, my cousin Arthur, and I were crossing a meadow. Arthur's interest in some little white mushrooms that were growing there led to this (9)_____:

"These mushrooms look so good," said Arthur. "Did you ever use them, Nate?"

"Yep," said Nate. "My ma used to cook 'em up."

"Great!" said Arthur. Nate's words seemed to (10)_____ Arthur's desire for those mushrooms. He gathered about a hundred of them. "How'd she fix them?" he asked Nate.

"Cooked 'em up in sugar water."

"Really? And then you ate them that way?"

"Ate 'em?" Nate was horrified. "You crazy? We used to put 'em in a bowl on the table to kill flies!"

| Scores | Sentence Check 2 _____% | Final Check _____% |

Enter your scores above and in the **Vocabulary Performance Chart** on the inside back cover of the book.

delete	menace
impartial	morale
integrity	naive
legitimate	overt
lenient	undermine

Ten Words in Context

In the space provided, write the letter of the meaning closest to that of each **boldfaced** word. Use the context of the sentences to help you figure out each word's meaning.

1 delete
(dĭ-lēt′)
-*verb*

- When I accidentally **deleted** several paragraphs of my research paper from the computer, it took ten minutes to retype them.
- The invitation list is too long. Unless we **delete** a few names, the party will be too crowded.

C Delete means   A. to type.   B. to add.   C. to get rid of.

2 impartial
(ĭm-pär′shəl)
-*adjective*

- Too much publicity before a trial makes it difficult for lawyers to find **impartial** jurors, people with no opinion about the case.
- "I'm an **impartial** judge of character," Dolores joked. "I distrust all people equally, without prejudice."

B Impartial means   A. not whole.   B. fair.   C. friendly.

3 integrity
(ĭn-tĕg′rə-tē)
-*noun*

- Our boss trusts Ramon with the key to the cash register because she knows that he has **integrity**.
- I thought our senator had **integrity**, so I was shocked to hear that she had taken a bribe.

A Integrity means   A. honesty.   B. talent.   C. a good memory.

4 legitimate
(lĕ-jĭt′ə-mĭt)
-*adjective*

- "A need to see the final episode in your favorite soap opera," said the teacher, "is not a **legitimate** excuse for missing class."
- Any company that guarantees to make all investors millionaires can't possibly be **legitimate**.

B Legitimate means   A. safe.   B. legal.   C. healthy.

5 lenient
(lē′nē-ənt)
-*adjective*

- Ms. Hall is very **lenient** about late papers. If you hand one in even a week late, she doesn't lower your grade.
- Mom wouldn't let us feed our poodle during dinner. But Dad, who was more **lenient**, would look the other way when we slipped the dog something under the table.

B Lenient means   A. heartless.   B. easygoing.   C. honest.

6 menace
(mĕn′ĭs)
-*noun*

- Acid rain is the biggest **menace** to the survival of freshwater fish.
- Ron's impatient attitude and his fast, zigzag driving make him a **menace** on the road.

C Menace means   A. a puzzle.   B. something noticeable.   C. a danger.

7 morale
(mə-răl′)
-noun

● Art class was good for Tyrone's **morale**. Each time the teacher praised his drawings, his confidence and enthusiasm increased.

● The workers' **morale** was so low that they constantly complained about the job. The only good part of the day was quitting time.

A *Morale means*   A. spirit.   B. pay.   C. sense of right and wrong.

8 naive
(nī-ēv′)
-adjective

● Though young, Rhoda is not **naive**. Being on her own for so long has made her streetwise.

● Having had little experience with salespeople, my younger sister is so **naive** that she believes everything they tell her.

A *Naive means*   A. lacking experience.   B. generous.   C. questioning.

9 overt
(ō-vûrt′)
-adjective

● Sometimes **overt** racism is easier to deal with than the hidden kind. You can better fight what is out in the open.

● Maya's love of reading was **overt**—books spilled over the shelves in every room of her apartment.

A *Overt means*   A. obvious.   B. fair.   C. harmful.

10 undermine
(ŭn′dər-mīn′)
-verb

● Leroy tried to **undermine** the coach's authority by making jokes about him behind his back.

● Numerous floods had **undermined** the foundation so greatly that the house was no longer safe.

C *Undermine means*   A. to reach.   B. to explore.   C. to weaken.

Matching Words with Definitions

Following are definitions of the ten words. Clearly write or print each word next to its definition. The sentences above and on the previous page will help you decide on the meaning of each word.

1. __impartial__   Fair; not biased; without prejudice

2. __menace__   A threat

3. __legitmate__   In accordance with accepted laws, rules, and standards

4. __morale__   State of mind with respect to confidence and enthusiasm; spirit

5. __delete__   To cross out or erase; remove

6. __undermine__   To gradually weaken or damage

7. __overt__   Obvious; not hidden

8. __lenient__   Not strict or harsh in disciplining or punishing; merciful

9. __naive__   Lacking worldly experience; unsuspecting; unsophisticated

10. __integrity__   Honesty; strong moral sense

CAUTION: Do not go any further until you are sure the above answers are correct. Then you can use the definitions to help you in the following practices. Your goal is eventually to know the words well enough so that you don't need to check the definitions at all.

Sentence Check 1

Using the answer line provided, complete each item below with the correct word from the box. Use each word once.

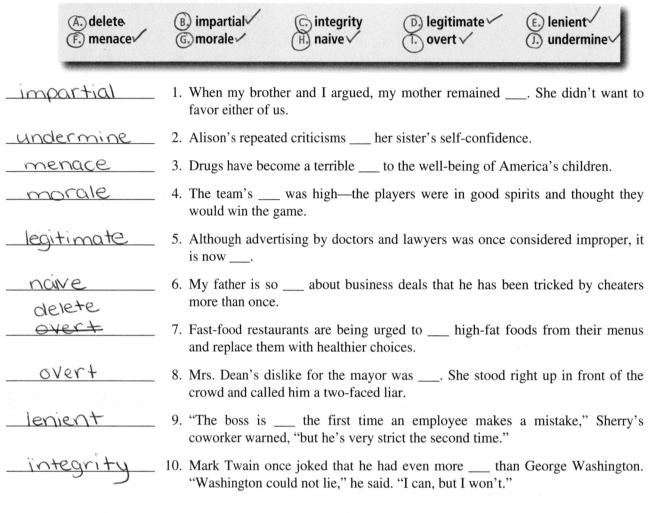

(A.) delete	(B.) impartial ✓	(C.) integrity	(D.) legitimate ✓	(E.) lenient ✓
(F.) menace ✓	(G.) morale ✓	(H.) naive ✓	(I.) overt ✓	(J.) undermine ✓

impartial   1. When my brother and I argued, my mother remained ___. She didn't want to favor either of us.

undermine   2. Alison's repeated criticisms ___ her sister's self-confidence.

menace   3. Drugs have become a terrible ___ to the well-being of America's children.

morale   4. The team's ___ was high—the players were in good spirits and thought they would win the game.

legitimate   5. Although advertising by doctors and lawyers was once considered improper, it is now ___.

naive   6. My father is so ___ about business deals that he has been tricked by cheaters more than once.

delete ~~*overt*~~   7. Fast-food restaurants are being urged to ___ high-fat foods from their menus and replace them with healthier choices.

overt   8. Mrs. Dean's dislike for the mayor was ___. She stood right up in front of the crowd and called him a two-faced liar.

lenient   9. "The boss is ___ the first time an employee makes a mistake," Sherry's coworker warned, "but he's very strict the second time."

integrity   10. Mark Twain once joked that he had even more ___ than George Washington. "Washington could not lie," he said. "I can, but I won't."

NOTE: Now check your answers to these items by turning to page 177. Going over the answers carefully will help you prepare for the next two practices, for which answers are not given.

Sentence Check 2

Using the answer lines provided, complete each item below with **two** words from the box. Use each word once.

overt
naive   1–2. Nick's interest in Janice's money is ___ enough for all her friends to notice. But Janice is so ___ that she has no idea about the real reason for Nick's attention.

morale
legitimate   3–4. The employees' ___ quickly fell when they learned that some of the company's earnings were put into a business that was not ___ and that was being investigated by the police.

integrity
delete   5–6. To give her essay ___, Isabel ___(e)d some statements that were not entirely true.

menace

undermine

impartial

lenient

7–8. Donald is a real ___ in the classroom. It's not uncommon for him to ___ classroom order by shooting spitballs at other students.

9–10. My parents should be ___, but they're much more ___ with my sisters than with me. My sisters often get off with a scolding. In contrast, I'm often compelled° to stay home for a night.

Final Check: *Who's on Trial?*

Here is a final opportunity for you to strengthen your knowledge of the ten words. First read the following selection carefully. Then fill in each blank with a word from the box at the top of the previous page. (Context clues will help you figure out which word goes in which blank.) Use each word once.

It would be nice to think every trial involved a(n) (1) _impartial_ judge and jury who wanted only to decide a case fairly. However, we would be (2) _naive_ to believe the world is always fair and just. Two famous trials in history show us that when accusers have no (3) _legitmate_ charges, they sometimes invent some.

The first trial was that of Socrates, a teacher in ancient Greece. Socrates did not give lectures or write books. Instead, he wandered around the marketplace in Athens, starting a discussion with anyone he met. Socrates was a man of great (4) _integrity_: he lived an honest life in search of truth. But by pointing out the faults of some upper-class Athenians, he made enemies. The Greek authorities feared he would (5) _undermine_ their ability to rule. Eventually Socrates was arrested and tried for being a(n) (6) _menace_ to the youth of Athens. He was found guilty and sentenced to death. His friends urged him to escape, but Socrates said he had to comply° with the court's decree. He carried out the sentence by drinking a cup of poison.

Jesus of Nazareth was another teacher who lived a life of great honesty. He, too, frightened the authorities of his time. More and more people flocked to hear the words of this carpenter who spoke of God as a loving father. Afraid he might encourage people to turn against them, the authorities invented charges against him. They said he hurt the (7) _morale_ of the country, making people unhappy and restless. The authorities' illegal treatment of Jesus was (8) _delete_: they allowed no lawyer or advisers to help him; they took him from his friends late at night, beat him, and dragged him into court the next morning. He was brought before the Roman governor Pontius Pilate. Pilate made some attempt to be (9) _lenient_ with Jesus, at one point making this concise° statement to the crowd, "I find no guilt in this man." However, Pilate lacked the courage to act on his belief. He had Jesus beaten yet again and sent him to be executed.

The evidence is clear and should not be (10) _overt_ (e)d from the history books: In some trials, society itself is the guilty party.

| Scores | Sentence Check 2 _____ % | Final Check _____ % |

38/40

Enter your scores above and in the **Vocabulary Performance Chart** on the inside back cover of the book.

agenda	prospects
antidote	radical
apathy	reinforce
bland	relevant
propaganda	ruthless

Ten Words in Context

In the space provided, write the letter of the meaning closest to that of each **boldfaced** word. Use the context of the sentences to help you figure out each word's meaning.

1 agenda
(ə-jĕn′də)
-noun

- There are two items on the **agenda** for today's office meeting: the company's new product and the holiday party.
- Ralph's daily **agenda** includes driving his granddaughter to school, working at the soup kitchen, and walking his dog after dinner.

A *Agenda* means A. a schedule. B. a desk. C. work.

2 antidote
(ăn′tĭ-dōt′)
-noun

- Because there was no **antidote** for the snake's poison, the cat that was bitten died.
- For me, a good **antidote** to feeling low is to bake a batch of brownies.

C *Antidote* means A. a short story. B. a cause. C. a cure.

3 apathy
(ăp′ə-thē)
-noun

- Determined to shock her students out of their **apathy**, the history teacher showed up for class one day dressed as Joan of Arc.
- Voter **apathy** was high, causing a low turnout on election day.

C *Apathy* means A. pity. B. understanding. C. lack of interest.

4 bland
(blănd)
-adjective

- The addition of a bright red scarf changed Linda's grey outfit from **bland** to striking.
- Mexicans, accustomed to hot and spicy foods, often find American dishes **bland** by comparison.

B *Bland* means A. old. B. dull. C. bitter.

5 propaganda
(prŏp′ə-găn′də)
-noun

- Until recently, the **propaganda** put out by cigarette companies said that nicotine didn't harm people's health.
- The political candidates ran TV ads made up largely of **propaganda** directed against their opponents.

B *Propaganda* means A. research. B. complaints. C. publicity.

6 prospects
(prŏs′pĕkts′)
-noun

- The movie's **prospects** for doing well at the box office were harmed by several bad reviews in the newspapers and on TV.
- What are my **prospects** of finding a hotel room in this town during Super Bowl weekend?

B *Prospects* means A. reasons. B. chances. C. fears.

7 radical
(răd′ĭ-kəl)
-adjective

- I won't vote for the **radical** candidate—his beliefs are too extreme for me.
- Most students tried to change school policy through peaceful compromise, but a **radical** group wanted to take over the president's office by force.

_A_ _Radical_ means   (A.) extreme.   B. average.   C. young.

8 reinforce
(rē′ĭn-fôrs′)
-verb

- Jonathan's wisecrack **reinforced** the teacher's opinion that he was interested only in fooling around.
- Some socks are **reinforced** at the heels and toes with extra layers of material so they won't develop holes.

_B_ _Reinforce_ means   A. to ruin.   (B.) to make stronger.   C. to repeat.

9 relevant
(rĕl′ə-vənt′)
-adjective

- History is always **relevant** to our lives because it shows us what results can follow certain actions.
- "The weather is not **relevant** to this conversation," Yvonne's mother said. "Don't change the subject when I bring up your speeding tickets."

_B_ _Relevant_ means   A. known.   (B.) related.   C. threatening.

10 ruthless
(rooth′lĭs)
-adjective

- My English teacher is a **ruthless** grader. He shows no mercy for weak reasoning or faulty grammar, so I've had to work extra hard on my papers.
- Barry is so **ruthless** that he would step on coworkers to advance himself.

_C_ _Ruthless_ means   A. sweet.   B. confusing.   (C.) without mercy.

Matching Words with Definitions

Following are definitions of the ten words. Clearly write or print each word next to its definition. The sentences above and on the previous page will help you decide on the meaning of each word.

1. _prospects_ Chances of success

2. _apathy_ Lack of interest and concern

3. _reinforce_ To strengthen; add support to

4. _agenda_ ✓ A list of things to be done; a schedule

5. _ruthless_ Lacking pity; merciless

6. _bland_ Dull; not interesting or exciting

7. _relevant_ Related to the matter at hand; to the point

8. _radical_ ✓ Favoring extreme changes, especially in politics and government

9. _antidote_ Something that reduces the effects of a poison; anything that relieves a harmful situation

10. _propaganda_ Ideas spread to support or oppose a cause; distorted information

CAUTION: Do not go any further until you are sure the above answers are correct. Then you can use the definitions to help you in the following practices. Your goal is eventually to know the words well enough so that you don't need to check the definitions at all.

Sentence Check 1

Using the answer line provided, complete each item below with the correct word from the box. Use each word once.

| A. agenda | B. antidote ✓ | C. apathy | D. bland ✓ | E. propaganda |
| F. prospects | G. radical | H. reinforce | I. relevant ✓ | J. ruthless ✓ |

j. ruthless 1. There are ___ drivers who make no effort to avoid hitting animals on the road.

d. bland 2. Carlos's personality is so ___ and unexciting that people tend not to notice him.

i. relevant 3. Your statement isn't ___; it has nothing to do with our conversation.

~~X~~. reinforce 4. Victoria will ___ the plant by tying its thin stem to a strong stick.

_~~X~~_ 5. My sister's ___ of passing Accounting II aren't good. She hasn't studied all term.

b. antidote 6. All medicine cabinets should contain a general ___ for accidental poisoning.

~~X~~. prospects 7. Every morning Lin writes out her ___, jotting down what she needs to accomplish that day.

~~C~~. apathy 8. Because my science teacher wants to do away with grading in his courses, many of the other teachers consider his views too ___.

_~~X~~_ 9. Sidewalk litter is a sign of ___, showing that people don't care about a clean environment.

~~X~~ E. propaganda 10. Advertisements are an important part of the ___ used by companies to persuade us to buy their products.

NOTE: Now check your answers to these items by turning to page 177. Going over the answers carefully will help you prepare for the next two practices, for which answers are not given.

Sentence Check 2

Using the answer lines provided, complete each item below with **two** words from the box. Use each word once.

antidote
apathy   1–2. Working at top speed, the doctors injected the poisoned woman with a powerful ___. Everyone in the emergency room seemed anxious and tense except the woman's husband. We couldn't understand his apparent ___.

agenda
ruthless   3–4. Gang members are a menace° to our neighborhoods. The only items on their ___ are theft and violence. Their ___ methods—threats and smashed windows—cause terror among local businesspeople.

bland
relevant   5–6. Mr. Turner's lectures would not seem so ___ to students if he didn't speak in such a dull tone of voice and if he included information that seemed ___ to their lives.

propaganda 7–8. The German Nazi Party used ___ in booklets, speeches, and films to spread
radical   its lies. Eventually this ___ group took over the German government, causing
                    many German citizens to leave the country and seek refuge° elsewhere.

prospects 9–10. If Henry starts exercising, his ___ for getting into shape will be very good.
reinforce   His desire to exercise was ___(e)d by the fact that he gained ten pounds last
                    year.

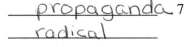

Final Check: *Students and Politics*

Here is a final opportunity for you to strengthen your knowledge of the ten words. First read the following selection carefully. Then fill in each blank with a word from the box at the top of the previous page. (Context clues will help you figure out which word goes in which blank.) Use each word once.

During the 1960s, the country's morale° was weakened by the Vietnam war and social problems. At that time, many young people were attracted to (1) _radical_ political groups. The groups all had similar long lists of things they wanted to accomplish. Their extensive° (2) _agenda_ included ending the war, feeding the hungry, and doing away with social prejudice. In universities, they demanded courses that were more (3) _bland_ ~~to the times: women's studies, African American literature, and world religions. These activists hoped such classes would serve as a(n) (4) _relevant_ to the "traditional" thinking of the 1950s they found so harmful. But in some cases, students also insisted that universities stop offering classical literature courses, saying such courses were nothing more than (5)_____ for an outdated way of life. Many small "underground" newspapers of the time helped to (6)_____ the idea that the past had nothing worthwhile to offer.

Today, some '60s activists are concerned by the (7)_____ that they believe they see among today's young people. These former activists fear today's students are, at best, so lacking in spirit as to be (8)_____ and harmless. At worst, they are so money-hungry and so (9)_____ that they genuinely don't care about people who are poverty-stricken. However, others believe the (10)_____ for social progress are bright. Many of today's students do volunteer work as a way of helping bring about social change.

40
-12
28

28/40

| Scores | Sentence Check 2 _____% | Final Check _____% |

Enter your scores above and in the **Vocabulary Performance Chart** on the inside back cover of the book.

endorse	illusion
erode	impact
gruesome	imply
hypocrite	novice
idealistic	obstacle

Ten Words in Context

In the space provided, write the letter of the meaning closest to that of each **boldfaced** word. Use the context of the sentences to help you figure out each word's meaning.

1 endorse
(ĕn-dôrs′)
-verb

- "If you **endorse** the new shopping mall," said the speaker, "you're supporting a large increase in neighborhood traffic."
- Some athletes earn more money **endorsing** such products as cereal and footwear than they do playing their sport.

_B_ _Endorse_ means   A. to buy.   B. to support.   C. to see.

2 erode
(ĭ-rōd′)
-verb

- As water **eroded** the topsoil, the tree roots beneath it became more and more visible.
- The team's confidence in its coach was **eroded** by his increasingly wild accusations against its opponents.

_A_ _Erode_ means   A. to wear away.   B. to build up.   C. to escape.

3 gruesome
(groo′səm)
-adjective

- The automobile accident was so **gruesome** that I had to look away from the horrible sight.
- The young campers sat around the fire and scared each other with **gruesome** horror stories.

_C_ _Gruesome_ means   A. unfair.   B. boring.   C. frightening.

4 hypocrite
(hĭp′ə-krĭt′)
-noun

- Dominic is such a **hypocrite**. He cheats his customers while complaining about how hard it is to be an honest, struggling salesman.
- I feel that the worst **hypocrites** are those who preach love and then attack anyone of a different culture or faith.

_A_ _Hypocrite_ means   A. an insincere person.   B. a religious person.   C. a loud person.

5 idealistic
(ī-dē′ə-lĭs′tĭk)
-adjective

- Very **idealistic** people are drawn to professions like teaching or the ministry, in which they feel they can help make the world a better place.
- My sister is too **idealistic** ever to marry for wealth or fame—she would marry only for love.

_B_ _Idealistic_ means   A. full of ideas.   B. emphasizing principles.   C. young.

6 illusion
(ĭ-loo′zhən)
-noun

- People lost in the desert sometimes experience the **illusion** that there is a lake right in front of them.
- The idea that the sun sets and rises is an **illusion**. It is really the Earth that is turning away from and then toward the sun.

_C_ _Illusion_ means   A. a fact.   B. a new idea.   C. a false impression.

7 impact
(ĭm′păkt′)
-noun

- When birds accidentally fly into windows, the **impact** of hitting the glass often kills them.
- That boxer punches with such power that the **impact** of his uppercut can knock out most opponents.

A *Impact* means   A. a force.   B. a possibility.   C. a sight.

8 imply
(ĭm-plī′)
-verb

- To Sherlock Holmes, the clues **implied** that the murderer was an elderly man who carried a cane.
- When my friend asked me, "Do you feel all right?" she **implied** that I did not look well.

C *Imply* means   A. to hide.   B. to overlook.   C. to suggest.

9 novice
(nŏv′ĭs)
-noun

- Because my father has never played tennis, he will join the class for **novices**.
- "Don't buy an expensive camera for a **novice**," said the saleswoman. "Let your son first get some experience with a cheaper camera."

B *Novice* means   A. a child.   B. a beginner.   C. a friend.

10 obstacle
(ŏb′stə-kəl)
-noun

- I'd better clean my apartment soon. There are too many **obstacles** on the floor between my bed and the refrigerator.
- The major **obstacle** to Hal's getting a promotion is his laziness.

C *Obstacle* means   A. something hidden.   B. something helpful.   C. something that prevents movement.

Matching Words with Definitions

Following are definitions of the ten words. Clearly write or print each word next to its definition. The sentences above and on the previous page will help you decide on the meaning of each word.

1. _imply_ — To express indirectly; suggest
2. _obstacle_ — Something that gets in the way; a barrier
3. _hypocrite_ — One who claims to be something he or she is not; an insincere person
4. _illusion_ — A false impression; a mistaken view of reality
5. _endorse_ — To support; express approval of; to state in an ad that one supports a product or service, usually for a fee
6. _gruesome_ — Horrible; shocking; frightful
7. _novice_ — A beginner; someone new to a field or activity
8. _impact_ — The force of one thing striking another
9. _erode_ — To gradually wear (something) away
10. _idealistic_ — Tending to emphasize ideals and principles over practical concerns

CAUTION: Do not go any further until you are sure the above answers are correct. Then you can use the definitions to help you in the following practices. Your goal is eventually to know the words well enough so that you don't need to check the definitions at all.

Sentence Check 1

Using the answer line provided, complete each item below with the correct word from the box. Use each word once.

A. endorse	**B.** erode ✓	**C.** gruesome ✓	**D.** hypocrite	**E.** idealistic
F. illusion	**G.** impact ✓	**H.** imply ✓	**I.** novice	**J.** obstacle

gruesome 1. The horror movie became too ___ for me to watch when the monster started eating people.

erode 2. Year after year, the waves continue to ___ the beach, wearing it away by constantly beating against it.

imply
endorse 3. Poems often ___ an idea. That is, they hint at the idea rather than state it directly.

novice 4. I was such a(n) ___ at computers that I didn't even know how to send an e-mail.

idealistic 5. Karen is the least ___ person I know. She is guided only by a desire to get ahead.

hypocrite 6. Don't be such a(n) ___! If you don't like Anitra, then you shouldn't pretend that you do.

endorse 7. An actress hired to ___ meat products on TV was fired when the producer learned she was a vegetarian.

impact 8. Ballet dancers sometimes break their toes when they land with too great a(n) ___ after a leap.

obstacles 9. We can never drive straight into our driveway because there are always ___s there—tricycles, garbage cans, or toys.

illusion 10. When the moon is low in the sky, it looks much larger than when it is overhead. This difference in size, however, is only a(n) ___.

NOTE: Now check your answers to these items by turning to page 177. Going over the answers carefully will help you prepare for the next two practices, for which answers are not given.

Sentence Check 2

Using the answer lines provided, complete each item below with **two** words from the box. Use each word once.

imply
_____ 1–2. "Just because I let them meet in the church basement," said Reverend Lucas, "does not ___ that I ___ everything the group stands for."

_____
impact 3–4. When the first soldier to fly in an airplane took off in 1908, he had no ___s about the danger—he knew flying was risky. However, he never expected to die from the ___ of crashing into a cemetery wall.

_____ 5–6. The first Peace Corps volunteers may have been ___, but they were tough

_____obstacle_____   about their dreams. No ___ would keep them from working for a better world.

_____ 7–8. Because she was just out of college, Faye was a(n) ___ at interviewing job
_____   applicants. Nevertheless, she could see that Perry was a(n) ___ who boasted
                                   about job skills he didn't have.

_____erode_____   9–10. Ten years in the soil had ___(e)d the body down to a mere skeleton. But
_____gruesome_____   when a gardener's shovel uncovered the ___ remains of the murder victim,
                                   she could still be identified by a gold locket around her neck.

Final Check: *Night Nurse*

Here is a final opportunity for you to strengthen your knowledge of the ten words. First read the following selection carefully. Then fill in each blank with a word from the box at the top of the previous page. (Context clues will help you figure out which word goes in which blank.) Use each word once.

I'm no (1)_____, so I'll acknowledge° I should never have taken the job of nurse on the midnight shift in a hospital emergency room. Not a single person in my family would (2)___endores___ my career decision, and maybe my family was right. I wasn't naive°; I had no (3)_____s about the difficulty of the work. I knew the emergency room would be tough, but I wasn't going to let that be a(n) (4)___obstacle___. Still, I did start out more (5)_____ about helping the world than I am now, ten months later. I don't mean to (6)_____ that I've given up on nursing, because I haven't. But when I first rushed a stretcher off an ambulance—as a(n) (7)_____ at the job—disappointment and regret had not yet started to (8)_____ my hopeful outlook.

I work at one of the biggest urban° hospitals in the state. More often than not, each shift brings a series of (9)___gruesome___ injuries, caused by everything from shootings to household accidents, but mostly by car crashes. One effect of my job has been to make me always wear a seat belt—I've seen first-hand the damage caused by the (10)___impact___ of a human head thrown against a windshield.

Emergency-room workers seem to follow one of two routes. Either they become accustomed to the difficult sights and stay in the field for years, or they quickly burn out and find refuge° in another line of work. I'm in the second category. Next week, I'm applying for a job in a doctor's office.

| Scores | Sentence Check 2 _____% | Final Check _____% |

Enter your scores above and in the **Vocabulary Performance Chart** on the inside back cover of the book.

6

auto-	re-
ex-	super-
-ful	un-
multi-	uni-
pre-	vis, vid

Ten Word Parts in Context

Common word parts—also known as *prefixes, suffixes,* and *roots*—are used in forming many words in English. Figure out the meanings of the following ten word parts by looking *closely* and *carefully* at the context in which they appear. Then, in the space provided, write the letter of the meaning closest to that of each word part.

1 auto-

- Years ago, in restaurants called **automats**, people served themselves by putting coins in slots and removing food from behind small glass doors.

- It is possible to hypnotize yourself through a process called **autohypnosis**.

_B_ The word part *auto-* means   A. see.   (B.) self.   C. above.

2 ex-

- "Inhale as you lower your head," called out the exercise instructor, "and **exhale** as you do the sit-up."

- My uncle isn't a very good businessman. He once tried to **export** rice to China and perfume to France.

_A_ The word part *ex-* means   (A.) before.   B. out.   C. not.

3 -ful

- Even though the movie and the meal were pretty bad, I had a **delightful** evening because the company was so good.

- Many children, **fearful** of the dark, feel comforted by a night-light.

_B_ The word part *-ful* means   A. not.   (B.) full of.   C. again.

4 multi-

- Luan is **multilingual**—she speaks English, French, and Chinese.

- Ours is a **multiracial** neighborhood. In fact, the area attracts people who want their children to grow up among many ethnic groups.

_A_ The word part *multi-* means   (A.) many.   B. one.   C. out.

5 pre-

- People who believe in fate think our lives are mainly **predetermined** and that we therefore can't do much to change things.

- I like to get to the theater in time to see the **previews** of coming movies.

_C_ The word part *pre-* means   A. again.   B. one.   (C.) before.

6 re-

- I don't recommend saving leftover coffee. **Reheated** coffee tastes like mud.

- Publishers sell books to bookstores, which then **resell** the books to customers.

_A_ The word part *re-* means   (A.) again.   B. above.   C. see.

7 super-
- Oprah Winfrey is such a **superstar** that "ordinary" stars are eager to appear on her show.
- The **superintendent** of schools is the highest-ranking official in a school system.

_C_ The word part *super-* means
A. out.   B. see.   (C.) above.

8 un-
- Our history teacher has an **unusual** approach to teaching. He often wears costumes to class and lectures as one of the historical people we're learning about.
- When I am involved in reading a good novel, I am totally **unaware** of the world around me.

_B_ The word part *un-* means
A. before.   (B.) not.   C. many.

9 uni-
- The company combined crayons, paints, and paper into a **unit** and sold it as a children's art kit.
- The dancers in the chorus line kicked their legs up and down in perfect **unison**, as if they were one body.

_A_ The word part *uni-* means
(A.) one.   B. not.   C. before.

10 vis, vid
- Our teacher prefers that our oral reports include **visual** aids such as PowerPoint presentations, which will appeal to students' eyes as well as ears.
- I always make a **videotape** of our annual family reunion. It's fun to see how everyone looked five, ten, or twenty years ago.

_C_ The word part *vis* or *vid* means
A. again.   B. before.   (C.) see.

Matching Word Parts with Definitions

Following are definitions of the ten word parts. Clearly write or print each word part next to its definition. The sentences above and on the previous page will help you decide on the meaning of each word part.

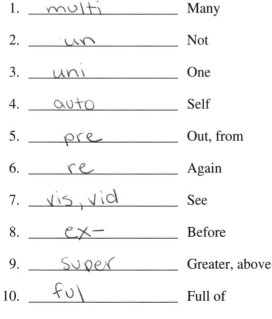

1. _multi_ Many

2. _un_ Not

3. _uni_ One

4. _auto_ Self

5. _pre_ Out, from

6. _re_ Again

7. _vis, vid_ See

8. _ex−_ Before

9. _super_ Greater, above

10. _ful_ Full of

CAUTION: Do not go any further until you are sure the above answers are correct. Then you can use the definitions to help you in the following practices. Your goal is eventually to know the word parts well enough so that you don't need to check the definitions at all.

Sentence Check 1

Using the answer line provided, complete each *italicized* word below with the correct word part from the box. Use each word part once.

A. auto- ✓	B. ex- ✓	C. -ful ✓	D. multi-	E. pre-
F. re- ✓	G. super- ✓	H. un- ✓	I. uni-	J. vis-

_____re_____ 1. After the hurricane, the city was (. . . *built*) ___ further inland, in a safer location.

_____vis_____ 2. Bees and butterflies can see certain colors that are not (. . . *ible*) ___ to the human eye.

_____super_____ 3. It is difficult for neighborhood food stores to compete with (. . . *markets*) ___, which offer more choices and lower prices.

_____pre_____ 4. Jurors must not (. . . *judge*) ___ a case. They must listen to all the evidence before coming to a conclusion.

_____ful_____ 5. I find it (*rest* . . .) ___ to vacation at home, where I can relax and catch up on reading and movies.

_____uni_____ 6. The legendary (. . . *corn*) ___, a horse-like animal with one horn, is often shown as having a lion's tail and a goat's beard.

_____ex_____ 7. My grandfather used to (. . . *tract*) ___ my loose baby teeth by tying each to a string and then yanking the string.

_____auto_____ 8. In her (. . . *biography*) ___, *Blackberry Winter*, the famous sociologist Margaret Mead writes about her childhood, her three marriages, and her career.

_____multi_____ 9. My bedroom is really a(n) (. . . *purpose*) ___ room. I read, watch TV, eat snacks, talk on the phone, do push-ups, daydream, and sleep there.

_____un_____ 10. Anyone who bumps into a stonefish is really (. . . *lucky*) ___, for it has thirteen poisonous spines sticking out of its body.

NOTE: Now check your answers to these items by turning to page 177. Going over the answers carefully will help you prepare for the next two practices, for which answers are not given.

Sentence Check 2

Using the answer line provided, complete each *italicized* word in the sentences below with the correct word part from the box. Use each word part once.

_____un_____
_____ful_____ 1–2. The magician (. . . *folded*) ___ a small red cloth and held it up so that we could see all of it. Then, in a flash, he had a (*hand* . . .) ___ of flowers.

_____ex_____
_____auto_____ 3–4. Students caught drinking anywhere on the school grounds are (. . . *pelled*) ___ from school (. . . *matically*) ___.

_____vis_____ 5–6. Unless we learn to be more accepting of each other, I cannot (_en . . . ion_) ___
_____ful_____   a time when this family will be peaceful and (_. . . fied_) ___.

_____super_____ 7–8. Todd painted the company president's office last week, but his (_. . . visor_)
_____re_____   ___ said he would have to (_. . . paint_) ___ it in a different color. The
      president thought the gray Todd used was too bland°.

_____multi_____ 9–10. A psychic (_. . . dicted_) ___ an improvement in my financial situation. She
_____re_____   was right: my debts have (_. . . plied_) ___.

Final Check: _Theo's Perfect Car_

Here is a final opportunity for you to strengthen your knowledge of the ten word parts. First read the following selection carefully. Then complete each _italicized_ word in the parentheses below with a word part from the box at the top of the previous page. (Context clues will help you figure out which word part goes in which blank.) Use each word part once.

My young son Theo wants to be a(n) (_. . . mobile_) (1)_____auto_____ designer some day. Until then, he feels he can best (_. . . pare_) (2)_____pre_____ for that profession by working on his own design of a (_. . . ior_) (3)_____vis_____ car.

So far, this great car of his runs on air. Theo says that means future gas stations will need only air pumps, for both the tank and the tires. In addition, his car has the ability to become (_in . . . ible_) (4)_____vis_____. (Theo feels it would be (_help . . ._) (5)_____ful_____ for a car to disappear whenever the driver is chased by bad guys.) The car will also have trays for candy instead of ashes and an (_. . . tended_) (6)_____in_____ trunk, to hold lots of luggage, toys, and plastic bags for people who get carsick. The front of the car will have an electric eye to warn the driver when obstacles° are on the road and a third headlight to help illuminate° very dark roads and tunnels. The tires will be (_. . . colored_) (7)_____un_____, with circles of red, yellow, purple, and blue.

I tell Theo that his car is imaginative and (_. . . que_) (8)_____uni_____; surely there is none other like it in the world. But then I (_. . . mind_) (9)_____re_____ him that if he doesn't do his math homework, it's (_. . . likely_) (10)_____un_____ that any automobile company will hire him as a designer.

| Scores | Sentence Check 2 _____% | Final Check _____% |

The box at the right lists twenty-five words from Unit One. Using the clues at the bottom of the page, fill in these words to complete the puzzle that follows.

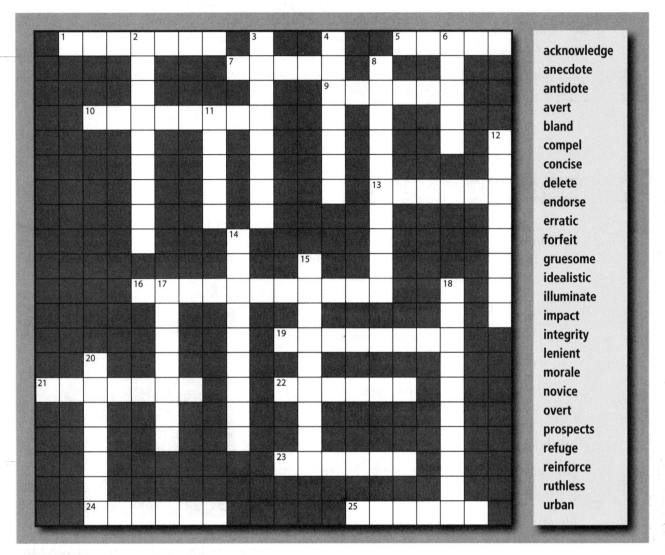

acknowledge
anecdote
antidote
avert
bland
compel
concise
delete
endorse
erratic
forfeit
gruesome
idealistic
illuminate
impact
integrity
lenient
morale
novice
overt
prospects
refuge
reinforce
ruthless
urban

ACROSS

1. Not strict or harsh in punishing; merciful
5. Dull; not interesting or exciting
7. Of or in a city
9. To cross out or erase; remove
10. An entertaining short story about an event
13. The force of one thing striking another
16. To admit or confess
19. Something that reduces the effects of a poison or relieves a harmful situation
21. To lose through some fault; to be forced to give up by way of penalty
22. State of mind with respect to confidence and enthusiasm; spirit
23. Shelter; protection
24. To force
25. A beginner; someone new to a field or activity

DOWN

2. Honesty; strong moral sense
3. Horrible; shocking; frightful
4. To support; express approval of; to state in an ad that one supports a product or service, usually for a fee
6. To prevent; to avoid
8. To light up
11. Obvious; not hidden
12. Lacking pity; merciless
14. Chances of success
15. To strengthen; add support to
17. Saying much in a few clear words; brief
18. Tending to emphasize ideals and principles over practical concerns
20. Not consistent

PART A

Choose the word that best completes each item and write it in the space provided.

anecdote 1. There are hunters who dip their arrows in the poison from a tiny frog—a deadly poison for which there is no ___.

  A. anecdote   B. integrity   C. antidote   D. obstacle

undermine 2. Smoking and drinking ___ your health.

  A. fortify   B. undermine   C. reinforce   D. isolate

avert 3. To ___ disaster in river rafting, you must steer clear of rocks.

  A. avert   B. erode   C. compel   D. endorse

extensive 4. Damage to the old car was so ___ that repairs would have cost more than the car was worth.

  A. bland   B. extensive   C. impartial   D. concise

endorse 5. The nurses asked the local union to ___ their strike by signing a letter of support.

  A. comply   B. undermine   C. endorse   D. isolate

alternative 6. After I failed my first two algebra quizzes, I decided that the sensible ___ to flunking was to get some tutoring.

  A. alternative   B. agenda   C. impact   D. morale

gruesome 7. Although the movie is titled *Tears of Blood*, it isn't ___; it contains no violence or blood.

  A. erratic   B. candid   C. gruesome   D. relevant

novice 8. On the first day of school, the kindergarten students met their new teacher, a 21-year-old ___ who was probably more nervous than they were.

  A. hypocrite   B. novice   C. menace   D. refuge

urban 9. One advantage of ___ living is the city's wealth of live entertainment, including plays and concerts.

  A. erratic   B. idealistic   C. ruthless   D. urban

agenda 10. The ___ of our Humor Club meetings usually consists of two activities: swapping funny stories and then doing humorous imitations of actors or politicians.

  A. propaganda   B. dialog   C. agenda   D. apathy

(Continues on next page)

PART B

On the answer line, write the letter of the choice that best completes each item.

_A_   11. Although the pizza shop appeared to be **legitimate**, it in fact
      A. ran an illegal gambling business.   C. was losing money.
      B. was not well-known.   D. was busy and popular.

_C_   12. The **appropriate** response when someone says, "How are you?" is to
      A. remain silent.   C. say, "Fine, thank you. And you?"
      B. say, "How am I what?"   D. say, "It's none of your business."

_A_   13. The **ruthless** dictator
      A. often lied to his people.   C. had children executed.
      B. was loved by his people.   D. wasn't biased.

_B_   14. "The speaker will answer only **relevant** questions," the chairwoman said. "So before you ask, make sure your question is
      A. brief."   C. interesting."
      B. on the topic."   D. clear."

_B_   15. My mother **implied** that she didn't like my new haircut when she said,
      A. "You look terrific!"   C. "Whoever cut your hair is talented."
      B. "I hate your new haircut."   D. "Did a student cut your hair this time?"

_C_   16. If my brother were really **idealistic**, he would
      A. give me cash for my birthday.   C. find out which careers paid the most money.
      B. spend more time doing volunteer work.   D. get married.

_A_   17. Our **radical** principal typically did such things as
      A. donating thirty dollars to the Red Cross.   C. being quite boring.
      B. coming to school early.   D. firing a teacher for no reason.

_A_   18. Jenna's dislike of Barry is **overt**; she
      A. insults him openly whenever she sees him.
      B. pretends to like him.
      C. likes most things about him, but a few things bother her.
      D. can't understand why she dislikes him.

_D_   19. We are **compelled** to
      A. relax at the end of a day.
      B. apologize whenever we hurt someone's feelings.
      C. volunteer to help the homeless.
      D. stop the car we're driving at red lights and stop signs.

_A_   20. When I came poorly prepared for my piano lesson, my teacher's **candid** comment was
      A. "You're wasting your money on lessons if you don't practice."
      B. "You're making excellent progress."
      C. "You're ready to go on to a new piece."
      D. "In music, practice is not important."

Score   (Number correct) _____ x 5 = _____ %

PART A

Complete each item with a word from the box. Use each word once.

A. acknowledge	B. delete	C. dialog	D. drastic	E. fortify
F. hypocrite	G. integrity	H. isolate	I. morale	J. propaganda
K. prospects	L. refuge	M. reminisce		

fortify   e 1. The old wooden beams in the barn were so weak that we had to ___ them with metal rods.

prospects   K 2. I'd say Bruno's ___ of getting the job are excellent—his father owns the company.

drastic   d. 3. In the 1870s one man took ___ action when his wife refused to serve him breakfast: he divorced her.

acknowledge
~~exit~~   a 4. Americans ___ that they have a great fear of cancer. When surveyed, most report that they fear this disease more than any other.

refuge   L 5. There is no hunting in the state park, which serves as a(n) ___ for wildlife.

propaganda   j 6. A large part of war is ___: spreading information that makes the enemy look bad.

morale   i 7. ___ is so low in my father's office that he comes home depressed almost every night.

delete   b. 8. When a formerly top-secret document was shown on TV, all names and places were ___(e)d. As a result, nearly every sentence had gaps.

isolate   h 9. People who work alone in toll booths must often feel their job ___s them too much, especially late at night.

dialog   C 10. Westerns are shown throughout the world. Still, it's odd to think of cowboys speaking their ___ in German, French, or Japanese.

integrity   g 11. Tarik has ___. When he accidentally backed into a parked car and smashed one of its lights, he was honest enough to leave a note with his name and number.

hypocrite   F 12. That woman is a(n) ___. She gives speeches about the evils of cruelty to animals, but she eats meat and owns two fur coats.

reminisce   m 13. I listened to my grandparents ___ about all the crazy fads they've seen come and go, including T-shirts that gave off a smell of chocolate, garlic, or fish when scratched.

(Continues on next page)

PART B

Write **C** if the italicized word is used **correctly**. Write **I** if the word is used **incorrectly**.

C 14. The *impact* of the baseball was so great that my hand stung even though I was wearing a mitt.

I 15. In seventeenth-century Massachusetts, one *lenient* jury hanged a dog accused of being a witch.

C 16. Since he wanted to borrow the car that night, Harry decided to *comply* with his mother's request that he clean his room.

I 17. My little sister is *naive* about basketball. She knows the names and records of dozens of players.

I 18. When his team won the game, Doug was filled with such *apathy* that he jumped up and down shouting "Yeah!" until he sprained his ankle.

C 19. In fifteenth-century France and Spain, a doctor was required to leave a cash deposit before caring for a patient. If the patient lived, the doctor got his money back. If the patient died, the doctor *forfeited* the deposit.

PART C

On the answer line, write the letter of the word that is the **synonym** of the boldfaced word.

Example: _B_ **delete**   A. restore   B. erase   C. insult

B 20. **erode**   A. build up   B. wear away   C. cover up

C 21. **concise**   A. old   B. wordy   C. brief

A 22. **impartial**   A. fair   B. prejudiced   C. small

PART D

On the answer line, write the letter of the word that is the **antonym** of the boldfaced word.

Example: _A_ **delete**   A. restore   B. erase   C. insult

C 23. **obstacle**   A. mistake   B. barrier   C. assistance

C 24. **erratic**   A. irregular   B. wrong   C. steady

B 25. **reinforce**   A. push   B. weaken   C. strengthen

Score   (Number correct) _____   x 4 = _____%

Enter your scores above and in the **Vocabulary Performance Chart** on the inside back cover of the book.

Each item below starts with a pair of words in CAPITAL LETTERS. For each item, figure out the relationship between these two words. Then decide which of the choices (A, B, C, or D) expresses a similar relationship. Write the letter of your choice on the answer line.

C 1. ANECDOTE : TELL ::
    A. lecture : sing
    B. television : delay
    C. letter : write
    D. garden : read

C 2. CONCISE : WORDY ::
    A. apologize : explain
    B. exist : live
    C. offer : suggest
    D. arrive : leave

B 3. CANDID : HONESTY ::
    A. joyful : pain
    B. powerful : strength
    C. doubtful : certainty
    D. confused : smoke

A 4. DRASTIC : HARSH ::
    A. frightening : scary
    B. late : later
    C. difficult : simple
    D. different : interesting

D 5. DIALOG : CONVERSATION ::
    A. telephone : e-mail
    B. radio : book
    C. letter : envelope
    D. lecture : speech

D 6. ERRATIC : IRREGULAR ::
    A. unusual : often
    B. odd : typical
    C. expected : event
    D. unexpected : surprising

C 7. ILLUMINATE : LIGHTBULB ::
    A. water : oil
    B. paint : picture
    C. heat : furnace
    D. cool : mixer

C 8. REFUGE : BOMB SHELTER ::
    A. dwelling : apartment
    B. airport : traveler
    C. train : station
    D. mosque : religion

C 9. DELETE : INSERT ::
    A. erase : cross out
    B. pronounce : word
    C. outline : write
    D. subtract : add

B 10. MENACE : RECKLESS DRIVER ::
    A. danger : loaded gun
    B. medicine : common cold
    C. food : plastic bag
    D. rescue : shark attack

(Continues on next page)

B   11. MORALE : TEAM ::
    A. navy : army   C. goodwill : business
    (B.) group : family   D. arrow : goal

C   12. OVERT : HIDDEN ::
    A. valuable : worthless   (C.) immediate : quick
    B. over : above   D. educational : program

A   13. AGENDA : MEETING ::
    (A.) grades : test   C. recipe : cookbook
    B. shopping list : carrots   D. outline : essay

B   14. ANTIDOTE : POISON ::
    A. evil : hate   C. illness : cure
    (B.) medicine : infection   D. pills : liquid

A   15. BLAND : MILK ::
    (A.) spicy : pepper   C. bitter : ice cream
    B. sour : chocolate   D. salty : peach

D   16. PROPAGANDA : ADVERTISING ::
    A. humor : audience   C. statistics : newspaper
    B. countries : atlas   (D) reference book : dictionary

C   17. ERODE : WEAR AWAY ::
    A. create : imagine   (C.) assist : help
    B. push : pull   D. view : enjoy

D   18. GRUESOME : HORROR MOVIE ::
    A. colorful : garden   C. final : beginning
    B. heavy : newspaper   (D) quiet : airport

A   19. ILLUSION : MAGICIAN ::
    (A.) textbook : student   C. election : candidate
    B. dinner : chef   D. movie : audience

B   20. OBSTACLE : OVERCOME ::
    A. detour : ignore   C. movie : delay
    (B.) target : miss   D. puzzle : solve

Score   (Number correct) _____   x 5 = _____%

Enter your scores above and in the **Vocabulary Performance Chart** on the inside back cover of the book.

PART A

Listed in the left-hand column below are ten common word parts, followed by words in which the parts are used. In each blank, write in the letter of the correct definition on the right.

Word Parts		Examples	Definitions
_i_	1. **auto-**	automat, autohypnosis	A. Before
_f_	2. **ex-**	exhale, export	B. See
_g_	3. **-ful**	delightful, fearful	C. Full of
_C_	4. **multi-**	multilingual, multiracial	D. Many
_A_	5. **pre-**	predetermined, previews	E. One
_H_	6. **re-**	reheated, resell	F. Not
_D_	7. **super-**	superstar, superintendent	G. Greater, above
_j_	8. **un-**	unusual, unaware	H. Again
_e_	9. **uni-**	unit, unison	I. Self
_B_	10. **vis, vid**	visual, videotape	J. Out, from

PART B

Using the answer line provided, complete each *italicized* word in the sentences below with the correct word part from the box. Not every word part will be used.

A. auto-	B. ex-	C. -ful	D. multi-	E. pre-
F. re-	G. super-	H. un-	I. uni-	J. vis

_____re_____ 11. If the tail of a certain lizard is cut off, the tail will (. . . *grow*) ___ to full size.

_____vis_____ 12. According to surveys, Americans consider the worst physical handicap to be a loss of (. . . *ion*) ___ .

_____uni_____ 13. In some marriage ceremonies, the bride and groom "tie the knot" by having their sleeves tied together, as a symbol of their (. . . *on*) ___ .

_____multi_____ 14. Bacteria are constantly (. . . *plying*) ___—one splits into two, two split into four, and so on. In a single day, one bacteria cell can turn into 16 million cells.

_____ex_____ 15. My girlfriend says my problem is not that my income is too low but that my (. . . *penses*) ___ are too high.

(Continues on next page)

PART C

Use your knowledge of word parts to determine the meaning of the **boldfaced** words. On the answer line, write the letter of each meaning.

_B_   16. In our garden, weeds are **plentiful**.

    A. lacking   (B) numerous   C. spread out

_A_   17. Factories are increasingly **automated**.

    (A) self-running   B. high-speed   C. complicated

_A_   18. The teacher thinks Tiffany writes **superlative** essays.

    (A) wordy   B. poor   C. of the highest quality

_C_   19. When I opened the damaged carton, I was relieved to find the china **unbroken**.

    A. broken in half   B. broken to bits   (C) not broken

_A_   20. My decision to get a new job was **premature**.

    (A) made before the right time   B. made at exactly the right time   C. made after the right time

Score   (Number correct) _____ x 5 = _____%

Unit Two

Chapter 7

concede	disclose
conservative	scapegoat
contrary	superficial
denounce	sustain
deter	transition

Chapter 8

compensate	moderate
conceive	supplement
derive	surpass
diversity	tentative
inhibit	verify

Chapter 9

alter	optimist
ample	pretense
blunt	prolong
chronic	refrain
chronological	remorse

Chapter 10

acute	donor
anonymous	phobia
apprehensive	prominent
arrogant	prudent
bestow	recipient

Chapter 11

absurd	compile
adhere	contempt
affluent	defect
alienate	doctrine
assess	dogmatic

Chapter 12

anti-	-less
bi-	phon
en-, em-	post-
graph, gram	spect
inter-	sub-

concede	disclose
conservative	scapegoat
contrary	superficial
denounce	sustain
deter	transition

Ten Words in Context

In the space provided, write the letter of the meaning closest to that of each **boldfaced** word. Use the context of the sentences to help you figure out each word's meaning.

1 concede
(kən-sēd')
-verb

- Our aunt hates to admit an error. She will never **concede** that she might be wrong.
- After pretending it was easy learning to use the new computer, Ross had to **concede** that he was struggling and ask for help.

_B_ _Concede_ means   A. to forget.   B. to admit.   C. to prove.

2 conservative
(kən-sûr'və-tĭv)
-adjective

- Lauren's **conservative** relatives were shocked when she broke with tradition and wore a rose-colored wedding gown.
- When the mayor suggested a new method of recycling garbage, a **conservative** member of the audience called out, "What we've done in the past is good enough. Why change things?"

_C_ _Conservative_ means   A. playful.   B. amused.   C. traditional.

3 contrary
(kŏn'trĕr-ē)
-adjective

- Claire's father insists that she share his views. He doesn't allow her to express an opinion **contrary** to his.
- Tisha and her husband have **contrary** ideas on how to spend a vacation. He wants to sleep on the beach for a week, but she prefers visiting museums.

_A_ _Contrary_ means   A. different.   B. favorable.   C. similar.

4 denounce
(dĭ-nouns')
-verb

- In Nazi Germany, anyone who publicly **denounced** Hitler as cruel or mad risked imprisonment, torture, and death.
- When Eugene said he saw me steal from another student's locker, I **denounced** him as a liar.

_C_ _Denounce_ means   A. to imitate.   B. to defend.   C. to condemn.

5 deter
(dĭ-tûr')
-verb

- No one is sure how much the threat of capital punishment **deters** murder.
- Beth's parents disapproved of her dating someone from a different culture, but their prejudice didn't **deter** her—she still dated Po-Yen.

_A_ _Deter_ means   A. to discourage.   B. to encourage.   C. to change.

6 disclose
(dĭs-klōz')
-verb

- When I applied for financial aid, I had to **disclose** my family's annual income. But it embarrassed me to reveal this information.
- The police don't **disclose** all the facts of a murder to the newspapers. That way, there will be some information which only the murderer would know.

_A_ _Disclose_ means   A. to reveal.   B. to deny.   C. to replace.

7 scapegoat
(skāp′gōt′)
-noun

- Several girls put dye into their high school swimming pool. In need of a **scapegoat**, they blamed another student who knew nothing about the prank.
- Because the manager wanted a **scapegoat** for his own mistake, he fired an innocent employee.

C *Scapegoat* means
    A. a correction.   B. a punishment.   C. someone to blame.

8 superficial
(soo′pər-fĭsh′əl)
-adjective

- Sal and Anita are interested only in appearances. They are so **superficial** that it's impossible to have a deep friendship with them.
- My teacher said my essay on divorce was too **superficial** because I didn't go into the subject in detail.

A *Superficial* means
    A. lacking depth.   B. complicated.   C. satisfactory.

9 sustain
(sə-stān′)
-verb

- My diets usually last three days at the most. I can't **sustain** my willpower any longer than that.
- An opera singer can **sustain** a high note for a long period of time.

C *Sustain* means
    A. to remember.   B. to delay.   C. to continue.

10 transition
(trăn-zĭsh′ən)
-noun

- Mark's parents were amazed at how easily he made the **transition** from full-time student to full-time employee.
- "The **transition** from being childless to being a parent is extreme," said the new father. "Last week, only two quiet people lived at our house. Suddenly, we're sharing space with a third, noisy person."

C *Transition* means
    A. an explanation.   B. a trip.   C. a change.

Matching Words with Definitions

Following are definitions of the ten words. Clearly write or print each word next to its definition. The sentences above and on the previous page will help you decide on the meaning of each word.

1. superficial — Lacking depth or meaning; shallow
2. contrary — Totally different; opposite; conflicting
3. transition — A change from one activity, condition, or location to another
4. scapegoat — Someone blamed for the mistakes of others
5. concede — To admit to something
6. deter — To prevent or discourage
7. disclose — To reveal; make known
8. denounce — To openly condemn; express disapproval of
9. sustain — To keep something going; continue; maintain
10. conservative — Tending to resist change; favoring traditional values and views

CAUTION: Do not go any further until you are sure the above answers are correct. Then you can use the definitions to help you in the following practices. Your goal is eventually to know the words well enough so that you don't need to check the definitions at all.

Sentence Check 1

Using the answer line provided, complete each item below with the correct word from the box. Use each word once.

| A. concede | B. conservative | C. contrary | D. denounce | E. deter |
| F. disclose | G. scapegoat | H. superficial | I. sustain | J. transition |

g *Scapegoat*   1. The teenagers who smashed the window made an innocent bystander the ___, claiming he had thrown the rock.

i *Sustain*   2. To ___ a high grade-point average throughout college requires much studying.

d *denounce*   3. The environmental group ___ (e)d a local chemical company for polluting the river.

a *concede*   4. Even after Stuart listed scientific facts that support his theory, the teacher refused to ___ that Stuart might be right.

e *deter*   5. A childhood stutter didn't ___ Leo. He overcame his speech handicap and reached his goal of being a radio announcer.

h *superficial*   6. I try to judge people by their character, not by something as ___ as physical appearance.

f *disclose*   7. Knowing my passion for chocolate, my mother refused to ___ the location of the bite-size Hershey bars, which she was saving for company.

j *transition*   8. Making the ___ from her own apartment to a nursing home has been difficult for my grandmother.

c *contrary*   9. Though Geena and Tom are happily married, they cast ___ votes in almost every election—she's a Republican and he's a Democrat.

b *conservative*   10. When Dawn brought home a boyfriend with a Mohawk and several body piercings, her ___ parents, who prefer everything old-fashioned and traditional, nearly fainted.

NOTE: Now check your answers to these items by turning to page 177. Going over the answers carefully will help you prepare for the next two practices, for which answers are not given.

Sentence Check 2

Using the answer lines provided, complete each item below with **two** words from the box. Use each word once.

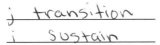

j *transition*
i *Sustain*

1–2. Starting with the ___ from home to college, some students neglect high-school friendships which they had vowed always to ___.

h *superficial*
e *deter*

3–4. Stan is more interested in how much money people have than in who they are. He is a ___ person, and that quality ___s people from becoming his friends.

g disclose ✗

d denounce

5–6. The owners of the unsafe factory used their employees as ___s. They ___(e)d the workers, claiming that their work was erratic° and that the explosion at the factory was entirely their fault.

b conservative

a concede

7–8. Mayor Jones was ___, preferring traditional solutions. So it was hard for him to ___ that some of the radical° ideas of his opponent might work.

f disclose

c contrary

9–10. Once Sandy ___(e)d her true values in the course of our conversation, I realized they were quite ___ to what I had supposed. She was a hypocrite°—not the type of person that I had believed her to be.

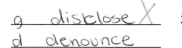

Final Check: *Relating to Parents*

Here is a final opportunity for you to strengthen your knowledge of the ten words. First read the following selection carefully. Then fill in each blank with a word from the box at the top of the previous page. (Context clues will help you figure out which word goes in which blank.) Use each word once.

As I look back at my relationship with my parents, I realize that we have gone through an interesting cycle together. When I was a kid, my parents were everything to me—the smartest, most interesting, most loving people in the world. But when I turned 13, there was a drastic° change—I suddenly developed a very (1) c. contrary view of them. I thought they were unreasonably strict. While I loved everything new in music, hairstyles, and clothes, they seemed boringly (2) b. conservative , wanting everything to remain the same. Our conversations, which used to be so deep and satisfying, became (3) h. superficial chats. I felt as if I had nothing to say to them anymore. If we (4) i sustain (e)d a conversation for any length of time, I quickly lost patience with what I considered their silly, old-fashioned ideas. To my friends, I often (5) d denounce (e)d them as hopelessly out of touch with the modern world.

But now, as I'm making the (6) j transition from my teen years to adulthood, I've had to (7) a concede that I was wrong. My parents are the same patient, loving, wise people they always were. I see that I used them as (8) g scapegoat s for my own uncertainties and for problems I had caused myself. I assumed they had their own agenda° and would not listen to opinions different from their own. Now I know that I can (9) f disclose my plans and dreams to them, and they will listen with respect. I hope I will never again let my own interests (10) e deter me from recognizing my parents' genuine love and concern for me.

Scores   Sentence Check 2 _____%   Final Check _____%

39/40

Enter your scores above and in the **Vocabulary Performance Chart** on the inside back cover of the book.

compensate	moderate
conceive	supplement
derive	surpass
diversity	tentative
inhibit	verify

Ten Words in Context

In the space provided, write the letter of the meaning closest to that of each **boldfaced** word. Use the context of the sentences to help you figure out each word's meaning.

1 compensate
(kŏm′pən-sāt′)
-verb

- Some companies still don't **compensate** women for their work as much as they pay men who do similar work.
- When an oil rig explosion killed Sam, the company **compensated** his widow with $100,000. However, nothing could really repay her for his loss.

_B_ *Compensate* means   A. to notice.   B. to pay.   C. to hire.

2 conceive
(kən-sēv′)
-verb

- When studying Australia in school, I **conceived** an interesting class project— each student could write to an Australian pen pal.
- Most people in the 1800s could not have imagined such things as TV and heart transplants. What will the next hundred years bring that we cannot yet **conceive** of?

_A_ *Conceive* means   A. to think of.   B. to expect.   C. to remember.

3 derive
(dĭ-rīv′)
-verb

- We **derive** plastics from oil. As a result, when oil prices go up, so do the prices of plastic products.
- Sarah **derived** pleasure from visiting and reading to old people after school. She enjoyed their company and felt she was doing something worthwhile.

_B_ *Derive* means   A. to recognize.   B. to get.   C. to want.

4 diversity
(dĭ-vûr′sĭ-tē)
-noun

- There's a great **diversity** of breakfast cereals at the supermarket. There are so many different kinds that they take up half an aisle.
- "One thing I'm looking for in a college," Janelle told her counselor, "is **diversity**. I want to meet many different kinds of people."

_C_ *Diversity* means   A. sameness.   B. need.   C. variety.

5 inhibit
(ĭn-hĭb′ĭt)
-verb

- Steve wanted to drive fast in his new car, but the fact that he had already gotten two speeding tickets **inhibited** him.
- Many people believe exercise makes one eat more, but I find that exercise **inhibits** my urge to snack.

_A_ *Inhibit* means   A. to hold back.   B. to get into the habit.   C. to satisfy.

6 moderate
(mŏd′ər-ĭt)
-adjective

- The trail was neither flat nor extremely steep—it was **moderate**, suitable for the average hiker.
- The prices at this restaurant aren't dirt cheap, but they are **moderate**. So we should be able to have a nice dinner without spending too much.

_B_ *Moderate* means   A. modern.   B. average.   C. difficult.

7 supplement
(sŭp′lə-mənt)
-verb

- Many people **supplement** their diet with vitamins.
- At busy times of the year, the department store **supplements** its sales staff with temporary workers.

B *Supplement* means   A. to replace.   (B.) to add to.   C. to reduce.

8 surpass
(sər-păs′)
-verb

- With hard work, you can reach and even **surpass** many of your highest goals.
- Denise was disappointed that she had only matched Rhonda's record leap in the high jump—she had hoped to **surpass** it.

A *Surpass* means   (A.) to go beyond.   B. to avoid.   C. to equal.

9 tentative
(tĕn′tə-tĭv)
-adjective

- My parents' wedding anniversary party date is **tentative**. Before we finalize the date, we have to be sure that everyone can be with us that weekend.
- Class membership was **tentative** because many students were still dropping and adding courses.

B *Tentative* means   A. clear.   (B.) uncertain.   C. early.

10 verify
(vĕr′ə-fī′)
-verb

- Race officials **verified** who the winner was by checking a photo of the horses at the finish line.
- We'd love to come to the party, but I have to check my calendar to **verify** that we're free that evening.

C *Verify* means   A. to predict.   B. to deny.   (C.) to make sure.

Matching Words with Definitions

Following are definitions of the ten words. Clearly write or print each word next to its definition. The sentences above and on the previous page will help you decide on the meaning of each word.

1. _diversity_ — Variety
2. _compensate_ — To make suitable payment to; pay; repay
3. _surpass_ — To do better than; go beyond in achievement or quality
4. _verify_ — To test or check the truth or accuracy of something; prove
5. _supplement_ — To add to, especially to make up for the lack of something
6. _derive_ — To receive from a source; get
7. _tentative_ — Not definite; not final
8. _moderate_ — Medium; average; not extreme in quality, degree, or amount
9. _concieve_ — To think of; imagine
10. _inhibit_ — To hold back; prevent

CAUTION: Do not go any further until you are sure the above answers are correct. Then you can use the definitions to help you in the following practices. Your goal is eventually to know the words well enough so that you don't need to check the definitions at all.

Sentence Check 1

Using the answer line provided, complete each item below with the correct word from the box. Use each word once.

A. compensate	B. conceive	C. derive	D. diversity	E. inhibit
F. moderate	G. supplement	H. surpass	I. tentative	J. verify

c derive   1. The Mississippi River ___s its name from Native American words meaning "big river."

j verify   2. To ___ that his checkbook balance was correct, Craig added the numbers again.

f moderate   3. If you aren't very hungry, then take only a ___ helping of food.

i tentative   4. The exact cast of the movie remains ___ until the director finds out if Will Smith is available.

h surpass   5. Babe Ruth's record number of home runs in a single baseball season was ___(e)d first by Roger Maris in 1961, then by Mark McGwire in 1998, and most recently by Barry Bonds in 2001.

g supplement   6. The Motor Vehicle Bureau now ___s its driver's manual with an attached publication on the new driving laws.

e inhibit   7. Even with her relatives, shy Yoko didn't feel free to be herself. Their noisy talk ___(e)d her.

b conceive   8. Artists feel frustrated when what they ___ in their minds fails to appear on the painted canvas.

d diversity   9. "Hearing a ___ of opinions is fine," said Lynn. "But it would be nice if everyone in this family could agree once in a while."

a compensate   10. When my uncle helped me pay for college, he said I could ___ him by helping someone else pay for college when I can afford to.

NOTE: Now check your answers to these items by turning to page 177. Going over the answers carefully will help you prepare for the next two practices, for which answers are not given.

Sentence Check 2

Using the answer lines provided, complete each item below with **two** words from the box. Use each word once.

b conceive
e inhibit   1–2. My sister cannot ___ of being in a relationship with someone who would ___ her personal growth.

i tentative
j verify   3–4. I have ___ plans to meet Cesar at the Midtown Theatre at eight, but first I have to ___ the show time and call him back.

a compensate
h surpass   5–6. When the company offered to ___ its employees well for working on Saturdays, the number of volunteers ___(e)d all expectations.

derive   C

Supplement   g

diversity   d

moderate   f

7–8. I ___ great pleasure from having my paintings in an art show, and I can ___ my income by selling some of them.

9–10. City College offers a ___ of courses and majors at a ___ price. Many students don't realize they have an extensive choice of courses at a lower cost than at many other colleges.

Final Check: *Job Choices*

Here is a final opportunity for you to strengthen your knowledge of the ten words. First read the following selection carefully. Then fill in each blank with a word from the box at the top of the previous page. (Context clues will help you figure out which word goes in which blank.) Use each word once.

After job-hunting for two months, Jessica had to choose between two alternatives° for employment—a fashion magazine and a clothing store. She already had (1)*i tentative* job offers from both employers. They planned to make the offers definite after they were able to (2)*j verify* the information on her job application.

In the meantime, Jessica thought about the good and bad points of the two jobs. Both offered the (3)*d diversity* that she liked; she hated doing the same thing every day. Both had good benefits, such as sick leave and vacation time. However, the two companies would not (4)*a compensate* her equally. At the clothing store, Jessica would start out at a (5)*f moderate* salary—not as much as she had hoped for. With her many expenses, she might even have to find a part-time job in the evenings to (6)*g supplement* this salary. But there were other reasons for taking this job. Working for the store, Jessica would be free to put her many ideas into practice right away. Her manager said he would not (7)*e inhabit* any attempts she might make to move up in the company. In fact, he promised that if her work was good, he would endorse° a promotion for her within a few months. At the fashion magazine, Jessica's starting salary would far (8)*h surpass* what she would get paid at the clothing store—she wouldn't have to worry about money at all. But the prospects° of getting promotions and raises were not so definite. Jessica could (9)*b conceive* of both jobs as learning experiences and also felt she could (10)*c derive* much satisfaction from either one. This would not be an easy decision.

Scores	Sentence Check 2 _____%	Final Check _____%

alter	optimist
ample	pretense
blunt	prolong
chronic	refrain
chronological	remorse

Ten Words in Context

In the space provided, write the letter of the meaning closest to that of each **boldfaced** word. Use the context of the sentences to help you figure out each word's meaning.

1 alter
(ôl′tər)
-verb

- Many inventions have changed the course of history. Television **altered** the world, for example, by making it smaller.
- Fern's dramatic weight loss and new hairstyle so **altered** her appearance that we barely recognized her.

_B_ _Alter_ means   A. to surprise.   B. to change.   C. to emphasize.

2 ample
(ăm′pəl)
-adjective

- Surprisingly, my compact car has **ample** space inside. Even Mario, who is six feet tall, never feels cramped in it.
- My parents believe that the most important requirement of any celebration is **ample** food, so that no one will be hungry.

_C_ _Ample_ means   A. little.   B. healthy.   C. plenty of.

3 blunt
(blŭnt)
-adjective

- "I'll be **blunt**," Phyllis said, as plainspoken as ever. "This movie is boring."
- My best friend is so **blunt** that he never softens the truth. He always states his opinion in a painfully straightforward way.

_B_ _Blunt_ means   A. very smart.   B. honest to the point of rudeness.   C. wordy.

4 chronic
(krŏn′ĭk)
-adjective

- My little brother is a **chronic** complainer—all we hear from him is whining, day in and day out.
- Leon has been chain-smoking for so long that he has developed a **chronic** cough, heard daily by everyone in the office.

_A_ _Chronic_ means   A. constant.   B. rare.   C. harmless.

5 chronological
(krŏn′ə-lŏj′ĭ-kəl)
-adjective

- I could have followed the movie better if it had presented events in **chronological** order, instead of jumping back and forth in time.
- In your resumé, list your jobs in reverse **chronological** order—begin with the most recent job and go backward.

_C_ _Chronological_ means   A. brief.   B. mixed-up.   C. arranged as the events happened.

6 optimist
(ŏp′tə-mĭst)
-noun

- My sister is a true **optimist**. When her friends get out their umbrellas, she puts on suntan lotion.
- Alonso is such an **optimist** that when he lost his job, he said only, "I bet I'll find a better one now."

_B_ _Optimist_ means   A. a friendly person.   B. a hopeful person.   C. a troublemaker.

7 pretense
(prē′tĕns′)
-noun

- The robber entered people's houses under the **pretense** of being a repairman.
- I asked several questions about Dean's illness, with the **pretense** of being concerned. In truth, I've never even liked Dean.

_A_   _Pretense_ means   (A.) a false claim.   B. a true statement.   C. a threat.

8 prolong
(prə-lông′)
-verb

- Pulling off a bandage always hurts, but pulling it off slowly **prolongs** the pain.
- My online registration for fall classes was **prolonged** because the school computer system crashed.

_C_   _Prolong_ means   A. to avoid.   B. to wear away.   (C.) to make longer.

9 refrain
(rĭ-frān′)
-verb

- I **refrained** from saying what I really thought about Anne's haircut because I didn't want to hurt her feelings.
- Since she's on a diet, Stella **refrained** from eating a second piece of carrot cake.

_A_   _Refrain_ means   (A.) to stop oneself.   B. to return.   C. to keep going.

10 remorse
(rĭ-môrs′)
-noun

- After she yelled at Russell, his mother was filled with **remorse**. She always regrets her outbursts of temper.
- Feeling **remorse** over losing her iPod, I apologized to my friend and promised to buy her a new one.

_C_   _Remorse_ means   A. excitement.   B. ambition.   (C.) regret.

Matching Words with Definitions

Following are definitions of the ten words. Clearly write or print each word next to its definition. The sentences above and on the previous page will help you decide on the meaning of each word.

1. _chronic_   Continuing; lasting a long time; constant

2. _pretense_   A false show or claim

3. _optimist_   Someone who expects a good outcome

4. _alter_   To change

5. _refrain_   To hold oneself back from doing something

6. _ample_   More than enough; plenty of

7. _remorse_   A strong feeling of regret and guilt

8. _chronological_   In the time order in which events happened

9. _blunt_   Straightforward and brief, often rudely so

10. _prolong_   To make something last longer

CAUTION: Do not go any further until you are sure the above answers are correct. Then you can use the definitions to help you in the following practices. Your goal is eventually to know the words well enough so that you don't need to check the definitions at all.

Sentence Check 1

Using the answer line provided, complete each item below with the correct word from the box. Use each word once.

A. alter ✓	B. ample ✓	C. blunt ✓	D. chronic ✓	E. chronological ✓
F. optimist ✓	G. pretense ✓	H. prolong	I. refrain ✓	J. remorse ✓

refrain   i   1. I couldn't ___ from laughing when Laurie bent over to pick up her pencil and split her tight jeans.

optimist   f.   2. My father always expects the worst, but my mother is a(n) ___.

alter   A   3. I used to dislike my neighbor, but learning that he delivered meals to elderly shut-ins ___(e)d my opinion of him.

prolong   H   4. The sporting-goods store will ___ its "One Day Only" sale to two days, since a storm kept people away the first day.

ample   B   5. Use a deep pan when baking the cake, so there will be ___ room for it to rise.

remorse   j   6. Immediately after calling her sister an idiot, Lydia felt ___. So she hugged her and said, "I didn't mean that."

blunt   C   7. If the teacher had been ___, she would have told Kevin his essay was terrible. Instead, she politely said, "It could use much more work."

chronological   e   8. A story in which early events are hidden until the end is often more dramatic than one told in exact ___ order.

chronic   d.   9. Although Pilar's back pain was ___, having lasted for five years, she refused to undergo surgery.

pretense   g.   10. With the ___ of being attracted to Paula, Marcus asked her to dance; but his real reason was to make his ex-girlfriend jealous.

NOTE: Now check your answers to these items by turning to page 178. Going over the answers carefully will help you prepare for the next two practices, for which answers are not given.

Sentence Check 2

Using the answer lines provided, complete each item below with **two** words from the box. Use each word once.

pretense   g.   1–2. Although her marriage was unhappy, Nell chose to ___ it. Because she was
optimist   f.   a(n) ___, she kept thinking her relationship with her husband would improve. Eventually, however, she realized their relationship had eroded° too much for the marriage to be sustained°.

refrain   i   3–4. Sylvester can't ___ from sniffling and blowing his nose because he suffers
chronic   d.   all summer from ___ hay fever.

remorse ;
chronologicale

5–6. During his trial for a long string of robberies, the ruthless° criminal showed no ___. As the lawyers described his many crimes in ___ order, he remained calm and even looked a little bored.

blunt C
alter A

7–8. ___ criticism is rarely the best way to ___ someone's behavior. Gentle suggestions tend to bring about more change.

prolong h.
ample b

9–10. Always dressed in shabby clothes, Darren made a(n) ___ of being poor. His neighbors, misled by his superficial° appearance, didn't know he had ___ money to live well.

Final Check: *No Joking*

Here is a final opportunity for you to strengthen your knowledge of the ten words. First read the following selection carefully. Then fill in each blank with a word from the box at the top of the previous page. (Context clues will help you figure out which word goes in which blank.) Use each word once.

My poor mother is the worst joke teller I've ever met. She has a(n) (1)_optimist_ inability to remember anecdotes° and punchlines—she's been like that for years. She begins a story in (2)_chronological_ order and then interrupts herself to say, "No, wait a minute. That's not the way it goes." In this way she manages to (3)_prolong_ jokes, making them

more lengthy than funny. Still, she can't (4)_refrain_ from trying to tell them. And she has (5)_ample_ opportunity to try when our family gets together. My uncle derives° amusement from seeing her embarrass herself, so he makes a(n) (6)_pretense_ of thinking she is funny. My father is more (7)_blunt_; he tells Mother outright that she has ruined the joke. After each failure, she is filled with (8)_remorse_ and swears she'll never tell another joke. But I don't believe she'll ever (9)_alter_ her behavior. A(n) (10)_chronic_, she always believes her next joke will be her best, and nothing will deter° her from trying again.

Scores   Sentence Check 2 _____%   Final Check _____%

Enter your scores above and in the **Vocabulary Performance Chart** on the inside back cover of the book.

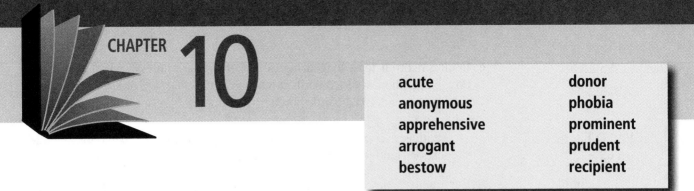

acute	donor
anonymous	phobia
apprehensive	prominent
arrogant	prudent
bestow	recipient

Ten Words in Context

In the space provided, write the letter of the meaning closest to that of each **boldfaced** word. Use the context of the sentences to help you figure out each word's meaning.

1 acute
(ə-kyōot′)
-adjective

- My headache pains were so **acute** that they felt like needles in my head.
- Gil joked, "This painting looks like something my two-year-old son would do." Then he felt **acute** regret when he learned the artist was standing behind him.

A *Acute* means   A. very great.   B. mild.   C. slow.

2 anonymous
(ə-nŏn′ə-məs)
-adjective

- Many **anonymous** works are very famous. For example, the author of the Christmas carol "God Rest Ye Merry, Gentlemen" is unknown.
- Laura tore up an **anonymous** note that said that her teenage daughter had cheated on a test. "If the writer was too ashamed to sign the note," said Laura, "why should I believe it?"

B *Anonymous* means   A. short.   B. having an unknown author.   C. poorly written.

3 apprehensive
(ăp′rĭ-hĕn′sĭv)
-adjective

- Ginny was **apprehensive** as she approached the cow, not knowing if it would try to bite or kick her.
- It is natural to be **apprehensive** when making a major purchase, such as a car or a home. Only the wealthy can afford to be calm at such times.

A *Apprehensive* means   A. fearful.   B. irritated.   C. confident.

4 arrogant
(ăr′ə-gənt)
-adjective

- Having been a very spoiled child, Becky turned out to be a very **arrogant** grownup.
- One of the most **arrogant** people I know paid the state extra money to get a custom license plate that reads "IMBEST."

C *Arrogant* means   A. polite.   B. quiet.   C. showing too much self-importance.

5 bestow
(bĭ-stō′)
-verb

- The Manhattan School of Music **bestowed** an honorary degree on a famous musician who had never gone to college.
- At the science fair, the judges **bestowed** the first prize on Vincent, whose experiment showed that dogs are colorblind.

C *Bestow* means   A. to take.   B. to prepare.   C. to award.

6 donor
(dō′nər)
-noun

- Our soccer team is seeking **donors** to contribute money for new uniforms.
- The man's twin sister was the **donor** of his new kidney.

B *Donor* means   A. one who receives.   B. one who gives.   C. one who doubts.

7 phobia
(fō′bē-ə)
-noun

● My roommate has joined a group that helps people with **phobias** because she wants to overcome her extreme fear of even the smallest spiders.

● Ned's fear of flying is so severe that he won't even step onto an airplane. But he says he's in no rush to cure his **phobia**, since driving is cheaper anyway.

_B_ *Phobia* means   A. an illness.   (B.) an extreme fear.   C. a bad temper.

8 prominent
(prŏm′ə-nənt)
-adjective

● Crystal's long black hair is so **prominent** that it's the first thing you notice about her.

● The Big Bird balloon was the most **prominent** one in the parade because it was so large and such a bright yellow.

_C_ *Prominent* means   A. cheerful.   B. expensive.   (C.) obvious.

9 prudent
(prōōd′ənt)
-adjective

● Sidney has learned the hard way that it's not **prudent** to tease our ill-tempered dog.

● **Prudent** as always, Meg thought carefully before finally deciding which of the used cars would be the best buy.

_C_ *Prudent* means   A. relaxed.   B. courageous.   (C.) careful and wise.

10 recipient
(rĭ-sĭp′ē-ənt)
-noun

● The actress Katharine Hepburn was the **recipient** of four Academy Awards. She received the fourth one nearly fifty years after the first one.

● Rashid was the annoyed **recipient** of forty pieces of spam on the same day.

_B_ *Recipient* means   A. one who gives.   (B.) one who receives.   C. one with good luck.

Matching Words with Definitions

Following are definitions of the ten words. Clearly write or print each word next to its definition. The sentences above and on the previous page will help you decide on the meaning of each word.

1. ___donor___   A person who gives or contributes

2. ___apprehensive___   Frightened; uneasy; anxious

3. ___phobia___   A continuing, abnormally extreme fear of a particular situation or thing

4. ___prudent___   Cautious; careful; wise

5. ___accute___   Severe; sharp; intense

6. ___arrogant___   Filled with self-importance; overly proud and vain

7. ___prominent___   Very noticeable; obvious

8. ___recipient___   A person who receives

9. ___anonymous___   Created or given by an unknown or unidentified person

10. ___bestow___   To give, as an honor or a gift; award

CAUTION: Do not go any further until you are sure the above answers are correct. Then you can use the definitions to help you in the following practices. Your goal is eventually to know the words well enough so that you don't need to check the definitions at all.

Sentence Check 1

Using the answer line provided, complete each item below with the correct word from the box. Use each word once.

a. acute	b. anonymous	c. apprehensive	d. arrogant	e. bestow
f. donor	g. phobia	h. prominent	i. prudent	j. recipient

phobia   g   1. Because of her ___, Martha will walk up twenty floors to avoid taking an elevator.

anonymous   b   2. The unsigned letter to the editor was not published because it was the newspaper's policy never to print ___ letters.

acute   a   3. Since I didn't eat all day, I began to feel ___ hunger pains in my stomach by early evening.

arrogant   d   4. The secretary to the president of the company behaves in a very ___ way. She thinks she's more important than the other secretaries.

recipient   j   5. Kendra was so popular that each year she was the ___ of dozens of Valentines.

bestow   e   6. When he retires, the biology professor will ___ on the school his collection of animal skeletons.

prudent   i   7. "Your decision to wait to marry until after graduation seems ___ to me," Devan's father said, pleased that his son was acting so wisely.

apprehensive c 8. Cliff became more and more ___ about his driver's test. He was afraid he'd forget to signal, fail to park correctly, or even get into an accident.

donor   f   9. Because the new tax laws limit certain deductions, art museums have fewer ___s.

prominent   h   10. The most ___ plants in Dwayne's garden are giant lilies. Some of them are eight feet tall.

NOTE: Now check your answers to these items by turning to page 178. Going over the answers carefully will help you prepare for the next two practices, for which answers are not given.

Sentence Check 2

Using the answer lines provided, complete each item below with **two** words from the box. Use each word once.

arrogant   d   1–2. The millionaire was so ___ that he refused to be a major ___ to the new town
donor   f   library unless it was named for him.

prudent   i   3–4. It's ___ to keep medication on hand if anyone in the family is subject to ___
acute   a   asthma attacks.

apprehensive c 5–6. Joey is very ___ when he has to give a speech, and his stutter becomes
prominent   h   especially ___. As a result, he refrains° from raising his hand in class.

recipient   j

anonymous   b

bestow   e

phobia   g

7–8. The famous actress was sometimes the ___ of ___ letters from fans too shy to sign their names.

9–10. Carlotta felt her therapist had ___ed upon her the greatest of gifts: freedom from fear of open spaces. Before her treatment, Carlotta's ___ had kept her a prisoner in her own home. It had inhibited° her from even walking into her own front yard.

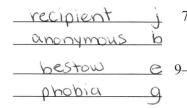

Final Check: *Museum Pet*

Here is a final opportunity for you to strengthen your knowledge of the ten words. First read the following selection carefully. Then fill in each blank with a word from the box at the top of the previous page. (Context clues will help you figure out which word goes in which blank.) Use each word once.

"I've got great news!" the museum director shouted as he ran into the employees' lunchroom. "Someone wants to (1) _e bestow_ five million dollars on the museum."

"Who?" one staff member asked excitedly.

"I don't know. He wishes his gift to remain (2) _b anonymous_. There's just one obstacle°," he added.

The employees' optimistic° smiles faded, and they began to look (3) _c apprehensive_.

"It seems our mystery (4) _f donor_ has a strange (5) _g phobia_: he's terribly afraid of cats."

Everyone turned to look at Willard, who had been the museum pet since he'd wandered in as a tiny kitten more than seven years ago. As usual, the large orange cat was stretched out in a (6) _h. prominent_ spot near the lunchroom entrance. He continued licking himself, not aware that he was the (7) _j. recipient_ of everyone's attention.

"I'm afraid Willard will have to go," the director said sadly. "This contributor isn't just a little afraid of cats; his fear is really (8) _a acute_. Apparently, he panicked when he saw Willard the last time he came. We can't risk frightening him again. It just wouldn't be (9) _i prudent_. Remember, he might give us more money in the future."

"I think it's pretty (10) _d arrogant_ of this contributor, whoever he is, to ask us to give up poor old Willard for him, even if he does want to give us the money," one employee said angrily. "How can any amount of money compensate° for the loss of a beloved pet?"

"I know you'll miss Willard," the director said, "but it would be a shame to forfeit° the money. And I'll be glad to have him come live at my house. You can all visit him whenever you like." And so Willard found a new home, where he still lives happily. The museum used the five million dollars to build a new addition, which is known as the Willard Wing.

| Scores | Sentence Check 2 _____% | Final Check _____% |

absurd	compile
adhere	contempt
affluent	defect
alienate	doctrine
assess	dogmatic

Ten Words in Context

In the space provided, write the letter of the meaning closest to that of each **boldfaced** word. Use the context of the sentences to help you figure out each word's meaning.

1 absurd
(ăb-sûrd′)
-adjective

- When six-foot Randy came to the costume party in only a diaper, he looked so **absurd** that everyone burst into laughter.
- It seemed **absurd** to Helen that she had more cooking experience than the teacher of her cooking class.

_C_ _Absurd_ means   A. responsible.   B. challenging.   Ⓒ ridiculous.

2 adhere
(ăd-hēr′)
-verb

- Beware of sitting on a hot car seat in shorts—your thighs may **adhere** to the vinyl.
- Angie used bubble gum to make the poster of Justin Timberlake **adhere** to her bedroom wall.

_C_ _Adhere_ means   A. to belong.   B. to grow.   Ⓒ to stick.

3 affluent
(ăf′lōō-ənt)
-adjective

- Some people live an **affluent** lifestyle by overcharging on their credit cards—a bad habit that can lead to a mountain of debts.
- Why should tax regulations benefit **affluent** people more than poor people?

_C_ _Affluent_ means   A. careless.   B. friendly.   Ⓒ rich.

4 alienate
(ā′lē-ə-nāt′)
-verb

- The coach often insulted Maria. His rude behavior began to **alienate** the other players, who had once thought of him as a friend.
- Bill and Joanne thought their marriage could survive while they worked in different cities. But being apart so much eventually **alienated** them from each other.

_B_ _Alienate_ means   A. to push away.   Ⓑ to frighten.   C. to comfort.

5 assess
(ə-sĕs′)
-verb

- It is harder for teachers to **assess** answers to essay questions than to grade multiple-choice items.
- After the fire, insurance representatives came to **assess** the damage.

_B_ _Assess_ means   A. to judge.   Ⓑ to think of.   C. to avoid.

6 compile
(kəm-pīl′)
-verb

- Before writing her essay, Sharon **compiled** a list of the points she wanted to make.
- The teacher asked students to **compile** reports on their family histories by interviewing parents and grandparents.

_C_ _Compile_ means   A. to read carefully.   B. to divide.   Ⓒ to put together.

7 contempt
(kən-tĕmpt')
-noun

- Vera pitied the beggar, but her boyfriend felt only **contempt**, saying, "He's too lazy to get a job."
- Molly expressed her **contempt** for Art's clumsy dancing by leaving him in the middle of the dance floor.

A *Contempt* means   (A.) disrespect.   B. acceptance.   C. curiosity.

8 defect
(dē'fĕkt')
-noun

- The only **defect** in the actor's good looks was that his ears stuck out. Careful camera angles and a longer haircut hid the problem.
- "Check these peaches for **defects**, Tom," said the grocer to his new employee. "Remove any with dark spots, bruises, or other imperfections."

A *Defect* means   (A.) a fault.   B. a strength.   C. a pattern.

9 doctrine
(dŏk'trĭn)
-noun

- Dr. Martin Luther King, Jr. followed the **doctrine** of fighting for social change without violence.
- Many people sincerely practice their faith without understanding all of its **doctrines**. The fine points of religion do not interest everyone.

B *Doctrine* means   A. a prediction.   (B.) a teaching.   C. a schedule.

10 dogmatic
(dôg-măt'ĭk)
-adjective

- The boss's **dogmatic** style bothered me. He listened to only one person's opinions—his own.
- A **dogmatic** teacher demands that students accept what is taught without question.

C *Dogmatic* means   A. wild.   B. very patient.   (C.) one-sided.

Matching Words with Definitions

Following are definitions of the ten words. Clearly write or print each word next to its definition. The sentences above and on the previous page will help you decide on the meaning of each word.

1. __contempt__   Disrespect; a feeling that a person or thing is inferior and undesirable

2. __assess__   To evaluate; to decide on the quality or value of

3. __dogmatic__   Opinionated; stating an opinion as if it were a fact

4. __adhere__   To stick firmly

5. __defect__   A fault; imperfection; flaw

6. __alienate__   To cause to become unfriendly; to separate emotionally

7. __affluent__   Wealthy

8. __absurd__   Ridiculous; opposed to common sense

9. __compile__   To gather together in an organized form, such as a list

10. __doctrine__   The strict teachings of a religious, political, or other group

CAUTION: Do not go any further until you are sure the above answers are correct. Then you can use the definitions to help you in the following practices. Your goal is eventually to know the words well enough so that you don't need to check the definitions at all.

Sentence Check 1

Using the answer line provided, complete each item below with the correct word from the box. Use each word once.

A. **absurd**	B. **adhere**	C. **affluent**	D. **alienate**	E. **assess**
F. **compile**	G. **contempt**	H. **defect**	I. **doctrine**	J. **dogmatic**

_____ 1. You cannot always ___ a student's progress by looking just at his or her grades.

_____ 2. Many of the houses in ___ neighborhoods have burglar alarms. Residents know there have been problems with robberies.

_____ 3. Margo's parents' constant arguments began to ___ her from them.

_____ 4. When Jerry cheated on the exam and then bragged about it as well, Eva felt ___ for him.

_____ 5. To ___ an encyclopedia takes many years. A huge number of facts need to be arranged into entries.

_____ 6. If you study the ___s of several religions, you may be surprised by the similarity of some of their teachings.

_____ 7. Something in a spider's thread makes bugs that touch it ___ to the web.

_____ 8. Vivian was about to buy a red dress when she noticed a small ___: some threads were loose on the collar.

_____ 9. The boss has a(n) ___ way of running things—he wants workers to do exactly what he tells them, without asking any questions.

_____ 10. Jasmin thought Hiroshi was ___ to do a rain dance on their dry front lawn— until she saw the sky blacken and lightning flash immediately afterward.

NOTE: Now check your answers to these items by turning to page 178. Going over the answers carefully will help you prepare for the next two practices, for which answers are not given.

Sentence Check 2

Using the answer lines provided, complete each item below with **two** words from the box. Use each word once.

_____
_____ 1–2. To ___ a patient's health, a doctor must ___ an extensive° record that includes all the medical tests that have been given.

_____
_____ 3–4. I have ___ for any ___ that teaches hatred of groups having different principles and beliefs.

_____
_____ 5–6. Stubborn, ___ parents who deny their children freedom to make some of their own decisions may eventually ___ those children. Helping children learn to think for themselves contributes to a healthy transition° from childhood to adulthood.

_____   7–8. My little sister thought the roll of tape that is sticky on both sides had a(n)

_____   ___, but I told her the tape was actually meant to ___ on both sides.

_____   9–10. It seems ___ that anyone should go hungry in a country as ___ as ours.

_____   Shouldn't there be a way to provide food to families in acute° need of it?

Final Check: _Unacceptable Boyfriends_

Here is a final opportunity for you to strengthen your knowledge of the ten words. First read the following selection carefully. Then fill in each blank with a word from the box at the top of the previous page. (Context clues will help you figure out which word goes in which blank.) Use each word once.

I will acknowledge° that I am an extremely organized person. I see no reason why everything in my life shouldn't be perfectly planned. For instance, my CDs are arranged according to the year they came out and alphabetized within that year. The cans on my kitchen shelves are placed in order of height. My clothes and accessories are perfectly organized, thanks to labels that (1)_____ to my dresser drawers. To me, being well-organized is a positive thing. But recently, a friend bluntly° told me that she thinks I am a control freak. She said this after reading a list I had (2)_____(e)d. It was a list of characteristics that my future boyfriend must have. According to her, my list would (3)_____ any half-decent guy who might otherwise be interested in me. I think her accusation is (4)_____. Why shouldn't my love life be as well planned as the rest of my existence? But I'll let you be the judge. You (5)_____ my list and tell me if it's unreasonable.

To begin with, my future boyfriend must be (6)_____. I plan to make a lot of money, and I wouldn't want him to feel bad about being less well-off than I am. Politically, he should be as conservative° as I am—I simply couldn't put up with anyone whose political (7)_____ calls for social change. He can't have any physical (8)_____s, of course—I deserve someone extremely handsome and physically fit. Because I am an urban° girl, he must want to live in the city. He has to like Thai food and dislike Mexican food, like tropical fish and hate cats and dogs, enjoy classical music and look with (9)_____ at any music written after 1850. He must enjoy beach vacations, and he must dislike camping, the mountains, bowling, suspense movies, hiking, novels, four-wheel-drive vehicles, foreign travel, and children.

My girlfriend has the nerve to call me (10)_____, saying that my list shows I'm close-minded and too opinionated. She says that every man I meet will be unacceptable in some way. I think she's just plain wrong. Be candid°—tell me the truth. What do you think?

| Scores | Sentence Check 2 _____% | Final Check _____% |

anti-	-less
bi-	phon
en-, em-	post-
graph, gram	spect
inter-	sub-

Ten Word Parts in Context

Figure out the meanings of the following ten word parts by looking *closely* and *carefully* at the context in which they appear. Then, in the space provided, write the letter of the meaning closest to that of each word part.

1 anti-
- **Antifreeze** prevents the water in a car radiator from freezing.
- Many students in the 1960s who disapproved of the United States' involvement in the Vietnam War took part in **antiwar** marches.

B The word part *anti-* means   A. for.   (B) against.   C. two.

2 bi-
- In addition to the expected pair of wheels, a **bicycle** built for two also has two seats.
- "You can have only one wife at a time," Judge Graves told the **bigamist**, "not two at once."

A The word part *bi-* means   (A) two.   B. look.   C. speech.

3 en-, em-
- On the boss's door were two signs: "**Enter**" and "Exit."
- A brief kiss, a quick **embrace**, and she was gone—leaving me wondering if I had really held her in my arms.

C The word part *en-* or *em-* means   A. sound.   B. below.   (C) in, into.

4 graph, gram
- My little sister practices her handwriting so that if she becomes famous, her **autograph** will look good.
- The **diagram** in my biology book shows that, strange as it may seem, an earthworm has two hearts.

B The word part *-graph* or *-gram* means   A. under.   (B) something written or drawn.   C. three.

5 inter-
- When my brother tries to speak while chewing gum, it's impossible to understand him without an **interpreter**.
- "Driving cross-country along the **interstate** highway was great," said Telly. "I got to eat in about twenty different states!"

B The word part *inter-* means   A. something written.   (B) between.   C. under.

6 -less
- The mayor spoke sadly about the **homeless**, but he did nothing to build low-income housing.
- The Smiths' marriage was **loveless**. They stayed together for the sake of their children, but the constant tension in their house was difficult for everyone to bear.

A The word part *-less* means   (A) without.   B. with.   C. look.

7 phon

- Alexander Graham Bell invented not only the **telephone** but also a kite that could carry a person.
- Whenever Wayne played the **saxophone**, dogs howled, cats screamed, and lovebirds got divorced.

☞ The word part *phon* means   A. under.   (B.) sound.   C. watch.

8 post-

- Why are baseball games **postponed** because of a light rain, but football games not called off even if it rains heavily?
- My playful sister included a **postscript** after her letter that said, "P.S. I don't have anything else to say."

☞ The word part *post-* means   A. half.   B. speech.   (C.) after.

9 spect

- Detective Blake amazed everyone by **inspecting** the tuna casserole the thief was baking and then fishing the stolen jewels out with a fork.
- **Spectators** at a tennis match tend to watch the ball, not the players.

☞ The word part *spect* means   A. hear.   (B.) look.   C. not.

10 sub-

- Some people won't travel by **subway** because they fear being trapped underground.
- On the **submarine** ride at Disneyland, passengers can see models of such underwater life as seahorses and sharks.

☞ The word part *sub-* means   (A.) under.   B. new.   C. over.

Matching Word Parts with Definitions

Following are definitions of the ten word parts. Clearly write or print each word part next to its definition. The sentences above and on the previous page will help you decide on the meaning of each word part.

1. _____post-_____ After
2. _____graph, gram_____ Something written or drawn
3. _____anti-_____ Against, acting against
4. _____en-, em-_____ Into, in
5. _____sub-_____ Under, below
6. _____bi-_____ Two
7. _____inter-_____ Between, among
8. _____spect_____ Look, watch
9. _____-less_____ Without
10. _____phon_____ Sound, speech

CAUTION: Do not go any further until you are sure the above answers are correct. Then you can use the definitions to help you in the following practices. Your goal is eventually to know the word parts well enough so that you don't need to check the definitions at all.

Sentence Check 1

Using the answer line provided, complete each *italicized* word below with the correct word part from the box. Use each word part once.

A. anti-	**B. bi-**	**C. en-, em-**	**D. graph, gram**	**E. inter-**
F. -less	**G. phon**	**H. post-**	**I. spect**	**J. sub-**

_____ 1. Out on the ocean, sunsets can be (. . . *acular*) ___ displays of color really worth seeing.

_____ 2. The French have trouble with English (. . . *etics*) ___, especially the sound of *er*, as in *anger* and *later*.

_____ 3. "We (. . . *rupt*) ___ this program to bring you a special news bulletin," the announcer said.

_____ 4. You can keep brown sugar moist by (. . . *closing*) ___ it in a container with a piece or two of apple.

_____ 5. In her (*autobio* . . . *y*) ___, *The Story of My Life*, Helen Keller tells how she was able to learn despite her blindness and deafness.

_____ 6. Clark was (. . . *social*) ___ in high school, but he became very outgoing in college.

_____ 7. Bird watchers prefer rubber-coated (. . . *noculars*) ___ because if they hit trees or equipment, they don't make a noise that scares birds away.

_____ 8. A (*cord* . . .) ___ phone allows a parent to talk to a caller while following a wandering child around the house.

_____ 9. Prenatal care for birds means sitting on the eggs. (. . . *natal*) ___ care involves almost constant feeding during the day.

_____ 10. When we saw what appeared to be a floating log (. . . *merge*) ___ and then slide under the water toward our canoe, we knew two things: one, it wasn't a log; two, it wanted to eat us.

NOTE: Now check your answers to these items by turning to page 178. Going over the answers carefully will help you prepare for the next two practices, for which answers are not given.

Sentence Check 2

Using the answer line provided, complete each *italicized* word in the sentences below with the correct word part from the box. Use each word part once.

_____
_____ 1–2. Because I'm allergic to all kinds of perfumes, my (. . . *perspirant*) ___ must be (*odor* . . .) ___.

_____
_____ 3–4. At the company luncheon, every new (. . . *ployee*) ___ was invited up to the (*micro* . . .) to say a few introductory words.

_____   5–6. Years ago, people sent (*tele . . . s*) ___ when they wanted messages to arrive
_____   quickly. They knew that recipients° would open and (*in . . .*) ___ them
immediately.

_____   7–8. No one (*. . . fered*) ___ with the mad scientist's plans because he worked
_____   in a hidden lab in a(n) (*. . . basement*) ___, under the laundry room in his
basement.

_____   9–10. As part of her recovery from an auto accident, my mother has (*. . . weekly*)
_____   ___ appointments with a physical therapist. The therapist is a wonderful
person with ample° patience. Once, when my mother was short of cash, he
even allowed her to (*. . . date*) ___ the check she paid him with.

Final Check: *Coping with Snow*

Here is a final opportunity for you to strengthen your knowledge of the ten word parts. First read the
following selection carefully. Then complete each *italicized* word in the parentheses below with a word
part from the box at the top of the previous page. (Context clues will help you figure out which word part
goes in which blank.) Use each word part once.

There are plenty of (*. . . joyable*) (1)_____

ways to keep your driveway free of snow. For example, you might

(*. . . vene*) (2)_____ between the snow

and the driveway by simply extending the roof of your house

until it covers the entire drive. Or you could paint the drive with

(*. . . freeze*) (3)_____, so that snowflakes will

melt as soon as they land, instead of adhering° to the surface.

Or, with just one quick (*tele . . . e*) (4)_____

call, you could order a plowing service to come shovel you out.

If there's only moderate° snow out there, attaching a plow to the

front of your (*. . . cycle*) (5)_____ and pedaling the snow away is another possibility.

This method will provide you with plenty of leg exercise. At the same time, you will make a(n) (*. . . acle*)

(6)_____ of yourself in front of the neighborhood children, who can (*photo . . .*)

(7)_____ you and keep the pictures to embarrass you later. Finally, since snow

remains only in (*. . . freezing*) (8)_____ temperatures, you can always (*. . . pone*)

(9)_____ your actions until a later time—say, May or June. See? There's no reason to

feel (*help . . .*) (10)_____ just because a blizzard piles a foot of snow on your driveway.

| Scores | Sentence Check 2 _____% | Final Check _____% |

The box at the right lists twenty-five words from Unit Two. Using the clues at the bottom of the page, fill in these words to complete the puzzle that follows.

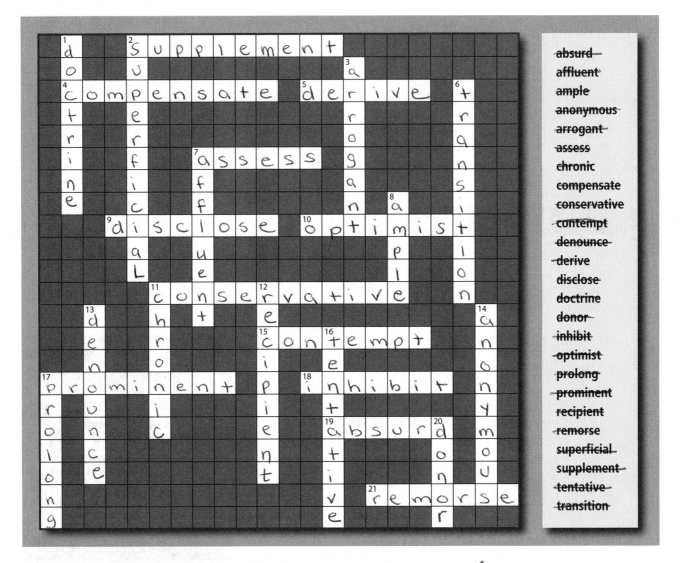

Word list:
absurd
affluent
ample
anonymous
arrogant
assess
chronic
compensate
conservative
contempt
denounce
derive
disclose
doctrine
donor
inhibit
optimist
prolong
prominent
recipient
remorse
superficial
supplement
tentative
transition

ACROSS

2. To add to, especially to make up for the lack of something
4. To pay or repay
5. To receive from a source; get
7. To evaluate; decide on the quality of or value of
9. To reveal; make known
10. Someone who expects a good outcome
11. Tending to resist change; favoring traditional values
15. Disrespect; a feeling that a person or thing is inferior
17. Very noticeable; obvious
18. To hold back; prevent
19. Ridiculous; opposed to common sense
21. A strong feeling of regret and guilt

DOWN

1. The strict teaching of a religious or political group
2. Lacking depth or meaning
3. Filled with self-importance; overly proud and vain
6. A change from one condition or location to another
7. Wealthy
8. More than enough; plenty of
11. Continuing; lasting a long time; constant
12. A person who receives
13. To openly condemn; express disapproval of
14. Written or given by an unknown person
16. Not definite; not final
17. To make something last longer
20. A person who gives or contributes

PART A

Choose the word that best completes each item and write it in the space provided.

_____ 1. My sister's ___ about snakes is so strong she actually faints if she sees one.

    A. phobia   B. doctrine   C. diversity   D. transition

_____ 2. In 1986, a small ___ in the space shuttle *Challenger* caused it to explode.

    A. pretense   B. remorse   C. phobia   D. defect

_____ 3. After you watch *Sesame Street* for a while, you forget how ___ the enormous, saucer-eyed Big Bird really looks.

    A. dogmatic   B. absurd   C. chronic   D. acute

_____ 4. Fred is a(n) ___ complainer—as soon as one problem is solved, he'll come up with another.

    A. affluent   B. prudent   C. moderate   D. chronic

_____ 5. I knew Jackie would do well in the pole vault, but her wonderful performance ___ even my expectations.

    A. assessed   B. bestowed   C. surpassed   D. sustained

_____ 6. I have to admire Mayor Moss for not being afraid to ___ some voters in order to do what he believes is right.

    A. prolong   B. verify   C. alienate   D. compile

_____ 7. We usually don't think about the fact that our books, newspapers, and wooden furniture are all ___ from trees.

    A. adhered   B. derived   C. disclosed   D. denounced

_____ 8. The new drug was taken off the market when it was learned that researchers had ___ test results to make it look as if the drug were safe.

    A. altered   B. deterred   C. bestowed   D. prolonged

_____ 9. Since kids sometimes call in orders to pizza parlors as a joke, some pizza clerks now call back to ___ that each order is genuine.

    A. alter   B. verify   C. prolong   D. bestow

_____ 10. At Gene's ten-year high-school reunion, he was struck by how many of his classmates seemed to have already made the ___ from a youthful to a middle-aged lifestyle.

    A. recipient   B. doctrine   C. transition   D. supplement

(Continues on next page)

PART B

On the answer line, write the letter of the choice that best completes each item.

_____ 11. Ross **conceded** to his boss that he had made the error, saying,
     A. "Sorry. My error."   C. "That's not an error."
     B. "Lee did it."   D. "You told me to do it."

_____ 12. Katya **sustained** her no-smoking effort by
     A. sneaking a smoke now and then.   C. picturing herself healthier each day.
     B. saying, "I just can't quit!"   D. being with people who smoke.

_____ 13. One way to **inhibit** the growth of a plant or bush is to
     A. water it whenever it begins to look dry.   C. trim it daily.
     B. give it lots of plant food.   D. talk to it.

_____ 14. Tara loves to dance. When she hears music with a strong beat, she cannot **refrain** from
     A. singing along.   C. making the music louder.
     B. sitting still.   D. dancing.

_____ 15. To **assess** a diamond ring's value, a jeweler might
     A. add some small rubies.   C. lie about how much it's worth.
     B. examine the diamond for flaws.   D. replace the diamond with a fake.

_____ 16. Lydia was **apprehensive** about going to an Indian restaurant because she
     A. enjoyed all Indian foods.
     B. was afraid the food might be too spicy for her.
     C. was curious about new foods.
     D. didn't have to work that day.

_____ 17. A typical statement from a **dogmatic** person would be:
     A. "There's only one way to do this—my way."
     B. "I can't make up my mind."
     C. "Let's listen to everyone's opinion."
     D. "Let's try something different this time."

_____ 18. Our house has **ample** room for guests. We
     A. have three extra bedrooms and an extra bathroom.
     B. already have two people sleeping in every room.
     C. can have overnight guests if they don't mind sleeping on the floor in sleeping bags.
     D. have one small guest bedroom with a single bed in it.

_____ 19. When waking up to a dark and rainy spring day, an **optimist** is likely to say something like,
     A. "I guess I'd better wear my raincoat and carry an umbrella."
     B. "Why did this have to happen to me? My whole day is ruined."
     C. "It looks like the weather report was right."
     D. "Great! This will get the flowers off to a good start."

_____ 20. To **compile** her grocery shopping list, Mrs. Rodriguez needs to
     A. cash her paycheck.
     B. buy only what's on her list.
     C. leave it at home when she goes to the store.
     D. check the refrigerator and kitchen shelves to see what she needs to buy.

Score   (Number correct) _____ x 5 = _____ %

PART A

Complete each item with a word from the box. Use each word once.

A. adhere	B. affluent	C. arrogant	D. blunt	E. compensate
F. conservative	G. denounce	H. disclose	I. diversity	J. prudent
K. remorse	L. supplement	M. tentative		

_____ 1. I can't stand that ___ movie critic. He always speaks as if his reviews came directly from God.

_____ 2. Our family isn't ___ by American standards, but we're rich compared with people from many other countries.

_____ 3. Len wouldn't take a hint, so Rebecca finally had to be ___ and say she just didn't want to go out with him.

_____ 4. Because of all the steam in our bathroom, the wallpaper there no longer ___s very well.

_____ 5. Prisoners of war were tortured until they were willing to publicly ___ their own governments.

_____ 6. I hung my dress outside the dry-cleaning shop when the owner refused to ___ me for ruining it by running the colors together.

_____ 7. In order to make viewers tune in the next day, soap opera episodes often end just before a character ___s some shocking secret.

_____ 8. After running out of gas on the way to the hospital during an emergency, I decided it was ___ to keep the tank full at all times.

_____ 9. The Monahans are famous in town for their ___ ways. They have gone to the same church, eaten in the same restaurants, and read the same newspaper for three generations.

_____ 10. The mugger's victim made a(n) ___ identification of her attacker from a photo. However, she said she would have to see him in person to be sure.

_____ 11. The young mother was still giving her toddler only milk. The doctor explained that it was time for her to ___ the child's diet with solid food.

_____ 12. I like our women's group because of its ___. Among the African American, Latina, and white members are grandmothers, young mothers, and young single women.

_____ 13. My brother expressed ___ for having stolen my slice of chocolate pie, but I think he was just trying to avoid getting into trouble with Dad.

(Continues on next page)

PART B

Write **C** if the italicized word is used **correctly**. Write **I** if the word is used **incorrectly**.

_____ 14. A central *doctrine* of Native American religions is respect for all living things.

_____ 15. After being the *recipient* of seven speeding tickets in one month, Marylee lost her license.

_____ 16. Whenever my brother makes a mistake, he blames someone else. He loves being the *scapegoat*.

_____ 17. Dad got Jen to the house for her surprise party on the *pretense* that she had left a jacket there.

_____ 18. Owen bragged that when he got rich, he would buy his mother the most *moderate* diamond necklace in town. He wanted her to have the best.

_____ 19. I'm a little angry at our neighbor. I told him to take just a few tomatoes from our garden, not to *bestow* all the ripe ones.

PART C

On the answer line, write the letter of the word that is the **synonym** of the boldfaced word.

Example: _B_ absurd   A. lively   B. ridiculous   C. sensible

_____ 20. **deter**   A. encourage   B. prevent   C. admit

_____ 21. **prominent**   A. surprising   B. hidden   C. noticeable

_____ 22. **donor**   A. giver   B. receiver   C. manager

PART D

On the answer line, write the letter of the word that is the **antonym** of the boldfaced word.

Example: _C_ absurd   A. lively   B. ridiculous   C. sensible

_____ 23. **superficial**   A. shallow   B. lengthy   C. deep

_____ 24. **anonymous**   A. identified   B. threatening   C. nameless

_____ 25. **prolong**   A. lengthen   B. shorten   C. force

Score   (Number correct) _____ x 4 = _____%

Enter your scores above and in the **Vocabulary Performance Chart** on the inside back cover of the book.

Each item below starts with a pair of words in CAPITAL LETTERS. For each item, figure out the relationship between these two words. Then decide which of the choices (A, B, C, or D) expresses a similar relationship. Write the letter of your choice on the answer line.

_____ 1. CONTRARY : SIMILAR ::
    A. confusing : clear   C. opposite : different
    B. conflicting : clashing   D. heated : argument

_____ 2. DISCLOSE : CONCEAL ::
    A. close : shut   C. continue : stop
    B. know : remember   D. discover : explore

_____ 3. SCAPEGOAT : BLAME ::
    A. movie star : fame   C. aunt : cousin
    B. bird : robin   D. soldier : sailor

_____ 4. SUPERFICIAL : MAKEUP ::
    A. healthful : sugar   C. deep : ocean
    B. welcome : illness   D. fatal : twisted ankle

_____ 5. COMPENSATE : PAYCHECK ::
    A. recognize : sale   C. envelope : letter
    B. reward : tax   D. punish : fine

_____ 6. CONCEIVE : IDEA ::
    A. melt : mountain   C. build : hole
    B. paint : picture   D. drip : ship

_____ 7. DIVERSITY : VARIETY ::
    A. place : location   C. cause : effect
    B. similarity : twins   D. weight : height

_____ 8. VERIFY : DISPROVE ::
    A. surrender : resist   C. lose : compete
    B. select : know   D. explore : find

_____ 9. CHRONOLOGICAL : TIME ::
    A. spatial : place   C. geographical : outer space
    B. geological : flowers   D. alphabetical : news

_____ 10. OPTIMIST : HOPE ::
    A. drawing : photo   C. smile : grin
    B. tree : branches   D. night : day

(Continues on next page)

____ 11. PROLONG : LENGTHEN ::
   A. recommend : suggest
   B. protect : harm
   C. walk : speak
   D. provide : supplies

____ 12. REMORSE : WRONGDOING ::
   A. affection : hate
   B. confusion : clarity
   C. joy : sin
   D. satisfaction : achievement

____ 13. ACUTE : MILD ::
   A. delicious : taste
   B. new : expensive
   C. tall : height
   D. violent : peaceful

____ 14. DONOR : GIVE ::
   A. player : stay
   B. child : remain
   C. thief : steal
   D. musician : lead

____ 15. ANONYMOUS : NAME ::
   A. funny : humor
   B. strong : health
   C. tall : height
   D. poor : money

____ 16. PRUDENT : WISE ::
   A. vain : modest
   B. pretty : attractive
   C. strong : weights
   D. serious : joking

____ 17. ADHERE : GLUE ::
   A. whiten : bleach
   B. sharpen : pencil
   C. polish : silver
   D. boil : ice

____ 18. AFFLUENT : BILLIONAIRE ::
   A. healthy : invalid
   B. generous : miser
   C. childless : parent
   D. creative : composer

____ 19. ALIENATE : UNITE ::
   A. divorce : marry
   B. join : friendly
   C. learn : study
   D. travel : depart

____ 20. CONTEMPT : RESPECT ::
   A. sympathy : understanding
   B. anger : annoyance
   C. treason : loyalty
   D. envy : jealousy

Score   (Number correct) _____ x 5 = _____%

Enter your scores above and in the **Vocabulary Performance Chart** on the inside back cover of the book.

PART A

Listed in the left-hand column below are ten common word parts, followed by words in which the parts are used. In each blank, write in the letter of the correct definition on the right.

Word Parts	Examples	Definitions
____ 1. **anti-**	antifreeze, antiwar	A. Against, acting against
____ 2. **bi**	bicycle, bigamist	B. Without
____ 3. **en-, em-**	embrace, enter	C. Look, watch
____ 4. **graph, gram**	autograph, diagram	D. Something written or drawn
____ 5. **inter-**	interpreter, interstate	E. Under, below
____ 6. **-less**	homeless, loveless	F. Sound, speech
____ 7. **phon**	telephone, saxophone	G. After
____ 8. **post-**	postpone, postscript	H. Two
____ 9. **spect**	inspecting, spectator	I. Between, among
____ 10. **sub-**	subway, submarine	J. Into, in

PART B

Using the answer line provided, complete each *italicized* word in the sentences below with the correct word part from the box. Not every word part will be used.

A. **anti-**	B. **bi-**	C. **en-**	D. **graph**	E. **inter-**
F. **-less**	G. **phon**	H. **post-**	I. **spect**	J. **sub-**

_____ 11. "P.S." at the end of a note or letter stands for (. . . *script*) ___.

_____ 12. Our fifth-grade teacher, who tried to teach us good grooming, (*in . . . ed*) ___ our fingernails every Monday morning.

_____ 13. In Moscow, taking a (. . . *way*) ___ is a pleasant experience. The underground stations have marble floors, stained glass, and statues.

_____ 14. The flying squirrel is actually (*wing . . .*) ___. It "flies" by spreading folds of skin as it glides short distances.

_____ 15. Zulu tribesmen are not allowed to (. . . *act*) ___ directly with their mothers-in-law but may communicate with them only through another person.

(Continues on next page)

PART C

Use your knowledge of word parts to determine the meaning of the **boldfaced** words. On the answer line, write the letter of each meaning.

_____ 16. Drugs **enslave** people.

        A. arouse against slavery   B. put into slavery   C. come after slavery

_____ 17. My sister is learning **phonics** in her reading class.

        A. the study of speech sounds   B. the study of letters   C. the study of grammar

_____ 18. While my grandfather was in Europe, he sent my grandmother **aerograms**.

        A. tape-recorded messages   B. airmail gifts   C. airmail letters

_____ 19. The army experimented with several **antitank** weapons.

        A. with tanks   B. against tanks   C. in place of tanks

_____ 20. Fifty dollars seems a lot of money for a subscription to a magazine that is published **bimonthly**.

        A. every month   B. every two months   C. every three months

Score   (Number correct) _____ x 5 = _____%

Enter your scores above and in the **Vocabulary Performance Chart** on the inside back cover of the book.

Unit Three

Chapter 13

accessible	prevail
awe	propel
cite	rational
compatible	retort
exempt	retrieve

Chapter 14

dubious	fictitious
ecstatic	gullible
encounter	liable
evolve	miserly
fallacy	pessimist

Chapter 15

elapse	infer
evasive	lethal
fluent	obsession
futile	ordeal
harass	persistent

Chapter 16

convey	subtle
delusion	unique
devise	universal
savor	versatile
stimulate	vivid

Chapter 17

defer	inevitable
endeavor	malicious
equate	option
impose	passive
indignant	patron

Chapter 18

con-	script, scrib
dict	-ship
dis-	tele-
micro-	trans-
ped	tri-

accessible	prevail
awe	propel
cite	rational
compatible	retort
exempt	retrieve

Ten Words in Context

In the space provided, write the letter of the meaning closest to that of each **boldfaced** word. Use the context of the sentences to help you figure out each word's meaning.

1 accessible
(ăk-sĕs′ə-bəl)
-*adjective*

- The department store was not **accessible** from her side of the road, so Kristin looked ahead for a U-turn.
- We always hung the candy canes on the Christmas tree's highest branches, where they weren't **accessible** to the younger children.

Accessible means   A. good to look at.   B. within reach.   C. desirable.

2 awe
(ô)
-*noun*

- Nelson and Donna have different types of heroes. Although Nelson greatly admires Tom Brady, Donna is in **awe** of Oprah Winfrey.
- Sid is in **awe** of his gymnastics coach, whom he considers the greatest man he knows.

Awe means   A. anger.   B. respect.   C. hope.

3 cite
(sīt)
-*verb*

- Jamal was embarrassed but pleased when the teacher **cited** his essay as an example of good writing.
- Tired of picking up after her sister, Kim **cited** examples of her sloppiness: "stacks of papers, piles of dirty clothes, and unwashed dishes."

Cite means   A. to forget.   B. to mention.   C. to ignore.

4 compatible
(kəm-păt′ə-bəl)
-*adjective*

- My former girlfriend and I weren't very **compatible**; whenever she wasn't angry with me, I was angry with her.
- Some sweet and salty foods are **compatible**: for example, chocolate-covered pretzels are delicious.

Compatible means   A. well-known.   B. healthy.   C. able to work together.

5 exempt
(ĭg-zĕmpt′)
-*adjective*

- Since he had never been spanked, my little brother thought he was **exempt** from punishment—until he wrote on the walls in ink.
- Students with A averages were **exempt** from final exams, so the top three students began their vacation early while the rest of us sweated it out on exam day.

Exempt means   A. excused.   B. in fear.   C. hiding.

6 prevail
(prĭ-vāl′)
-*verb*

- Most Hollywood movies have a happy ending: good **prevails** over evil.
- Although Kennedy **prevailed** over Nixon in 1960, eight years later Nixon won the presidency.

Prevail means   A. to win.   B. to watch.   C. to lose.

7 propel
(prə-pĕl′)
-verb

- My brother gave me a shove, which **propelled** me into the lake fully clothed.
- When the wind failed to **propel** the boat, we lowered the sails and turned on the motor.

Propel means   A. to support.   B. to move forward.   C. to raise.

8 rational
(răsh′ə-nəl)
-adjective

- Mr. Tibbs isn't **rational**; in addition to believing he came from another planet, he does crazy things like shoveling snow in his pajamas.
- The belief that breaking a mirror brings seven years of bad luck isn't **rational**. The only bad luck it could really bring is stepping on a sharp piece of broken glass.

Rational means   A. helpful.   B. kind.   C. reasonable.

9 retort
(rĭ-tôrt′)
-noun

- Sue, who is slender, boasted, "Thin is in." So Pat, who is heavy, gave this **retort**: "Well, fat is where it's at."
- When Shelley's balding boyfriend made fun of her new perm, her **retort** was, "Jealous?"

Retort means   A. a wish.   B. an answer.   C. a fact.

10 retrieve
(rĭ-trēv′)
-verb

- My dog Floyd refuses to **retrieve** a thrown Frisbee. Instead of running to bring it back, he only tilts his head and gives me a questioning look.
- I can't **retrieve** my sweater from the library until tomorrow, since the library had closed by the time I realized the sweater was missing.

Retrieve means   A. to remember.   B. to touch.   C. to get back.

Matching Words with Definitions

Following are definitions of the ten words. Clearly write or print each word next to its definition. The sentences above and on the previous page will help you decide on the meaning of each word.

1. ___rational___   Reasonable; logical

2. ___cite___   To mention in support of a point; refer to

3. ___retort___   A sharp, clever, or angry reply

4. ___propel___   To provide the force that moves something; to move something forward

5. ___accessible___   Easily reached or entered

6. ___retrieve___   To get (something) back

7. ___compatible___   Able to get along well together; combining well

8. ___prevail___   To win or win out; triumph; defeat (someone or something)

9. ___awe___   Great respect mixed with wonder and amazement

10. ___exempt___   Free from some unpleasant duty or situation

CAUTION: Do not go any further until you are sure the above answers are correct. Then you can use the definitions to help you in the following practices. Your goal is eventually to know the words well enough so that you don't need to check the definitions at all.

Sentence Check 1

Using the answer line provided, complete each item below with the correct word from the box. Use each word once.

A. **accessible**	B. **awe**	C. **cite**	D. **compatible**	E. **exempt**
F. **prevail**	G. **propel**	H. **rational**	I. **retort**	J. **retrieve**

_____ 1. When I go bowling with Joan, she usually wins, but I always ___ in Scrabble.

_____ 2. Jet engines ___ a plane forward.

_____ 3. I ran back to the ladies' room to ___ my purse, but someone had already taken it.

_____ 4. In my family, a person is ___ from household chores on his or her birthday.

_____ 5. The cabinet above the refrigerator was ___ to Tanya but not to her roommate Mieko, who was much shorter.

_____ 6. The general's uniform and medals filled Scott with ___. However, Marla, who knew the general personally, felt only disrespect for him.

_____ 7. My father thinks everything combines well with peanut butter. He even thinks peanut butter and onions are ___ in a sandwich.

_____ 8. When Bridget writes up her experiment, she will ___ similar studies by other researchers, to show that her results match theirs.

_____ 9. Some people don't think in a(n) ___ way. Their thoughts are governed by emotion, not reason.

_____ 10. There are at least two versions of the joke in which a customer complains that a fly is in his soup. The waiter's ___ is either "That's okay—there's no extra charge" or "Don't worry—he won't drink much."

NOTE: Now check your answers to these items by turning to page 178. Going over the answers carefully will help you prepare for the next two practices, for which answers are not given.

Sentence Check 2

Using the answer lines provided, complete each item below with **two** words from the box. Use each word once.

_____
_____ 1–2. Luis was in ___ of his athletic friend Ben, who seemed to ___ in any contest of strength or speed.

_____
_____ 3–4. The speaker told his high-school audience, "I can ___ dozens of cases of adults who mistakenly thought they were ___ from the harm of cocaine. They all eventually lost their jobs and alienated° their families."

_____
_____ 5–6. Keith and Sara's matchmaking friends were so sure they'd be ___ that they tried everything to ___ the two into each other's arms.

_____   7–8. The prudent° and ___ thing to do is to ask Michael to return your sweater
_____   before you sneak into his room to ___ it behind his back.

_____   9–10. When I complained to my arrogant° landlord that the kitchen shelves were so
_____   high they were ___ only by ladder, his ___ was, "So get a ladder!"

Final Check: *Our Headstrong Baby*

Here is a final opportunity for you to strengthen your knowledge of the ten words. First read the following
selection carefully. Then fill in each blank with a word from the box at the top of the previous page.
(Context clues will help you figure out which word goes in which blank.) Use each word once.

Before our child was born, we truly believed we would be
(1)_____ from many of the restrictions of
our friends who were parents. Being novices° at parenthood,
we were sure a baby and a nicely decorated home could be
(2)_____. We thought we could just
explain to the baby in a calm, (3)_____
manner that certain objects in the house were not to be touched.
But now we are parents, and our illusions° about babies are gone.
Now we are in (4)_____ of a tiny infant's
amazing abilities. We've learned that when an adult and a baby
disagree, the baby will almost always (5)_____. We've learned, too, that a child who
can't even crawl can somehow (6)_____ her little body over to an object that attracts
her. Each day brought another "accident," for which, of course, we blamed our baby. It took us a while to
admit defeat—we could (7)_____ examples of vases broken and books chewed into
pulp. But we finally gave up and realized we had to stop turning our child into a scapegoat°. It was up to us,
not the baby, to avert° daily destruction. We look at our formerly attractive house now and see that every
surface which is (8)_____ to the baby has been cleared of everything but toys. So
now, when our childless friends laugh at us as we (9)_____ our belongings from the
uppermost shelves of the house, this is our (10)_____: "We'll listen to you when you
have a kid of your own."

| Scores | Sentence Check 2 _____ % | Final Check _____ % |

Enter your scores above and in the **Vocabulary Performance Chart** on the inside back cover of the book.

14

dubious	fictitious
ecstatic	gullible
encounter	liable
evolve	miserly
fallacy	pessimist

Ten Words in Context

In the space provided, write the letter of the meaning closest to that of each **boldfaced** word. Use the context of the sentences to help you figure out each word's meaning.

1 dubious
(do͞o′bē-əs)
-*adjective*

● Aretha lacked confidence in her math ability. Even after a long tutoring session, she was **dubious** about her ability to pass the geometry exam.

● Matt was **dubious** about graduate school as preparation for a career in clothing design. He felt work experience might be better.

__B__ *Dubious* means   A. certain.   B. unsure.   C. happy.

2 ecstatic
(ĭk-stăt′ĭk)
-*adjective*

● I wouldn't be just glad if I won the five-million-dollar lottery; I'd be absolutely **ecstatic**.

● The smallest thing, like an ice cream cone on a hot day, a train ride, or a ladybug in the grass, can make a child **ecstatic**.

__C__ *Ecstatic* means   A. active.   B. patient.   C. full of joy.

3 encounter
(ĕn-koun′tər)
-*verb*

● I never expected to **encounter** anyone I knew at the crowded concert, but my friend Jeff sat just two rows in front of me.

● I had a strange dream in which I **encountered** my old boyfriend while I was on my honeymoon.

__B__ *Encounter* means   A. to avoid.   B. to run into.   C. to go with.

4 evolve
(ĭ-vŏlv′)
-*verb*

● The women's club began as an informal get-together and then **evolved** into an educational and support group.

● How did the plan for a block party **evolve** into a citywide celebration?

__A__ *Evolve* means   A. to grow gradually.   B. to fall apart.   C. to shrink.

5 fallacy
(făl′ə-sē)
-*noun*

● It is a **fallacy** for people to think that they can drink and still manage to drive safely.

● To opponents of nuclear energy, the idea that nuclear power plants are safe for humans is a **fallacy**.

__B__ *Fallacy* means   A. a useful idea.   B. an error.   C. a goal.

6 fictitious
(fĭk-tĭsh′əs)
-*adjective*

● The characters in novels are usually totally **fictitious**, but some are based on real people.

● Violence in TV movies may frighten very young children, who have not learned the difference between true and **fictitious** events.

__A__ *Fictitious* means   A. unreal.   B. future.   C. active.

7 gullible
(gŭl'ə-bəl)
-adjective

- Candace is so **gullible** that she believed me when I told her the White House is really yellow.
- You might think I'm **gullible** enough to fall for that old line, but you can't fool me that easily.

C *Gullible* means
    A. suspicious.   B. mean.   C. easily fooled.

8 liable
(lī'ə-bəl)
-adjective

- If you lie to me once, I will think you're **liable** to lie to me again.
- I'm **liable** to start overeating again if I let myself have even one candy bar, cupcake, or cookie, so I'm careful not to give in, even for a moment.

A *Liable* means
    A. likely.   B. unable.   C. unlikely.

9 miserly
(mī'zĕr-lē)
-adjective

- In Charles Dickens's *A Christmas Carol*, Scrooge at first hated to spend money, but he later regretted his **miserly** ways.
- My rich uncle was so **miserly** that he never gave money to charity.

B *Miserly* means
    A. lazy.   B. stingy.   C. bossy.

10 pessimist
(pĕs'ə-mĭst)
-noun

- A **pessimist** can see a bad side to even the best situation.
- My family is very balanced: my father sees the best in everything, but my mother is usually a **pessimist**.

B *Pessimist* means
    A. a pest.   B. one who expects the worst.   C. one who is wise.

Matching Words with Definitions

Following are definitions of the ten words. Clearly write or print each word next to its definition. The sentences above and on the previous page will help you decide on the meaning of each word.

1. _fictitious_   Imaginary; made-up

2. _evolve_   To change gradually; develop

3. _encounter_   To meet, especially unexpectedly

4. _ecstatic_   In a state of great joy; overjoyed

5. _liable_   Likely (to experience or do something unpleasant or dangerous)

6. _pessimist_   A person who tends to see the bad side of things

7. _dubious_   Doubtful

8. _miserly_   Stingy and greedy

9. _fallacy_   A mistaken idea

10. _gullible_   Easily fooled

CAUTION: Do not go any further until you are sure the above answers are correct. Then you can use the definitions to help you in the following practices. Your goal is eventually to know the words well enough so that you don't need to check the definitions at all.

Sentence Check 1

Using the answer line provided, complete each item below with the correct word from the box. Use each word once.

A. **dubious**	B. **ecstatic**	C. **encounter**	D. **evolve**	E. **fallacy**
F. **fictitious**	G. **gullible**	H. **liable**	I. **miserly**	J. **pessimist**

_____ 1. Our grandmother is so ___ that all she ever gives us for our birthdays is a card.

_____ 2. If you tease the dog too much, he's ___ to bite you.

_____ 3. Many children have ___ friends—people or animals who exist only in their imaginations.

_____ 4. I am ___ about Emmet's ability to do the job alone, but I am willing to give him a try.

_____ 5. As I stepped into the garage, I ___(e)d an unexpected visitor—a raccoon.

_____ 6. "I'm ___," said Christine on the day of her college graduation. "I wasn't this happy even on my wedding day."

_____ 7. Don't be such a(n) ___. Just because you did poorly on the midterm doesn't mean you won't pass the course.

_____ 8. It is a(n) ___ that reading without good light ruins your eyesight. Actually, reading in dim light does not harm your vision at all.

_____ 9. Surprising Miguel on his birthday was easy. He's so ___ that we knew he'd believe whatever story we told him.

_____ 10. Interest in the environment has ___(e)d from a simple love of nature into a troubled awareness that we might be destroying our planet.

NOTE: Now check your answers to these items by turning to page 178. Going over the answers carefully will help you prepare for the next two practices, for which answers are not given.

Sentence Check 2

Using the answer lines provided, complete each item below with **two** words from the box. Use each word once.

_____
_____
1–2. When my sister visited California, she ___(e)d Denzel Washington in a department store. Despite feelings of awe°, she managed to get up enough nerve to ask him for his autograph, and she has been ___ ever since.

_____
_____
3–4. Alma is so ___ that her friends often tell her totally ___ stories and then tease her about believing them.

_____
_____
5–6. A ___ person is ___ to end up with lots of money and few friends.

_____   7–8. An extreme ___ believes that bad luck can't be escaped and that it is a ___ to
_____   expect good luck. If such a person were the recipient° of a million dollars, he
    or she would complain about the taxes.

_____   9–10. At first I was ___ about the prospects° of our school's basketball team; I did
_____   not think that they would win even one game. But as the season progressed,
    the team surpassed° all my expectations and ___(e)d into championship
    material.

Final Check: *Mr. Perfect?*

Here is a final opportunity for you to strengthen your knowledge of the ten words. First read the following selection carefully. Then fill in each blank with a word from the box at the top of the previous page. (Context clues will help you figure out which word goes in which blank.) Use each word once.

Kathy was (1)_____ as she told me that she had (2)_____(e)d the "perfect man," as she called him. She insisted he didn't have one single defect°. But I was (3)_____ right from the start. Contrary° to Kathy's view, my own opinion is that "perfection" is a(n) (4)_____—I've never met anyone who was perfect. I must admit that, because of my own bad luck in dating, I am (5)_____ to be more of a (6)_____ than most on this subject. I dated one guy who was so (7)_____ that, when we went to the movies, we had to stay in the theater

after the film had ended so he could supplement° his income—by searching under the seats for dropped coins. Another was addicted to sausages. He ate sausages for breakfast, lunch, and dinner. His strange eating habits alienated° me, and our relationship quickly (8)_____(e)d from bad to "wurst." Then there were all those fellows who couldn't quite tell the truth. They disclosed° so many (9)_____ details about their lives that they should have been novelists. To cite° a few examples, they told me they were in college (they weren't), they had jobs (they didn't), and they had gotten perfect scores on their SATs (they hadn't). So you can see why I'm apprehensive° about encouraging Kathy, who is so (10)_____ that she believes anything anyone says. I can't wait to meet Mr. Perfect. He's probably either a liar or a lunatic. And I'm not sure which is worse.

Scores   Sentence Check 2 _____%   Final Check _____%

Enter your scores above and in the **Vocabulary Performance Chart** on the inside back cover of the book.

elapse	infer
evasive	lethal
fluent	obsession
futile	ordeal
harass	persistent

Ten Words in Context

In the space provided, write the letter of the meaning closest to that of each **boldfaced** word. Use the context of the sentences to help you figure out each word's meaning.

1 elapse
(ĭ-lăps′)
-verb

- Although four years had **elapsed** since I last saw Marian, we talked as if we'd never parted.
- When I'm busy with work I enjoy, I never notice how much time is **elapsing**.

C   *Elapse* means   A. to develop.   B. to go back.   C. to go by.

2 evasive
(ĭ-vā′sĭv)
-adjective

- The Rothmans worried that their son was hiding something when he became **evasive** about where he had been and what he'd been doing.
- We didn't want anyone at school to know our father was in the hospital, so we were **evasive** about him, saying only, "He has to be away for a while."

B   *Evasive* means   A. truthful.   B. indefinite.   C. detailed.

3 fluent
(flōō′ənt)
-adjective

- To work in a foreign country, it helps to be **fluent** in its language.
- Jamila wanted to hear what was wrong with her car in simple, everyday words. She was not **fluent** in the language of auto mechanics.

C   *Fluent* means   A. able to remember.   B. able to teach.   C. able to express oneself.

4 futile
(fyōōt′l)
-adjective

- My best friend is so stubborn that once he has made a decision, it is **futile** to try to change his mind.
- I'm convinced that washing machines eat socks, so it is **futile** to try to find matching pairs in a load of clean laundry.

A   *Futile* means   A. hopeless.   B. easy.   C. useful.

5 harass
(hə-răs′)
-verb

- A few students in the cafeteria like to **harass** everyone else by frequently clinking their silverware and stamping their feet.
- Sometimes it doesn't help to **harass** people about quitting smoking. Bothering them all the time may make them resist quitting.

B   *Harass* means   A. to injure.   B. to annoy.   C. to please.

6 infer
(ĭn-fûr′)
-verb

- The fact that the old man left his fortune to strangers led us to **infer** he was not fond of his children.
- Since you went hiking on Super Bowl Sunday, I **inferred** that you were not a football fan.

A   *Infer* means   A. to conclude.   B. to forget.   C. to conceal.

7 lethal
(lē′thəl)
-adjective

● My father is not alive today because of a **lethal** combination of driving and drinking.

● Jake is so good at karate that his hands are **lethal** weapons. Because he realizes he could kill somebody, he is very careful with his karate skills.

_B_ _Lethal_ means   A. rare.   (B.) deadly.   C. hopeful.

8 obsession
(əb-sĕsh′ən)
-noun

● Psychologists help people troubled by **obsessions** to gain control over their thinking, so they are not bothered by the same thoughts over and over.

● Going to garage sales was at first just a hobby. But bargain-hunting has become such an **obsession** that I can't seem to stop going to them.

___ _Obsession_ means   A. a helpful habit.   B. a possession.   C. a constant concern.

9 ordeal
(ôr-dēl′)
-noun

● Even if you are in good physical condition, running cross-country is an **ordeal**.

● Hannah came out of the difficult three-hour test, sighed, and said, "What an **ordeal**. I'm worn out."

___ _Ordeal_ means   A. a welcome event.   B. a sure success.   C. a difficult challenge.

10 persistent
(pər-sĭs′tənt)
-adjective

● At first Tony wouldn't go out with Lola, but she was **persistent** in asking him. Now they're engaged.

● I am a very **persistent** salesman. I work with customers for as long as it takes for them to buy something.

___ _Persistent_ means   A. stubborn.   B. useless.   C. late.

Matching Words with Definitions

Following are definitions of the ten words. Clearly write or print each word next to its definition. The sentences above and on the previous page will help you decide on the meaning of each word.

1. _____ To draw a conclusion from evidence

2. _____ An idea or feeling, often unreasonable, which completely fills someone's mind; fascination

3. _____ A very difficult or painful experience

4. _____ Deliberately unclear

5. _____ Useless; unable to succeed

6. _____ Able to cause death; deadly

7. _____ Refusing to quit; stubbornly continuing

8. _____ To pass or slip by (usually said of time)

9. _____ Able to express oneself with skill and ease

10. _____ To constantly irritate or disturb; bother

CAUTION: Do not go any further until you are sure the above answers are correct. Then you can use the definitions to help you in the following practices. Your goal is eventually to know the words well enough so that you don't need to check the definitions at all.

Sentence Check 1

Using the answer line provided, complete each item below with the correct word from the box. Use each word once.

A. elapse	B. evasive	C. fluent	D. futile	E. harass
F. infer	G. lethal	H. obsession	I. ordeal	J. persistent

_____   1. Roger knew a few Chinese phrases, but he was not ___ enough in Chinese to carry on a conversation.

_____   2. Photographers ___(e)d the movie star, photographing her even on a private beach.

_____   3. When I'm on a diet, the thought of eating pizza becomes an ___ for me.

_____   4. Reporters tried to pin the President down on his plan to rescue the hostages, but he always gave a(n) ___ answer.

_____   5. After ten seconds ___, a bell rings, and the game-show host reads the next question.

_____   6. Selling drugs can be a(n) ___ occupation—there is almost one drug-related murder a day in Philadelphia alone.

_____   7. Going to the veterinarian is a real ___ for our dog, who begins to shiver in fear at the sight of the vet's office.

_____   8. It is ___ to try to have a conversation with Manny when a football game is on television because his eyes are glued to the set.

_____   9. Eduardo had to work full-time to support his family, but he still earned his college degree by being ___ in his studies even when he was busy or tired.

_____   10. It was easy for the teacher to ___ that one of the students had copied the other's paper—both had the same wording in several paragraphs.

NOTE: Now check your answers to these items by turning to page 178. Going over the answers carefully will help you prepare for the next two practices, for which answers are not given.

Sentence Check 2

Using the answer lines provided, complete each item below with **two** words from the box. Use each word once.

_____
_____   1–2. Wild mushrooms were an ___ of my aunt, who picked and ate them whenever possible. Unfortunately, her abnormal interest proved ___, for she died after a meal of poisonous creamed mushrooms on toast.

_____
_____   3–4. The student hesitated and then gave a vague answer. "From your ___ answer," said the teacher, "I ___ that you haven't studied the chapter. In the future, maybe you could put a few minutes of homework on your daily agenda°."

_____   5–6. Five days ___(e)d before the forest fire was put out. It was an especially difficult ___ for the firefighters, who had to get by on very little sleep.

_____   7–8. You must be ___ in learning a language if you wish to become ___ in it. Study the textbook regularly, and then reinforce° what you've learned by practicing with language tapes or computer programs.

_____   9–10. Cats on my street have learned they can safely ___ the dog chained in my neighbor's yard. And they derive° much pleasure from doing so. The poor dog, however, hasn't seemed to learn that it is ___ to threaten the cats.

Final Check: *A Narrow Escape*

Here is a final opportunity for you to strengthen your knowledge of the ten words. First read the following selection carefully. Then fill in each blank with a word from the box at the top of the previous page. (Context clues will help you figure out which word goes in which blank.) Use each word once.

"We'll never escape. *Never.*" The gruesome° thought had become an (1)_____—I could think of nothing else.

When Craig and I had hopped into the truck to hitch a ride toward Frankfurt, Germany, the two truck drivers were very friendly. Although we were not (2)_____ in their language—we couldn't even figure out what language they were speaking, but we knew it wasn't German—they spoke a little English. So we could (3)_____ from their words and motions that they would take us to Frankfurt after they delivered a package. But they drove around for such a long time that we began to be dubious° they really were making a delivery.

As the hours (4)_____(e)d, we became worried. Our worry turned to fear as we realized the men were arguing, and it seemed to be about us. Occasionally the driver would ask us a question, like "Your parents rich Americans?" or "You their only child?" The men apologized for the delay and were (5)_____ in repeating their promise to get us to Frankfurt "very soon." But they became more and more (6)_____ about exactly when "very soon" would be, and that's when I started to think we might never escape.

Suddenly, they pulled up to an empty warehouse in the middle of nowhere. The driver showed us a long knife and said, "You give us your parents' address." This overt° threat told me we were being kidnapped. With the truck finally stopped, I grabbed the door handle and tried to get out. But my efforts were (7)_____; the door was locked. Knowing the driver had a (8)_____ weapon scared me badly, but trying to sound braver than I felt, I shouted, "Let us out NOW!" Craig joined me in shouting at the men. Suddenly they began arguing in their own language again; the second man seemed to be (9)_____ing the driver to do something. Finally the driver threw up his hands in disgust. The second man unlocked the door, opened it, and shouted "YOU OUT NOW." He didn't have to say it twice. We propelled° ourselves out of that truck and eventually found our way to a town. We could hardly believe that our (10)_____ was over and we were safe.

Scores   Sentence Check 2 _____%   Final Check _____%

Enter your scores above and in the **Vocabulary Performance Chart** on the inside back cover of the book.

convey	subtle
delusion	unique
devise	universal
savor	versatile
stimulate	vivid

Ten Words in Context

In the space provided, write the letter of the meaning closest to that of each **boldfaced** word. Use the context of the sentences to help you figure out each word's meaning.

1 convey
(kən-vā′)
-verb

- Using sign language, chimpanzees can **convey** such ideas as "Candy sweet" and "Give me hug."
- At my parents' twenty-fifth wedding anniversary celebration, I read a poem I had written for them to **convey** my congratulations and love.

___ *Convey* means   A. to think of.   B. to prevent.   C. to communicate.

2 delusion
(dĭ-loō′zhən)
-noun

- Alex clings to the **delusion** of being in total control even when drunk. In reality, he then lacks both judgment and muscle control.
- Chang holds the **delusion** that money is everything. Sadly, in seeking financial success, he neglects what is truly important, such as family and friends.

___ *Delusion* means   A. a pleasure.   B. a wrong belief.   C. an action.

3 devise
(dĭ-vīz′)
-verb

- In the 1880s an American woman **devised** a machine that sprayed dinnerware with hot, soapy water—the first automatic dishwasher.
- The police had **devised** a plan to catch the thief, but he escaped on the freight elevator.

___ *Devise* means   A. to create.   B. to forget.   C. to carry.

4 savor
(sā′vər)
-verb

- Katie **savored** the candy bar, eating it bit by bit so that the pleasure would last as long as possible.
- Given a rare chance to enjoy the beach, I **savored** every moment in the warm sun.

___ *Savor* means   A. to save for later.   B. to enjoy.   C. to ignore.

5 stimulate
(stĭm′yə-lāt′)
-verb

- The teacher hoped to **stimulate** her students' interest in reading by choosing books that related to their own lives.
- I tried to **stimulate** my sick rabbit's appetite by offering him choice bits of carrots and celery.

___ *Stimulate* means   A. to make active.   B. to recognize.   C. to discourage.

6 subtle
(sŭt′l)
-adjective

- Animal actors are trained to respond to human signals too **subtle** to be noticed by the audience.
- Although Yasmin was born in Alabama, she has lived in New York for many years. As a result, her Southern accent is so **subtle** that some of her friends don't even notice it.

___ *Subtle* means   A. obvious.   B. peaceful.   C. slight.

7 unique
(yoo-nēk′)
-adjective

● Any live musical performance is **unique**—the music will never again be played in exactly the same way.

● My talents are **unique** in my family. For example, I'm the only one who can whistle through my nose.

__ *Unique* means   A. active.   B. hardly noticeable.   C. one of a kind.

8 universal
(yoo′nə-vûr′səl)
-adjective

● The United Nations was founded to advance **universal** freedom and peace.

● The film had **universal** success—it was a hit in all parts of the United States and in other countries as well.

__ *Universal* means   A. limited.   B. throughout the world.   C. throughout time.

9 versatile
(vûr′sə-təl)
-adjective

● Our computer is **versatile**. It can balance the family checkbook, do word processing, keep tax records, and play against me in chess.

● Edie is the most **versatile** person I know: she paints, sings, does gymnastics, and is a math whiz.

__ *Versatile* means   A. having many abilities.   B. boring.   C. out of control.

10 vivid
(vĭv′ĭd)
-adjective

● To make the living room bright and dramatic, we decorated it in **vivid** shades of red.

● At funerals, most people wear black or dark gray clothing with little or no **vivid** color.

__ *Vivid* means   A. dull.   B. bright.   C. pale.

Matching Words with Definitions

Following are definitions of the ten words. Clearly write or print each word next to its definition. The sentences above and on the previous page will help you decide on the meaning of each word.

1. _____ Unlike any other; one of a kind

2. _____ To invent; think up; create

3. _____ Bright; brightly colored; striking

4. _____ Hardly noticeable; not obvious

5. _____ To communicate; make known

6. _____ To cause to become active or more active; arouse

7. _____ Worldwide; widespread

8. _____ To taste or smell with pleasure; to appreciate fully

9. _____ A false opinion or belief

10. _____ Able to do many things or serve many purposes well

CAUTION: Do not go any further until you are sure the above answers are correct. Then you can use the definitions to help you in the following practices. Your goal is eventually to know the words well enough so that you don't need to check the definitions at all.

Sentence Check 1

Using the answer line provided, complete each item below with the correct word from the box. Use each word once.

A. convey	B. delusion	C. devise	D. savor	E. stimulate
F. subtle	G. unique	H. universal	I. versatile	J. vivid

_____ 1. The chimp ___(e)d a way of reaching the banana that hung from the ceiling. She piled one box on top of another and climbed up.

_____ 2. The "terrible twos" is a ___ stage of childhood. In every culture, children start demanding independence at about this age.

_____ 3. Breathing deeply, I ___(e)d my favorite summer smell—freshly-cut grass.

_____ 4. Pam's eyes blinked a ___ message that only her husband saw: "I think we should get ready to leave before it gets any later."

_____ 5. The painting, with its bright stripes of shocking pink, green, and yellow, was so ___ that it glowed even in dim light.

_____ 6. Even if Mr. Pierce sang his lecture while dancing on his desk, he couldn't ___ my interest in geology. To me, it's the most boring of subjects.

_____ 7. When Geraldo saw the Grand Canyon, he made no attempt to describe it on a postcard. He felt that the glories of this natural wonder were too amazing to ___ in words.

_____ 8. "I thought she loved me, but it was only a ___," said Lawrence. "She was just a good friend."

_____ 9. This Egyptian bracelet is ___ since no other bracelet in the world is made with the same combination of gems and precious metals.

_____ 10. From a child's point of view, a simple cardboard box is very ___. It can be a dollhouse, a bucket, a desk, or even a funny hat.

NOTE: Now check your answers to these items by turning to page 178. Going over the answers carefully will help you prepare for the next two practices, for which answers are not given.

Sentence Check 2

Using the answer lines provided, complete each item below with **two** words from the box. Use each word once.

_____
_____ 1–2. When Jill applies for a job, it will be to her advantage to ___ to interviewers just how ___ she is. Employers will welcome her many different skills.

_____
_____ 3–4. I ___ the time I have alone with my brother, who is unlike anyone else. He has a ___ way of looking at things.

_____
_____ 5–6. I wish someone would ___ a way to ___ children's appetites so they will feel hungry for something besides pizza and peanut butter.

_____   7–8. Rosa enjoys wearing ___ colors, like red and purple, but I prefer more ___
_____   shades, such as pale pinks and blues.

_____   9–10. Denny truly believes that ___ peace will occur during his lifetime. Being a
_____   pessimist°, I think that the possibility of world harmony is a ___.

Final Check: *The Power of Advertising*

Here is a final opportunity for you to strengthen your knowledge of the ten words. First read the following selection carefully. Then fill in each blank with a word from the box at the top of the previous page. (Context clues will help you figure out which word goes in which blank.) Use each word once.

I am convinced that advertising agencies could sell people last week's garbage. Being masters of propaganda°, they make everything sound good. Using evasive° language, advertisers make such vague but impressive statements as "Professionals recommend our skin creams." (The careful consumer will ask, "Professionals in what field?") The agencies are also skilled at using richly appealing images. For example, newspaper ads never sell "brightly colored towels." Instead they sell "petal-soft bath sheets in a variety of (1)_____ rainbow colors." Perfumes in ads don't make you "smell good"; they "invite you to please that special man in your life with this (2)_____ yet unmistakable scent of tea

petal-soft bath sheets in a variety of vivid rainbow colors

roses." Food ads (3)_____ your appetite by offering "a sauce carefully blended to produce an unforgettable taste that you and your guests will (4)_____." Clothing ads (5)_____ the idea that if you wear a particular suit or dress, you will be classier than the next person. Other ads, such as those for computers, tell you how (6)_____ their products will make you, suggesting that they will give you more skills than others have. Advertisements must have (7)_____ appeal to attract millions of people. Yet they must also persuade all those people to accept the (8)_____ that they will be (9)_____ if they buy a particular product. Yes, I'll bet an advertising agency *could* sell last week's garbage to naive° or gullible° people. The agency would simply (10)_____ an ad saying, "Nowhere else can you find a gift with so powerful an aroma—one that overflows with bittersweet memories of yesterday, yet hints that it will grow stronger with each passing day."

| Scores | Sentence Check 2 _____% | Final Check _____% |

defer	inevitable
endeavor	malicious
equate	option
impose	passive
indignant	patron

Ten Words in Context

In the space provided, write the letter of the meaning closest to that of each **boldfaced** word. Use the context of the sentences to help you figure out each word's meaning.

1 defer
(dĭ-fûr′)
-verb

● The children showed great respect for their grandmother and **deferred** to her every wish.

● When it comes to fixing cars, I **defer** to my brother's judgment. He knows much more about auto mechanics than I do.

___ *Defer* means   A. to object.   B. to give in.   C. to want.

2 endeavor
(ĕn-dĕv′ər)
-verb

● Becky **endeavored** to raise money for Christmas presents by selling candy and cookies door to door.

● Your company would be wise to hire Jesse. He will **endeavor** to do his best at whatever jobs you give him.

___ *Endeavor* means   A. to try.   B. to pretend.   C. to step aside.

3 equate
(ĭ-kwāt′)
-verb

● It would be a mistake to **equate** the two teams just because they both have perfect records. One team has played much stronger opponents.

● Don't **equate** all homework assignments with busywork. Homework can increase one's understanding of a subject.

___ *Equate* means   A. to exchange.   B. to consider to be the same.   C. to enjoy.

4 impose
(ĭm-pōz′)
-verb

● Our neighbor pounded on our door as we were sitting down to eat. "I'm sorry to **impose** on you during dinner," he said, "but I need to borrow a fire extinguisher."

● Roy is always asking favors, yet people never seem to notice how much he **imposes** on them.

___ *Impose* means   A. to selfishly bother.   B. to improve.   C. to spy.

5 indignant
(ĭn-dĭg′nənt)
-adjective

● My mother becomes **indignant** when she sees parents treat their children with disrespect.

● When she was falsely accused of stealing a classmate's gold chain, the student became very **indignant**.

___ *Indignant* means   A. angry.   B. patient.   C. amused.

6 inevitable
(ĭn-ĕv′ĭ-tə-bəl)
-adjective

● I am such a chocoholic that if you put a brownie in front of me, it is **inevitable** that I will eat it.

● We try so hard to look and stay young, but aging is **inevitable**.

___ *Inevitable* means   A. unlikely.   B. surprising.   C. unavoidable.

7 malicious
(mă-lĭsh′əs)
-*adjective*

● Bullies are **malicious**—they take pleasure in hurting others.
● Raquel loves **malicious** gossip. The more spiteful it is, the more she likes it, and the more likely she is to repeat it.

__ *Malicious* means   A. mean.   B. ambitious.   C. common.

8 option
(ŏp′shən)
-*noun*

● When my overweight uncle was told, "Stop eating so much or you'll have a heart attack within five years," he didn't like either **option**.
● Noah thinks a multiple-choice test allows him to choose more than one **option**.

__ *Option* means   A. an opinion.   B. an advantage.   C. a choice.

9 passive
(păs′ĭv)
-*adjective*

● Taylor is very **passive**. He waits for things to happen instead of making them happen.
● Students learn more when they take part in class discussions instead of simply being **passive** listeners.

__ *Passive* means   A. insincere.   B. inactive.   C. flexible.

10 patron
(pā′trən)
-*noun*

● The punk-rock star was a good **patron** of the beauty shop. She came in at least once a week to change her hair color.
● Many of the diner's **patrons** were stagehands who worked at the theater across the street.

__ *Patron* means   A. an advertiser.   B. an owner.   C. a customer.

Matching Words with Definitions

Following are definitions of the ten words. Clearly write or print each word next to its definition. The sentences above and on the previous page will help you decide on the meaning of each word.

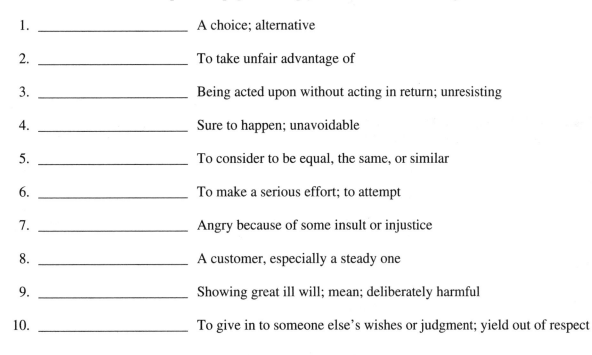

1. _____ A choice; alternative

2. _____ To take unfair advantage of

3. _____ Being acted upon without acting in return; unresisting

4. _____ Sure to happen; unavoidable

5. _____ To consider to be equal, the same, or similar

6. _____ To make a serious effort; to attempt

7. _____ Angry because of some insult or injustice

8. _____ A customer, especially a steady one

9. _____ Showing great ill will; mean; deliberately harmful

10. _____ To give in to someone else's wishes or judgment; yield out of respect

CAUTION: Do not go any further until you are sure the above answers are correct. Then you can use the definitions to help you in the following practices. Your goal is eventually to know the words well enough so that you don't need to check the definitions at all.

Sentence Check 1

Using the answer line provided, complete each item below with the correct word from the box. Use each word once.

A. defer	B. endeavor	C. equate	D. impose	E. indignant
F. inevitable	G. malicious	H. option	I. passive	J. patron

_____   1. When rats are crowded together, it's ___ they will fight with each other.

_____   2. I have only two ___s at work: I can do what my boss asks, or I can be fired.

_____   3. In our society, we too often ___ happiness with money.

_____   4. Mort isn't a(n) ___ football fan. He actively participates by jumping out of his seat and yelling until he's hoarse.

_____   5. I was the store's most loyal ___ until new management raised the prices, and then I started shopping elsewhere.

_____   6. Heidi is so ___ that she makes up lies to ruin other people's reputations.

_____   7. "I don't want to ___ on you," Scott said, "but if you're going to the post office, would you get me some stamps?"

_____   8. When his wife accused him of never helping around the house, Mac was ___. Hadn't he just built a deck off the kitchen?

_____   9. Our instructor doesn't expect us to ___ to his opinions just because he's the teacher; he wants us to think for ourselves.

_____   10. Many climbers who have ___(e)d to reach the top of Mount Everest have died on the way.

NOTE: Now check your answers to these items by turning to page 178. Going over the answers carefully will help you prepare for the next two practices, for which answers are not given.

Sentence Check 2

Using the answer lines provided, complete each item below with **two** words from the box. Use each word once.

_____
_____   1–2. ___ that the boys had thrown rocks at the monkeys, the zookeeper said, "Don't ___ being an animal with having no feelings." Feeling remorse°, the boys later wrote a note of apology.

_____
_____   3–4. Rita, a(n) ___ of Angelo's restaurant for several years, has ___(e)d without success to copy Angelo's delicious spaghetti sauce. Now she has given up. "I've learned it is futile° even to try," she says.

_____
_____   5–6. "If you remain so ___ that you don't object when Jean takes advantage of you, she'll just ___ on you more and more," my friend warned.

_____   7–8. Since Sam's family is so poor, it seems ___ that he'll work full-time
_____   as soon as he finishes high school. He won't have the ___ of going to college
                                 right away. However, he plans to be prudent° in handling the money he'll
                                 earn and then enroll in college in a couple of years.

_____   9–10. Jerome is so ___ that he goes out of his way to hurt anyone who won't ___
_____   to his wishes. I have great contempt° for people who are that mean and self-
                                 centered.

Final Check: *Waiter*

Here is a final opportunity for you to strengthen your knowledge of the ten words. First read the following selection carefully. Then fill in each blank with a word from the box at the top of the previous page. (Context clues will help you figure out which word goes in which blank.) Use each word once.

The loud voice of the young man at the next table startled me. He was (1)_____ about some undeserved criticism the waiter had received. He said to the waiter, "Why did you just stand there and let that woman denounce° you like that without sticking up for yourself? You were like a(n) (2)_____ little child."

"I beg your pardon, sir," the waiter answered. "That woman is a(n) (3)_____ of this restaurant. I (4)_____ to treat our customers with respect."

"Even those who (5)_____ on you by being as demanding as that woman was? Even those who think they're better than you because you're waiting on them?"

"You seem to (6)_____ my polite manner with weakness," the waiter answered. "I don't like arrogant° customers, but they're part of a waiter's territory. Standing up publicly to the woman may seem like a smart move to you, but it would have made two things (7)_____: an ugly scene and the loss of my job."

"But you have no (8)_____," the customer insisted. "You can't let people harass° you, ever—especially when they're being (9)_____, giving you a hard time for no good reason."

"You're giving me just as hard a time as that woman did," was the waiter's retort°. "Why should I (10) _____ to your opinion and not hers?"

| Scores | Sentence Check 2 _____% | Final Check _____% |

Enter your scores above and in the **Vocabulary Performance Chart** on the inside back cover of the book.

con-	script, scrib
dict	-ship
dis-	tele-
micro-	trans-
ped	tri-

Ten Word Parts in Context

Figure out the meanings of the following ten word parts by looking *closely* and *carefully* at the context in which they appear. Then, in the space provided, write the letter of the meaning closest to that of each word part.

1 con-

- Members of the **congregation** screamed when the minister fell down in the middle of his sermon.
- "You know," Mr. Warner told his band, "the trombones are supposed to play with the **conductor**, not against him."

___ The word part *con-* means   A. write.   B. together.   C. foot.

2 dict

- "The job of our country's **dictator** is to speak," said the general. "He does not have to listen."
- If I say no, Malik says yes. He loves to **contradict** me.

___ The word part *dict* means   A. speak.   B. with.   C. foot.

3 dis-

- It **displeases** Tai to hear his girlfriend say bad things about herself all the time.
- Before they **disappeared** from the earth, dinosaurs were around for 140 million years.

___ The word part *dis-* means   A. write.   B. by hand.   C. opposite of.

4 micro-

- In World War II, spies took **microphotographs** and then made them even smaller, the size of a printed period.
- **Microbiology** is the study of life forms so tiny they cannot be seen by the naked eye.

___ The word part *micro-* means   A. quality.   B. small.   C. far.

5 ped

- Humans and apes aren't the only **bipeds**. Birds also walk on two feet.
- I like to give myself a **pedicure** in the summer so my toes look neat and polished in open-toed shoes.

___ The word part *ped* means   A. over.   B. not.   C. foot.

6 script, scrib

- The author of the play didn't like it when actors spoke words that were not in the **script**.
- Travel writers use richly detailed language to **describe** the places they have visited.

___ The word part *script* or *scrib* means   A. time.   B. write.   C. remember.

7 -ship

- Does good **citizenship** require following all the rules all the time?
- The two elderly sisters live together to provide each other with help and **companionship**.

___ The word part *-ship* means

A. state of being.   B. across.   C. the opposite of.

8 tele-

- Through the **telephoto** lens, the distant eagle came clearly into view.
- Before the **telephone** was invented, people could not speak to faraway loved ones.

___ The word part *tele-* means

A. before.   B. three.   C. far.

9 trans-

- I had to **transfer** a large package from my right hand to my left in order to reach for my keys and open the door.
- It's hard to **translate** Zulu sounds into written English because the Zulu language includes clicks, ticks, and pops.

___ The word part *trans-* means

A. heat.   B. change.   C. again.

10 tri-

- Stan bought three rattles, three little blankets, and three knitted caps. He's the proud grandfather of **triplets**.
- Mara, Tod, and I have formed a guitar **trio**. Now all we need are three guitars.

___ The word part *tri-* means

A. beyond.   B. three.   C. good.

Matching Word Parts with Definitions

Following are definitions of the ten word parts. Clearly write or print each word part next to its definition. The sentences above and on the previous page will help you decide on the meaning of each word part.

1. _____ State, quality, or condition

2. _____ Three

3. _____ With, together

4. _____ Far; distant

5. _____ Speak

6. _____ Change, beyond, across

7. _____ Not; the opposite of

8. _____ Write

9. _____ Small

10. _____ Foot

CAUTION: Do not go any further until you are sure the above answers are correct. Then you can use the definitions to help you in the following practices. Your goal is eventually to know the word parts well enough so that you don't need to check the definitions at all.

Sentence Check 1

Using the answer line provided, complete each *italicized* word below with the correct word part from the box. Use each word part once.

A. con-	**B.** dict	**C.** dis-	**D.** micro-	**E.** ped
F. script, scrib	**G.** -ship	**H.** tele-	**I.** trans-	**J.** tri-

_____   1. The weather forecaster (*pre . . . ed*) ___ rain, but we got the opposite of what he'd said: a lovely sunny day.

_____   2. Only one foot is required to operate the piano (*. . . als*) ___.

_____   3. To hold her camera still, the photographer put it on a (. . . *pod*) ___, a three-legged support.

_____   4. The organ (. . . *plant*) ___ involved replacing the child's damaged kidney with a kidney from his father.

_____   5. In (*partner . . .*) ___ with local businesses, the mayor fought graffiti.

_____   6. "Teenagers don't like to be different. They desperately want to (. . . *form*) ___," said Mr. Gilbert, "but with their friends, not with their parents."

_____   7. Aisha and Hollis get along very well even though they strongly (. . . *agree*) ___ on politics.

_____   8. Libraries can store huge amounts of printed material in small spaces by photographing the material on (. . . *film*) ___.

_____   9. My grandfather is very religious; he reads the (. . . *ures*) ___ every morning.

_____   10. Because the presentation of Academy Awards is (. . . *vised*) ___ live, even people thousands of miles away can see it as it happens.

NOTE: Now check your answers to these items by turning to page 178. Going over the answers carefully will help you prepare for the next two practices, for which answers are not given.

Sentence Check 2

Using the answer line provided, complete each *italicized* word in the sentences below with the correct word part from the box. Use each word part once.

_____
_____   1–2. Many parents (. . . *approve*) ___ of their children's watching more than a couple of hours of (. . . *vision*) ___ each day. Watching TV is passive°, and they feel children should be active.

_____
_____   3–4. The text of a play is often greatly (. . . *formed*) ___ between the time the (*manu . . .*) ___ is first written and the first live performance is given. When an author actually hears the dialog° spoken, he or she is liable° to see many ways to improve the lines.

_____ 5–6. No matter how hard my persistent° little nephew (. . . *als*) ___ his (. . . *cycle*) ___, he can't keep up with his sister on a two-wheeler. But that doesn't deter° him from trying.

_____ 7–8. The word (*male . . . ion*) "___" means "curse." It (. . . *nects*) ___ two word parts meaning "badly" and "speak."

_____ 9–10. "The secret to (*scholar . . .*) ___ in biology," Professor Kant told Don, "is to spend your time looking at cells through a (. . . *scope*) ___, not staring at all the females in the class!"

Final Check: *Black Widow Spiders*

Here is a final opportunity for you to strengthen your knowledge of the ten word parts. First read the following selection carefully. Then complete each *italicized* word in the parentheses below with a word part from the box at the top of the previous page. (Context clues will help you figure out which word part goes in which blank.) Use each word part once.

If you stopped the average (. . . *estrian*) (1)_____ walking down the street and asked, "What creature do you fear most?" you might get this answer: "The black widow spider." However, it's a fallacy° that the black widow is very dangerous. Bees kill 120 times as many Americans as black widows do. In addition, there is an antidote° to the spider's poison. People can tolerate bees, but they can't (. . . *cend*) (2)_____ their fear of black widows. Perhaps that phobia° is fed by the knowledge of how the spiders got their name: the female, who has an hourglass-shaped red mark on her belly, sometimes eats the male.

My nephew, who lives in California, has repeatedly told me over the (. . . *phone*) (3)_____ of his war with black widows. And nearly every e-mail he sends (. . . *tains*) (4)_____ the (*post . . .*) (5)_____ "P. S. House still has black widows." When he finds the black spider with the double red (. . . *angles*) (6)_____ on her belly, the (*ver . . .*) (7)_____ is always "Guilty." With a can of insect spray, he blasts the almost (. . . *scopic*) (8)_____ little lady in her web. And when he has finished (. . . *honoring*) (9)_____ the defenseless spider in this way, he throws away any remaining chance of gaining her (*friend . . .*) (10)_____ by pounding her to death with a rolled-up magazine.

My nephew is dogmatic° on the subject of black widows. Whenever I tell him he's being unfair to them, he becomes indignant° and insists he has a legitimate° right to do away with them.

"Fine," I told him. "Let's just hope that in your next life, you don't come back as an eight-legged insect."

Scores	Sentence Check 2 _____%	Final Check _____%

The box at the right lists twenty-five words from Unit Three. Using the clues at the bottom of the page, fill in these words to complete the puzzle that follows.

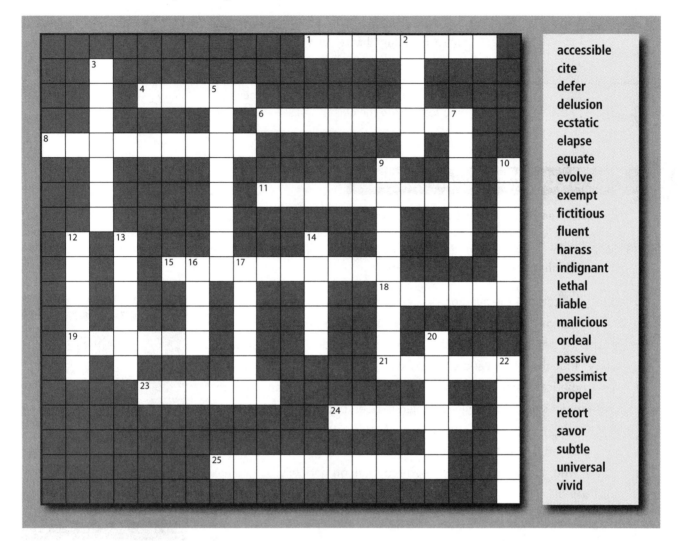

accessible
cite
defer
delusion
ecstatic
elapse
equate
evolve
exempt
fictitious
fluent
harass
indignant
lethal
liable
malicious
ordeal
passive
pessimist
propel
retort
savor
subtle
universal
vivid

ACROSS

1. A false opinion or belief

4. To give in to someone else's wishes or judgment

6. Showing great ill will; mean; deliberately harmful

8. A person who tends to see the bad side of things

11. Angry because of some insult or injustice

15. Easily reached or entered

18. A sharp, clever, or angry reply

19. To pass or slip by (usually said of time)

21. Likely (to experience or do something unpleasant or dangerous)

23. To consider to be equal, the same, or similar

24. A very difficult or painful experience

25. Imaginary; made-up

DOWN

2. To taste or smell with pleasure; to appreciate fully

3. Being acted upon without acting in return

5. In a state of great joy

7. Hardly noticeable; not obvious

9. Worldwide; widespread

10. Able to express oneself with skill and ease

12. To provide the force that moves something; to move something forward

13. Able to cause death; deadly

14. Bright; brightly colored; striking

16. To mention in support of a point; refer to

17. Free from some unpleasant duty or situation

20. To constantly irritate or disturb; bother

22. To change gradually; develop

PART A

Choose the word that best completes each item and write it in the space provided.

_____ 1. The air escaping from the balloon ___ it across the table and into the punch bowl.

A. propelled   B. devised   C. inferred   D. imposed

_____ 2. I used a fishing pole to ___ my hat from the duck pond.

A. savor   B. retrieve   C. infer   D. stimulate

_____ 3. When the usually peppy dog became ___ and wouldn't play, Marta knew he must be ill.

A. ecstatic   B. passive   C. unique   D. futile

_____ 4. Lisa, who is unusually short, had her kitchen built with cabinets low enough to be ___ to her.

A. subtle   B. indignant   C. accessible   D. vivid

_____ 5. Kia turned her ___ of being lost in the desert into good fortune by selling the story to a movie studio.

A. ordeal   B. pessimist   C. retort   D. patron

_____ 6. After denting his parents' car, Victor let several months ___ before he asked to borrow the car again.

A. evolve   B. prevail   C. devise   D. elapse

_____ 7. Using only gestures, Tina managed to ___ to Jerry the message that she would meet him at the Student Center at two o'clock.

A. impose   B. savor   C. cite   D. convey

_____ 8. The Broadway dancer dyed her hair a ___ red so she would stand out among all the blondes and brunettes in the chorus line.

A. vivid   B. versatile   C. futile   D. universal

_____ 9. My ___ uncle refuses to give money to charity, claiming that charity begins and ends at home.

A. exempt   B. miserly   C. liable   D. rational

_____ 10. Marjorie wanted her prom dress to be ___, and it was—no one else wore a yellow-and-black gown that looked like an overripe banana.

A. gullible   B. unique   C. dubious   D. lethal

(Continues on next page)

PART B

On the answer line, write the letter of the choice that best completes each item.

_____ 11. I **equate** our school's great basketball team
    A. with some professional teams.   C. by attending its games.
    B. in the newspaper each morning.   D. because I work on game nights.

_____ 12. Dena said she's **liable** to visit me this morning, so I
    A. will be surprised if I see her.   C. have no idea if she plans to visit.
    B. expect to see her.   D. know for a fact that she isn't coming.

_____ 13. My aunt's new kitchen appliance is truly **versatile**. It
    A. takes up a great deal of space.   C. makes toast, brews coffee, and fries
    B. squeezes oranges.   bacon.
                              D. cost more than $500.

_____ 14. To **defer** to my parents' wishes that I dress up for Thanksgiving dinner, I
    A. went barefoot.   C. wore a tie.
    B. wore a turkey costume.   D. skipped the dinner.

_____ 15. A **malicious** reply to the question "Will you go out with me on Friday?" is
    A. "No, thank you; I have other plans."   C. "I'd really like to go out with you."
    B. "Why would I do that? You're disgusting."   D. "I'm not sure if I'm free that night."

_____ 16. The mosquito was so **persistent** that it
    A. wouldn't stop buzzing around my head, no matter what I did.
    B. couldn't be found.
    C. weaved back and forth as it flew.
    D. flew away immediately.

_____ 17. I **inferred** that Julia and Roberto had had a fight when I
    A. saw them fighting.
    B. heard an untrue rumor that they had fought.
    C. saw they were holding hands.
    D. saw her pass right by him without speaking to him.

_____ 18. The change in Eleanor's hair color is so **subtle** that
    A. friends keep saying, "Holy cow, Eleanor—what did you do to your hair?"
    B. everyone comments on how good the new color looks.
    C. only her best friend noticed it.
    D. no one mentions it, for fear of embarrassing her by telling her how ugly it is.

_____ 19. I knew my girlfriend and I were **compatible** when
    A. we discovered we both love horror movies and smelly cheese.
    B. she groaned at my choices of novels and CDs.
    C. we learned we were both born in the summer.
    D. she refused to go to football games with me.

_____ 20. Which of the following famous scenes from Shakespeare's plays demonstrates an **obsession**?
    A. The fairy Puck turns one character into a donkey (in _A Midsummer Night's Dream_).
    B. Lady Macbeth washes her hands again and again to try to remove imaginary blood (in _Macbeth_).
    C. The two young lovers first meet at a ball given by Juliet's family (in _Romeo and Juliet_).
    D. The king decides to divide his kingdom among his three daughters (in _King Lear_).

Score   (Number correct) _____ x 5 = _____ %

PART A

Complete each item with a word from the box. Use each word once.

A. awe	B. cite	C. delusion	D. evolve	E. gullible
F. impose	G. indignant	H. lethal	I. option	J. rational
K. retort	L. savor	M. universal		

_____ 1. After recently lending Trisha money to help her pay her rent, I was ___ when I learned she had been using the money to buy herself expensive jewelry.

_____ 2. It's thrilling to watch LeBron James play basketball. His athletic ability fills me with ___.

_____ 3. We considered several ___s for dinner: cooking, going out, or having a pizza delivered.

_____ 4. The town's belief that the company was loyal to its workers proved to be a ___. The company laid everyone off and moved the plant to a country with cheaper labor.

_____ 5. Dad was embarrassed to admit he'd been ___ enough to buy a "genuine diamond wristwatch" from a stranger on the street.

_____ 6. As Gwen got to know Peter better, her feelings for him ___(e)d from interest to affection to love.

_____ 7. It's dangerous to mix chlorine bleach and other household cleaners. The combination can produce ___ fumes.

_____ 8. My sister ___s on her husband's good nature by having him run errands for her all the time.

_____ 9. Knowing the ice cream would be his last before beginning his diet, Jon took time to ___ every rich spoonful.

_____ 10. The German and American children didn't mind that they couldn't speak the same language. They all knew the ___ language of play.

_____ 11. Loni is overly ___ about her love life. She lists a guy's good and bad qualities before deciding if she'll date him again.

_____ 12. When someone is rude to me, I'd love to make a clever ___, but a snappy comeback never occurs to me until hours later.

_____ 13. To make my point that school can be as stressful as a full-time job, I ___(e)d the pressures of being a student.

(Continues on next page)

PART B

Write **C** if the italicized word is used **correctly**. Write **I** if the word is used **incorrectly**.

_____ 14. Pearl and I went to the same party, but it was so crowded that we never *encountered* each other.

_____ 15. At some health clinics, people with little income are *exempt* from all fees.

_____ 16. I think of myself as a *pessimist* because I can find something good in even the worst situation.

_____ 17. After Judy's wonderful performance in the play, friends rushed backstage to *harass* her with flowers and praise.

_____ 18. Lynn has repeatedly asked Brian exactly what he does for a living, but she always gets an *evasive* answer like "I work downtown."

_____ 19. My overactive young nephew takes medicine to *stimulate* his tendency to race around the house and throw things.

PART C

On the answer line, write the letter of the word that is the **synonym** of the boldfaced word.

Example: __A__ **malicious**   A. spiteful   B. kindly   C. eager

_____ 20. **prevail**   A. lose   B. triumph   C. happen

_____ 21. **dubious**   A. certain   B. foolish   C. doubtful

_____ 22. **fallacy**   A. error   B. prediction   C. truth

PART D

On the answer line, write the letter of the word that is the **antonym** of the boldfaced word.

Example: __B__ **malicious**   A. spiteful   B. kindly   C. eager

_____ 23. **futile**   A. useless   B. evil   C. effective

_____ 24. **ecstatic**   A. unhappy   B. clear   C. overjoyed

_____ 25. **inevitable**   A. avoidable   B. certain   C. injured

Score   (Number correct) _____ x 4 = _____%

Enter your scores above and in the **Vocabulary Performance Chart** on the inside back cover of the book.

Each item below starts with a pair of words in CAPITAL LETTERS. For each item, figure out the relationship between these two words. Then decide which of the choices (A, B, C, or D) expresses a similar relationship. Write the letter of your choice on the answer line.

____ 1. ACCESSIBLE : ENTER ::
    A. invisible : see   C. impossible : do
    B. lovable : hate   D. preventable : avoid

____ 2. AWE : RESPECT ::
    A. adoration : love   C. attraction : disgust
    B. anger : affection   D. amusement : sorrow

____ 3. PROPEL : BASEBALL ::
    A. float : rock   C. dig : deep
    B. hang : laundry   D. shake : television

____ 4. RETRIEVE : GET BACK ::
    A. remove : keep   C. recall : remember
    B. reward : punish   D. receive : repeat

____ 5. DUBIOUS : UNSURE ::
    A. cautious : careful   C. reasonable : talented
    B. serious : joyful   D. anxious : carefree

____ 6. ECSTATIC : HAPPY ::
    A. difficult : easy   C. interested : bored
    B. miserable : uncomfortable   D. heavy : tall

____ 7. FICTITIOUS : BATMAN ::
    A. weak : Superman   C. real : Martin Luther King, Jr.
    B. forgotten : Abraham Lincoln   D. movies : Marilyn Monroe

____ 8. MISERLY : GENEROUS ::
    A. first : number one   C. wide awake : alert
    B. fuzzy : smooth   D. stiff : board

____ 9. LETHAL : HEALTHFUL ::
    A. close : near   C. kind : mean
    B. useful : helpful   D. blue : navy

____ 10. FLUENT : SPEAKER ::
    A. warm : snow   C. long : cure
    B. graceful : dancer   D. green : skies

(Continues on next page)

_____ 11. FUTILE : USEFUL ::
     A. easy : simple   C. fatal : deadly
     B. slight : great   D. red : scarlet

_____ 12. ORDEAL : TERM PAPER ::
     A. conflict : conclusion   C. injury : full recovery
     B. trial : verdict   D. challenge : final exam

_____ 13. DELUSION : MIND ::
     A. disease : body   C. thorn : daisy
     B. heart : lungs   D. nutrition : health

_____ 14. DEVISE : INVENTION ::
     A. play : workplace   C. read : glasses
     B. write : essay   D. carve : skill

_____ 15. SUBTLE : OBVIOUS ::
     A. bright : light   C. factual : realistic
     B. written : pencil   D. hinted at : stated

_____ 16. UNIQUE : ONE ::
     A. multiple : many   C. two : three
     B. three : six   D. numerous : few

_____ 17. ENDEAVOR : SUCCEED ::
     A. know : fail   C. compete : win
     B. attack : defend   D. grow : shrink

_____ 18. INDIGNANT : ANGRY ::
     A. sorrowful : sad   C. regretful : satisfied
     B. hungry : thirsty   D. worried : confident

_____ 19. INEVITABLE : DEATH ::
     A. predictable : expected   C. believable : doubtful
     B. unlucky : guess   D. unforeseen : accident

_____ 20. PATRON : RESTAURANT ::
     A. client : lawyer   C. employee : worker
     B. child : adult   D. chairperson : committee

Score   (Number correct) _____   x   5   = _____%

PART A

Listed in the left-hand column below are ten common word parts, followed by words in which the parts are used. In each blank, write in the letter of the correct definition on the right.

Word Parts	Examples	Definitions
____ 1. **con-**	congregation, conductor	A. State, quality, or condition
____ 2. **dict**	dictator, contradict	B. Write
____ 3. **dis-**	displease, disappear	C. Speak
____ 4. **micro-**	microphotograph, microbiology	D. Foot
____ 5. **ped**	biped, pedicure	E. Three
____ 6. **script, scrib**	script, describe	F. Far; distant
____ 7. **-ship**	citizenship, companionship	G. Small
____ 8. **tele-**	telephoto, telephone	H. Change, beyond, across
____ 9. **trans-**	transfer, translate	I. Not; the opposite of
____ 10. **tri-**	triplets, trio	J. With, together

PART B

Using the answer line provided, complete each *italicized* word in the sentences below with the correct word part from the box. Not every word part will be used.

A. **con-**	B. **dict**	C. **dis-**	D. **micro-**	E. **ped**
F. **script**	G. **-ship**	H. **tele-**	I. **trans-**	J. **tri-**

_____ 11. The easiest way to catch a cold is through skin (. . . *tact*) ___.

_____ 12. Other kids fall from bicycles, but I was so clumsy as a child that I lost my balance even on a (. . . *cycle*) ___.

_____ 13. Lamar often brought Tamika flowers during their (*court* . . .) ___. After they got married, he planted a garden for her.

_____ 14. Is there anything more amazing than the (. . . *formation*) ___ of a creepy caterpillar into a gorgeous butterfly?

_____ 15. Allergy medicine bought with a doctor's (*pre* . . . *ion*) ___ is likely to cost much more than allergy medicines on the drugstore shelf.

(Continues on next page)

PART C

Use your knowledge of word parts to determine the meaning of the **boldfaced** words. On the answer line, write the letter of each meaning.

_____ 16. The newest computers contain dual-core **microchips**.

      A. very large chips   B. chips that carry sound   C. very small chips

_____ 17. The office worker was asked if he had ever used a **Dictaphone**.

      A. a machine that records spoken words
      B. a machine that has the ability to make copies
      C. a machine that is operated by foot

_____ 18. Wreaths had been placed around the **pedestal** of the statue.

      A. top   B. middle   C. foot

_____ 19. While trying to fix Elena's car, Rico **disabled** it.

      A. made it unable to run   B. improved its ability   C. wrote about its ability

_____ 20. In 1608, the **telescope** was invented by accident when the inventor happened to look through two lenses at once.

      A. an instrument which makes it easier to see distant things
      B. an instrument which makes it easier to see very small things
      C. an instrument which makes it easier to see writing

Score   (Number correct) _____ x 5 = _____%

Enter your scores above and in the **Vocabulary Performance Chart** on the inside back cover of the book.

Unit Four

Chapter 19

adapt	reciprocate
dismay	refute
exile	retain
gesture	revert
recede	ritual

Chapter 20

elaborate	indifferent
emerge	indulgent
exotic	liberal
frugal	mediocre
impulsive	notable

Chapter 21

affirm	essence
alleged	immunity
allude	impair
coerce	query
elite	sadistic

Chapter 22

plausible	ridicule
provoke	shrewd
recur	skeptical
reprimand	stereotype
revoke	tactic

Chapter 23

consequence	simultaneous
destiny	strategy
detain	tedious
diminish	transaction
procrastinate	vital

Chapter 24

-able	man
cent-, centi-	mem
in-	mono-, mon-
-logy, -ology	port
mal-	therm-, thermo-

adapt	reciprocate
dismay	refute
exile	retain
gesture	revert
recede	ritual

Ten Words in Context

In the space provided, write the letter of the meaning closest to that of each **boldfaced** word. Use the context of the sentences to help you figure out each word's meaning.

1 adapt
(ə-dăpt′)
-*verb*

● After many years of being a student, I found it hard to **adapt** to the schedule of a full-time job.

● Gina **adapted** well to California. She had no trouble adjusting to living so far from her family and friends.

___ *Adapt* means   A. to return.   B. to become accustomed.   C. to travel.

2 dismay
(dĭs-mā′)
-*verb*

● Aaron was **dismayed** when he realized that he wouldn't have enough money to buy a special birthday present for his girlfriend.

● The doctor knew it would **dismay** Karl to learn that his injured leg would never regain its previous strength.

___ *Dismay* means   A. to discourage.   B. to relieve.   C. to delay.

3 exile
(ĕg′zīl)
-*noun*

● The political rebel decided to end his five-year **exile** and return to his native land to oppose the government.

● Fernando fled his native country thirty years ago and has lived in **exile** ever since.

___ *Exile* means   A. a long vacation.   B. a bad attitude.   C. a separation from one's homeland.

4 gesture
(jĕs′chər)
-*noun*

● As a **gesture** of sympathy, the neighborhood association sent flowers to Milly when her husband died.

● The other workers' **gestures** of friendship made Vic feel at home on the first day of his new job.

___ *Gesture* means   A. a signal.   B. a request.   C. a report.

5 recede
(rĭ-sēd′)
-*verb*

● The heavy blanket of clouds finally began to **recede**, allowing the sun to warm the crowd at the football game.

● Walter had to wait until the flood waters **receded** before he could get to his house to see the damage.

___ *Recede* means   A. to grow.   B. to go back.   C. to return.

6 reciprocate
(rĭ-sĭp′rə-kāt′)
-*verb*

● I've done many favors for Anne, but she never **reciprocates** by doing a favor in return.

● Hakeem treated me to dinner, so I'm going to **reciprocate** by taking him to a movie.

___ *Reciprocate* means   A. to celebrate.   B. to pay back.   C. to disappoint.

7 refute
(rĭ-fyo͞ot′)
-verb

- The lawyer was able to **refute** the defendant's claim that she was home the night of the murder. He had found a witness who saw her in a mall store that night.
- Some science-fiction fans were disappointed when photos of Mars **refuted** the idea that intelligent life exists there.

___ *Refute* means   A. to support.   B. to repeat.   C. to show to be wrong.

8 retain
(rĭ-tān′)
-verb

- Plastic storage containers often **retain** the odors of foods. I have one that still smells like spaghetti sauce after ten washings.
- "I can usually **retain** my sense of humor," Janice said. "But I lose it totally when I'm laid off and break up with my boyfriend in the same week."

___ *Retain* means   A. to hold onto.   B. to adjust to.   C. to lose.

9 revert
(rĭ-vûrt′)
-verb

- After his release from jail, Sam **reverted** to his old habit of stealing and ended up in jail again.
- Helene gave up smoking while she was pregnant, but she **reverted** to a pack a day after her daughter was born.

___ *Revert* means   A. to go back.   B. to refer.   C. to say no.

10 ritual
(rĭch′o͞o-əl)
-noun

- **Rituals**—set practices that are repeated regularly—are important in most religious traditions.
- Each time Mary Ann must fly, she writes a check to a charity, brings it with her on the plane, and mails it at her destination. She believes this **ritual** guarantees a safe flight.

___ *Ritual* means   A. a lesson.   B. a ceremony.   C. a prayer.

Matching Words with Definitions

Following are definitions of the ten words. Clearly write or print each word next to its definition. The sentences above and on the previous page will help you decide on the meaning of each word.

1. _____ To return to a previous habit or condition

2. _____ Something said or done to show intention or attitude; indication; signal

3. _____ To do in return; pay back

4. _____ Separation from one's native country through force or choice

5. _____ A ceremony; any actions done regularly in a set manner

6. _____ To prove wrong or false

7. _____ To adjust to a situation

8. _____ To move back or away from a particular point or limit

9. _____ To keep

10. _____ To discourage; make fearful or uneasy

CAUTION: Do not go any further until you are sure the above answers are correct. Then you can use the definitions to help you in the following practices. Your goal is eventually to know the words well enough so that you don't need to check the definitions at all.

Sentence Check 1

Using the answer line provided, complete each item below with the correct word from the box. Use each word once.

A. **adapt**	B. **dismay**	C. **exile**	D. **gesture**	E. **recede**
F. **reciprocate**	G. **refute**	H. **retain**	I. **revert**	J. **ritual**

_____ 1. Getting a D on the first math test of the semester ___(e)d Sean. He was sure he'd done well.

_____ 2. If the shoreline continues to ___, there soon won't be any sandy beach at all.

_____ 3. Antonio tried to ___ my argument, but I was able to prove I was right.

_____ 4. In a(n) ___ of cooperation, the manager and the head of the union shook hands.

_____ 5. To ___ her strength and energy, Mrs. Green does push-ups, sit-ups, and leg-lifts three times a week.

_____ 6. My brother vowed to eat only one Oreo a day, but I'm afraid he'll ___ to his old habit of eating the entire bag of cookies at a sitting.

_____ 7. As the Ice Age ended, some animals were able to ___ to the new climate. Those who could not adjust failed to survive.

_____ 8. The country's new dictator feared having certain political enemies in the country, so he sent them into ___.

_____ 9. I always send Kiran a birthday card, but he doesn't bother to ___ with a card or phone call on my birthday.

_____ 10. Homer always goes through the same baseball ___ before he bats: he twirls his bat three times, stretches his arms, and says, "Okay, okay, this one will be good."

NOTE: Now check your answers to these items by turning to page 178. Going over the answers carefully will help you prepare for the next two practices, for which answers are not given.

Sentence Check 2

Using the answer lines provided, complete each item below with **two** words from the box. Use each word once.

_____
_____ 1–2. "I don't want to ___ you," Jack's lawyer told him. "And I will certainly endeavor° to do my best, but it's going to be difficult to ___ the testimony against you."

_____
_____ 3–4. The Reillys have been so kind to me that I want to ___ in some way. I don't have much money, so I hope they'll infer° that a small gift is meant as a(n) ___ of great appreciation.

_____

_____

5–6. A reader wrote, "My husband is afraid his hairline will ___, causing him to ___ to the bald head he was born with." The advice columnist responded, "Tell him that this obsession° of his shouldn't undermine° his self-confidence. He's the same great guy with or without hair."

_____

_____

7–8. Any customary ___, such as the Roman Catholic Mass, helps a church to ___ a sense of tradition.

_____

_____

9–10. The Howards had ___(e)d well to other cultures, but they were still pleased to retire from the Foreign Service and return to America after their long ___ in Europe and Asia. Now they love to reminisce° with their friends about their interesting worldwide adventures.

Final Check: *Adjusting to a New Culture*

Here is a final opportunity for you to strengthen your knowledge of the ten words. First read the following selection carefully. Then fill in each blank with a word from the box at the top of the previous page. (Context clues will help you figure out which word goes in which blank.) Use each word once.

When En-Mei first came to the United States from China, any little problem was enough to (1)_____ her. As a lonely student, she felt as if she were in forced (2)_____ from her native country. She didn't like American food and tried to limit her diet to Chinese dishes. Otherwise, however, she worked hard to (3)_____ to an unfamiliar country. Finding it difficult to express herself in English, En-Mei at first isolated° herself from others. But she kept working on her English and eventually became quite fluent° in it. This helped her to overcome her shyness and learn to (4)_____ other students' (5)_____s of friendship. When she was with her new friends, with whom she was completely compatible°, homesickness would (6)_____ into the background.

But En-Mei didn't try to become "all-American"; she wanted to (7)_____ her Chinese identity. She taught her new friends about modern China and tried to (8)_____ mistaken ideas they had about her country. She even found a group of friends willing to learn tai chi, an ancient Chinese exercise (9)_____ that benefits body and spirit. It involves a set series of movements which the group performs together.

Of course, living in America wasn't always easy. Sometimes En-Mei would miss her family so badly that she would (10)_____ to her former unhappiness. But such times were increasingly rare. By the end of her first year here, En-Mei even found she had started to savor° American food—she had become a devoted fan of pizza and apple pie.

Scores   Sentence Check 2 _____%   Final Check _____%

20

elaborate	indifferent
emerge	indulgent
exotic	liberal
frugal	mediocre
impulsive	notable

Ten Words in Context

In the space provided, write the letter of the meaning closest to that of each **boldfaced** word. Use the context of the sentences to help you figure out each word's meaning.

1 elaborate
(ĭ-lăb′ər-ĭt)
-adjective

- The dinner required **elaborate** preparation. Each course included a complicated favorite dish of one of the guests.
- Irma's quilt was very **elaborate**. She used tiny stitches to sew together hundreds of fabric pieces.

___ *Elaborate* means   A. easy and simple to do.   B. detailed.   C. ordinary.

2 emerge
(ĭ-mûrj′)
-verb

- Anna **emerged** from the dressing room, looking beautiful in a blue prom gown.
- When the chick **emerged** from its egg, it was tired and wet, but a day later it was a fluffy yellow ball of energy.

___ *Emerge* means   A. to come out.   B. to trip.   C. to call out.

3 exotic
(ĭg-zŏt′ĭk)
-adjective

- Orchids are grown in the United States, not just in foreign countries. So Americans really should not consider these flowers **exotic**.
- The kiwi fruit, grown in New Zealand, is one of several **exotic** fruits now commonly sold in supermarkets.

___ *Exotic* means   A. local.   B. foreign.   C. rare.

4 frugal
(frōō′gəl)
-adjective

- You can stretch your dollars by being **frugal**. For example, using store coupons and waiting for expensive items to be on sale can save a lot of money.
- Diane buys designer jeans, but because I need to be more **frugal**, I buy store-brand jeans, which are much cheaper.

___ *Frugal* means   A. hardworking.   B. lucky.   C. thrifty.

5 impulsive
(ĭm-pŭl′sĭv)
-adjective

- Ved is too **impulsive** to make plans. He always prefers to act on the spur of the moment.
- Kids are usually more **impulsive** than adults. Children will follow such sudden urges as the desire to climb a tree even if they are wearing their best clothes.

___ *Impulsive* means   A. fearful.   B. careful.   C. acting without planning.

6 indifferent
(ĭn-dĭf′ər-ənt)
-adjective

- Does our society have no interest in homeless children? Are we **indifferent** to the many families who can no longer afford to pay rent?
- Because her husband was **indifferent** to how the apartment would be decorated, Kaylin felt free to do the job any way she wanted.

___ *Indifferent to* means   A. interested in.   B. unconcerned with.   C. insulted by.

7 indulgent
(ĭn-dŭl′jənt)
-adjective

● Monica's grandparents are too **indulgent** with her. They don't scold her even when she splatters the walls with baby food.

● I'm surprised at Robin's self-**indulgent** attitude. It never occurs to her not to give in to every little desire she has.

___ *Indulgent* means   A. strict.   B. giving in.   C. not caring.

8 liberal
(lĭb′ər-əl)
-adjective

● Being a chocolate lover, Amos puts **liberal** amounts of chocolate chips in his Toll House cookies.

● Norma left the waiter a **liberal** tip because he had been especially friendly and helpful.

___ *Liberal* means   A. average.   B. frequent.   C. generous.

9 mediocre
(mē-dē-ō′kər)
-adjective

● The mystery movie was neither terrible nor great; it was just **mediocre**.

● Although Hank can be quite funny, his jokes are only **mediocre** compared with those of the best comedians.

___ *Mediocre* means   A. ordinary.   B. awful.   C. short.

10 notable
(nō′tə-bəl)
-adjective

● Winning the Nobel Prize can make a little-known scientist into a **notable** world figure.

● Abraham Lincoln's "Gettysburg Address" is surely his most **notable** speech, especially among the many Americans who memorized it in school.

___ *Notable* means   A. ineffective.   B. well-known.   C. generous.

Matching Words with Definitions

Following are definitions of the ten words. Clearly write or print each word next to its definition. The sentences above and on the previous page will help you decide on the meaning of each word.

1. _____   To rise up or come forth

2. _____   Famous; widely known

3. _____   Having no real interest; unconcerned

4. _____   Large in amount or quantity; generous

5. _____   Done with great attention to details; complicated

6. _____   Average; ordinary; neither very bad nor very good

7. _____   Tending to act on sudden urges; not in the habit of planning ahead

8. _____   Foreign; from a different part of the world; strange or different in an appealing way

9. _____   Thrifty; avoiding unnecessary expenses

10. _____   Giving in to someone's desires, often too much so; lenient

CAUTION: Do not go any further until you are sure the above answers are correct. Then you can use the definitions to help you in the following practices. Your goal is eventually to know the words well enough so that you don't need to check the definitions at all.

Sentence Check 1

Using the answer line provided, complete each item below with the correct word from the box. Use each word once.

A. **elaborate**	B. **emerge**	C. **exotic**	D. **frugal**	E. **impulsive**
F. **indifferent**	G. **indulgent**	H. **liberal**	I. **mediocre**	J. **notable**

_____ 1. Although my father didn't do badly in school, he wasn't a great student. So he's proof it's possible to have a successful career despite ___ grades.

_____ 2. Overly ___ parents, who let young children do whatever they please, will end up with problem teenagers.

_____ 3. The puppy ___(e)d from her bath much cleaner than when she entered it, but we doubted that she'd stay clean for long.

_____ 4. Tran is such a skilled public speaker that we all expect him to become a ___ politician one day.

_____ 5. The boss gave such ___ bonuses that Gail was able to buy a new sofa with the money.

_____ 6. Ella embroidered a(n) ___ design on the back of her sweatshirt. She used four colors in a complicated pattern of swirls and flowers.

_____ 7. People walked past the bleeding, moaning man without even pausing; they were ___ to his need for help.

_____ 8. "Gowns are so expensive," Cara said, "that I've decided to be ___ and rent a wedding dress instead of buying one."

_____ 9. Bruce, as ___ as ever, suddenly changed his mind about going to a restaurant and announced, "Let's have a picnic."

_____ 10. A Native American rain dance may seem ___ to many people in the United States, but it is actually more native to this country than square-dancing.

NOTE: Now check your answers to these items by turning to page 178. Going over the answers carefully will help you prepare for the next two practices, for which answers are not given.

Sentence Check 2

Using the answer lines provided, complete each item below with **two** words from the box. Use each word once.

_____
_____ 1–2. The actress, ___ for her great performance, deserved her Academy Award. Compared with her, all of the others appeared ___. Overjoyed, she said, "Thank you, thank you, thank you. This is my first Oscar, and I am too ecstatic° to think of anything else to say."

_____
_____ 3–4. Every time Sylvia shops, she manages to ___ from the store with only items that are on sale. I wish I could be such a(n) ___ shopper.

_____   5–6. The ___ meal, full of strange but delicious foods, involved ___ preparation
_____   that took up most of the afternoon. But all the work was worth it; we
                                  savored° every bite.

_____   7–8. When it comes to the suffering of others, Americans are idealistic°. When a
_____   disaster strikes, they find it difficult to be ___ to the victims, so they send ___
                                  donations to the Red Cross.

_____   9–10. Rafael is so ___ that he often decides he wants to go out for dinner or to a
_____   movie at the last minute. Overly ___, his wife agrees every time. She even
                                   defers° to his wish to eat out after she has already cooked dinner.

Final Check: _A Dream about Wealth_

Here is a final opportunity for you to strengthen your knowledge of the ten words. First read the following
selection carefully. Then fill in each blank with a word from the box at the top of the previous page.
(Context clues will help you figure out which word goes in which blank.) Use each word once.

In my student days, when I was very poor, I sometimes
daydreamed about being rich and having an amazingly affluent°
lifestyle. I imagined being such a(n) (1)_____
member of society that my name would turn up in the
newspaper columns every time I attended a party. I pictured
myself traveling to (2)_____ places in
faraway lands and being a patron° of the finest restaurants. I
would forget no detail when planning (3)_____
parties for five hundred of my closest friends. There would be
nothing (4)_____ in my life, not even an ordinary, average toaster. No, I would have the
finest toasters, the biggest houses, the most glamorous wardrobe—the best. And I would own a unique°
art collection—no prints for me—only one-of-a-kind masterpieces by famous artists. Of course, I would be
quite (5)_____: whenever I had the urge, I would buy diamond jewelry or jump into
my Olympic-size pool. But I promised myself that I wouldn't be totally self- (6)_____.
I'd also give (7)_____ amounts of money to help the poor and underprivileged. I would
not be (8)_____ to their needs. And being modest as well as generous, I'd always be an
anonymous° donor°.

After graduating, I began earning money, and I stopped daydreaming about being rich. Having some
wages to spend, I had finally (9)_____(e)d from a life of endless budgeting, a life in
which I was forced to be extremely (10)_____. Of course, I am still thrifty because I
don't want to waste my hard-earned money. But now that I have enough money to be comfortable, I no
longer need to create fictitious° situations in which I'm super-rich.

Scores	Sentence Check 2 _____%	Final Check _____%

CHAPTER

21

affirm	essence
alleged	immunity
allude	impair
coerce	query
elite	sadistic

Ten Words in Context

In the space provided, write the letter of the meaning closest to that of each **boldfaced** word. Use the context of the sentences to help you figure out each word's meaning.

1 affirm
(ə-fûrm′)
-verb

● The witness **affirmed** in court that he had seen the defendant commit the robbery.

● During the wedding ceremony, Lana did **affirm** that she would love and honor Joseph, but she did not state that she would obey him.

___ *Affirm* means
A. to fear.
B. to state.
C. to write.

2 alleged
(ə-lĕjd′)
-adjective

● The **alleged** killer was never proven guilty in court, but many people believe he committed the murder.

● Nan, who believed Luther was innocent of starting the fire, reminded her friends that his guilt was only **alleged**.

___ *Alleged* means
A. assumed.
B. admired.
C. harmless.

3 allude
(ə-lōōd′)
-verb

● Although the mayor won't use her opponent's name, she plans to **allude** to him by mentioning the scandal he's involved in.

● Tracy **alluded** to Santiago's weight gain by calling him "Santa."

___ *Allude to* means
A. to clearly mention.
B. to hint at.
C. to keep.

4 coerce
(kō-ûrs′)
-verb

● To **coerce** the general into giving up, the rebels kidnapped his daughter.

● Our gym teacher used to **coerce** us into doing fifty sit-ups by refusing to let anyone leave before we all had finished.

___ *Coerce* means
A. to talk.
B. to join.
C. to force.

5 elite
(ĭ-lēt′)
-adjective

● The 57th was the **elite** military unit. Its members were the toughest and the smartest and had trained the longest.

● The **elite** neighborhood in town is surrounded by a high fence and has a guard at its gates.

___ *Elite* means
A. worst.
B. best.
C. least important.

6 essence
(ĕs′əns)
-noun

● Trust is the **essence** of a good relationship; without it, the relationship won't last.

● Boiled down to its **essence**, the lecture can be stated in one short sentence: Much important work gets done in America by volunteers.

___ *Essence* means
A. the main part.
B. the opposite.
C. the sad part.

118

7 immunity
(ĭ-myōō'nĭ-tē)
-noun

- Foreign ambassadors often park in no-parking zones because they have **immunity** from parking fines.
- When the actor punched a police officer, even his wealth and fame didn't get him **immunity** from jail.

__ *Immunity* means   A. recognition.   B. freedom.   C. an income.

8 impair
(ĭm-pâr')
-verb

- Listening to very loud music for extended periods of time **impairs** hearing by damaging the inner ear.
- The auto accident **impaired** my ability to walk, leaving me with a limp.

__ *Impair* means   A. to involve.   B. to repair.   C. to harm.

9 query
(kwēr'ē)
-verb

- If no printed schedule is available, please **query** the person at the information booth to learn the time of your train's arrival or departure.
- Reporters repeatedly **queried** the candidate about whether he would raise taxes, but his only reply was "No comment."

__ *Query* means   A. to ask.   B. to quote.   C. to answer.

10 sadistic
(sə-dĭs'tĭk)
-adjective

- Cats seem to be naturally **sadistic**. Instead of killing their victims quickly, they like to make the process slow and drawn-out.
- Our **sadistic** science teacher had a strange way of teaching about electrical currents. First, he had us hold hands in a circle. Then he put one student's hand on a wire with a slight electrical charge.

__ *Sadistic* means   A. sad.   B. cruel.   C. rude.

Matching Words with Definitions

Following are definitions of the ten words. Clearly write or print each word next to its definition. The sentences above and on the previous page will help you decide on the meaning of each word.

1. _____ To damage; weaken

2. _____ To refer indirectly

3. _____ Taking pleasure from being cruel

4. _____ A fundamental characteristic or the most important quality of something; the heart of a matter

5. _____ Freedom from something unpleasant or something required of others

6. _____ To indicate to be true; state with certainty

7. _____ Being or intended for the best or most privileged; superior

8. _____ To force; compel°

9. _____ Supposed to be true or real, but not proved; assumed

10. _____ To question; ask

CAUTION: Do not go any further until you are sure the above answers are correct. Then you can use the definitions to help you in the following practices. Your goal is eventually to know the words well enough so that you don't need to check the definitions at all.

Sentence Check 1

Using the answer line provided, complete each item below with the correct word from the box. Use each word once.

A. affirm	B. alleged	C. allude	D. coerce	E. elite
F. essence	G. immunity	H. impair	I. query	J. sadistic

_____ 1. The Puritan colonists ___(e)d Native Americans into slavery by capturing and selling them to buyers in the West Indies.

_____ 2. The ___ war criminal had laughed while he tortured his victims.

_____ 3. Drugs and alcohol ___ a person's ability to drive.

_____ 4. The ___ of a paragraph is stated in its topic sentence.

_____ 5. As a child, I didn't enjoy total ___ from punishment, but my parents rarely spanked me.

_____ 6. During the spelling bee, the judge would ___ that a spelling was correct by nodding silently.

_____ 7. The ___ car thief could not possibly be guilty. Not only was he out of town on the day of the theft, but he cannot drive.

_____ 8. A(n) ___ group of doctors, including the country's top brain surgeons, met to discuss a new operation.

_____ 9. When two people are arrested for the same crime, the police ___ them separately to see if they give the same answers.

_____ 10. My brother and I used secret names to ___ to certain relatives. For example, if we wished to speak about Aunt Dotty, we instead spoke about "an old Chevy."

NOTE: Now check your answers to these items by turning to page 179. Going over the answers carefully will help you prepare for the next two practices, for which answers are not given.

Sentence Check 2

Using the answer lines provided, complete each item below with **two** words from the box. Use each word once.

_____
_____ 1–2. The senator would neither deny nor ___ that the ___, expensive country club he belonged to did not allow minority members. Nevertheless, to avoid any appearance of a problem, he decided it would be appropriate° to resign from the club.

_____
_____ 3–4. I need to ___ my teacher more closely about her views on protecting the environment. Although I've grasped the ___ of her position, I don't understand all the details yet.

_____
_____ 5–6. When my roommate wants to ___ me into doing her some favor, all she has to do is ___ to certain dark secrets of mine. The hint that she might tell them leaves me no option° but to help her out.

_____   7–8. Ava accuses her husband of being ___ when he turns the volume way up on
_____   the TV. She says he doesn't care that the noise bothers her. In addition, the
                                   sound is so loud that it could permanently ___ her hearing.

_____   9–10. Nobody is sure if the ___ bribery really took place. The person who would
_____   have been the chief suspect was given ___ from arrest by a powerful political
                                   figure.

Final Check: *Children and Drugs*

Here is a final opportunity for you to strengthen your knowledge of the ten words. First read the following
selection carefully. Then fill in each blank with a word from the box at the top of the previous page.
(Context clues will help you figure out which word goes in which blank.) Use each word once.

When I hear people talk about "harmless, recreational" drug use, it
makes me sick. It isn't only because I'm concerned about what the drug
users are doing to their own minds and bodies. It's because I've seen
the business that these people are supporting with their "recreational"
drug use. It's a business run by the scum of the earth—people so evil and
(1)_____ that they will gladly use children as human
shields between themselves and the law.

On a daily basis in our nation's cities, police pick up preteens who
are used as drug dealers' lookouts and delivery boys. When the police
(2)_____ them, the children often say that the dealers (3)_____ them
into doing these jobs. Because they are so afraid of the dealers, they usually don't say very much more.
They may (4)_____ to "bad things" happening to children who cooperate with police.
Police know that those "bad things" often include being beaten, tortured, and even killed.

Sadly, poor kids don't always need to be forced. They are naturally attracted to the money they
are offered, and they speak of the dealers with awe°. In neighborhoods where honest jobs are scarce,
the dealers, with their fancy cars and big rolls of money, seem to these children to be members of a(n)
(5)_____ club. According to the mother of one (6)_____ drug delivery
boy (the police could never prove he really was a drug runner), the dealers serve as "role models" to her son
and his friends.

The dealers, of course, take full advantage of these children and their poverty. The kids are useful to
the dealers because their age gives them (7)_____ from serious criminal charges. The
police (8)_____ that arresting the children doesn't (9)_____ the
dealers' business much. The loss of a child or two is not important to the dealers, because it doesn't inhibit°
other poor, eager kids who are ready to take the lost child's place. To the children, at least at first, serving as
lookouts and drug runners is almost a game. By the time they find out what kind of evil, malicious° people
they are working for, it is too late to get out.

As the "recreational" drug users sit safely in their comfortable homes, enjoying their "harmless" highs,
I hope they think of these children. The children's ruined lives clearly show that the (10)_____
of the drug trade is the abuse of people.

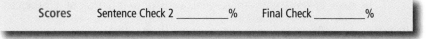

| Scores | Sentence Check 2 _____% | Final Check _____% |

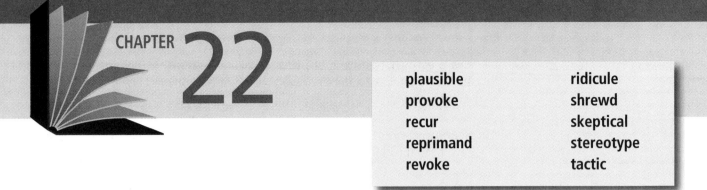

plausible	ridicule
provoke	shrewd
recur	skeptical
reprimand	stereotype
revoke	tactic

Ten Words in Context

In the space provided, write the letter of the meaning closest to that of each **boldfaced** word. Use the context of the sentences to help you figure out each word's meaning.

1 plausible
(plô′zə-bəl)
-*adjective*

● Was Buck's excuse for being late **plausible**? Or did he tell you some unbelievable story?

● "Some classic TV shows were just not **plausible**," said the producer. "Who ever heard of a flying nun or a teenage doctor?"

___ *Plausible* means   A. nice.   B. believable.   C. long enough.

2 provoke
(prə-vōk′)
-*verb*

● "Mr. Jackson **provoked** me by saying nasty things about my mother, so I hit him," Terry told the judge.

● My father is slow to anger, but this morning my sister's wisecracks began to **provoke** him.

___ *Provoke* means   A. to delay.   B. to confuse.   C. to anger.

3 recur
(rĭ-kûr′)
-*verb*

● Five-year-old Arnie's nightmare of ghosts chasing him tends to **recur** at least once a week.

● "If your headaches keep **recurring**," the doctor told Mrs. Lopez, "I'm going to recommend a lab test. We need to find out why you are having so much pain."

___ *Recur* means   A. to disappear.   B. to improve.   C. to happen again.

4 reprimand
(rĕp′rə-mănd′)
-*noun*

● If a boss wants to criticize a worker, the union requires that the **reprimand** be written.

● As a child, when I misbehaved, my father gave me verbal **reprimands**, but my mother would not hesitate to send me to my room for a time-out.

___ *Reprimand* means   A. praise.   B. a scolding.   C. an answer.

5 revoke
(rĭ-vōk′)
-*verb*

● Mrs. Byers said she would **revoke** Ken's privileges at the computer lab if he ever again squirted glue between the computer keys.

● To avoid having his driver's license **revoked**, Art paid the $467 he owed for all of his speeding tickets.

___ *Revoke* means   A. to cancel.   B. to make longer.   C. to recognize.

6 ridicule
(rĭd′ĭ-kyōōl′)
-*verb*

● Ignorant people often **ridicule** my brother because he is so overweight. Even if they had perfect bodies—which they do not—they have no right to tease him.

● Eugene knew his friends would **ridicule** him for wearing a shirt and shorts with two different plaids, but he had no other clean clothes to wear.

___ *Ridicule* means   A. to praise.   B. to notice.   C. to make fun of.

7 shrewd
(shrōōd)
-adjective

● Julio is a fine musician, but he's no good with money. So he hired a friend with a **shrewd** business sense to handle his financial affairs.

● Sherry is a **shrewd** chess player. She always surprises her opponents with clever winning moves.

__ *Shrewd* means   A. lucky.   B. loud.   C. smart.

8 skeptical
(skĕp′tĭ-kəl)
-adjective

● Vanessa's family is so rich that she is **skeptical** about any man who asks her out. She wonders if he's interested in her or in her money.

● I am **skeptical** about the articles on movie stars and space aliens in supermarket newspapers. My brother, however, believes every word he reads in those papers.

__ *Skeptical* means   A. economical.   B. doubtful.   C. believing.

9 stereotype
(stĕr′ē-ə-tīp′)
-noun

● Bev still accepts the **stereotype** of all athletes as stupid even though the school's star quarterback is her math tutor.

● Because not all members of a group are alike, **stereotypes** lead to inaccurate judgments of people.

__ *Stereotype* means   A. an oversimplified image.   B. a desired image.   C. a true image.

10 tactic
(tăk′tĭc)
-noun

● The teacher finally caught on to Greg's sneaky **tactic** for getting his homework done—having his sister do it.

● The best **tactic** for keeping young children from fighting is to separate them.

__ *Tactic* means   A. a method.   B. a result.   C. a reason.

Matching Words with Definitions

Following are definitions of the ten words. Clearly write or print each word next to its definition. The sentences above and on the previous page will help you decide on the meaning of each word.

1. _____ Doubting; questioning

2. _____ Clever; tricky

3. _____ Believable; appearing truthful or reasonable

4. _____ To stir up anger or resentment

5. _____ To take away or cancel

6. _____ A means to reach a goal; method

7. _____ A formal criticism; a harsh scolding

8. _____ To make fun of; mock

9. _____ To occur again; happen repeatedly

10. _____ A commonly accepted image that is oversimplified, with no individuality taken into account; label; generalization

CAUTION: Do not go any further until you are sure the above answers are correct. Then you can use the definitions to help you in the following practices. Your goal is eventually to know the words well enough so that you don't need to check the definitions at all.

Sentence Check 1

Using the answer line provided, complete each item below with the correct word from the box. Use each word once.

A. **plausible**	B. **provoke**	C. **recur**	D. **reprimand**	E. **revoke**
F. **ridicule**	G. **shrewd**	H. **skeptical**	I. **stereotype**	J. **tactic**

_____ 1. At first the other students ___(e)d Sofi for speaking with an accent, but they stopped teasing her once they got to know her better.

_____ 2. *Aesop's Fables* are charming stories based on ___s of animals. In the fables, foxes are always sly, lions are always fierce, and owls are always wise.

_____ 3. It takes great skill to make a science fiction film seem ___ to the audience.

_____ 4. It was ___ of Connie to move to California last year. Now she can pay in-state fees when she takes courses at San Bernardino Valley College.

_____ 5. Jordan has headaches that ___ as often as once a day.

_____ 6. Some divorced parents who want to see more of their children use an illegal ___: kidnapping.

_____ 7. The roofer's estimate was so low that we became ___ about the quality of his work.

_____ 8. The principal sent the gym teacher a written ___ for not having his class leave the gym right after the fire alarm rang.

_____ 9. Arturo usually doesn't let his older sister's teasing ___ him, but he gets angry whenever she calls him "baby."

_____ 10. Maggie's parents said she could not attend the prom because of her bad grades, but later they felt sorry for her and ___(e)d the punishment.

NOTE: Now check your answers to these items by turning to page 179. Going over the answers carefully will help you prepare for the next two practices, for which answers are not given.

Sentence Check 2

Using the answer lines provided, complete each item below with **two** words from the box. Use each word once.

_____
_____ 1–2. When it comes to preventing cheating, our science teacher is ___. His ___s include checking our hands before a test and having us sit in alternate seats during a test. And he puts students he's suspicious of in prominent° seats near the front of the room.

_____
_____ 3–4. Some ___s may get their start when certain behavior patterns ___ among members of a particular group.

_____   5–6. "Of course I'm ___ about your excuse," Mel's boss said. "You have to give
_____   me a more ___ reason for not compiling° the sales figures than that you
                          forgot how to turn your computer on."

_____   7–8. "It is both illegal and absurd° to park your hot-dog cart in a McDonald's
_____   driveway," said the judge to the owner of the cart. "This time you're getting
                          only a ___. Next time your license may be ___(e)d."

_____   9–10. When some boys teased and ___(e)d a learning-disabled student for being
_____   "dumb," the principal was greatly ___(e)d. So she kept the boys after school
                          and compelled° them to write "I am not as smart as I think" five hundred
                          times.

Final Check: *Party House*

Here is a final opportunity for you to strengthen your knowledge of the ten words. First read the following selection carefully. Then fill in each blank with a word from the box at the top of the previous page. (Context clues will help you figure out which word goes in which blank.) Use each word once.

The loud parties at the Phi Gamma fraternity house had (1)_____(e)d its neighbors all year. The neighbors complained to the college administration, but the Phi Gammas were (2)_____ enough to come up with a (3)_____ explanation each time. Each explanation, of course, was an elaborate° lie. For example, they once claimed that one of their members tended to have nightmares which would (4)_____ throughout finals week, making him cry out loudly throughout the night. This, they said,

woke up all of the other members, who had gone to bed early that evening. Again and again, the Phi Gammas were let off by the lenient° college dean with only a (5)_____. But members of the other fraternities were (6)_____ about Phi Gamma's excuses. They also disliked the way the group contributed to a negative (7)_____ of fraternities. So they decided on a (8)_____ to get back at Phi Gamma. They used a camera phone to secretly record one of the Phi Gamma meetings. During that meeting, the Phi Gamma members (9)_____(e)d the dean by mocking the way he always believed their excuses and granted them immunity° from punishment. And, still indifferent° to the comfort of their neighbors, they also made plans for more loud parties. When the dean heard the recording, he (10)_____(e)d Phi Gamma's campus license.

| Scores | Sentence Check 2 _____% | Final Check _____% |

consequence	simultaneous
destiny	strategy
detain	tedious
diminish	transaction
procrastinate	vital

Ten Words in Context

In the space provided, write the letter of the meaning closest to that of each **boldfaced** word. Use the context of the sentences to help you figure out each word's meaning.

1 consequence
(kŏn′sĭ-kwĕns)
-noun

- As a **consequence** of her heavy spending at the mall, Lily was short of cash until her next paycheck.
- Small children reach for hot things and sharp objects because they don't know the **consequences** of such actions.

___ *Consequence* means   A. an effect.   B. a cause.   C. a rule.

2 destiny
(dĕs′tə-nē)
-noun

- Believing in fate, the soldier wondered if his **destiny** was to die in the coming battle.
- Omar believes that he and Nadia were born for each other and that it was their **destiny** to meet.

___ *Destiny* means   A. a habit.   B. fate.   C. a hope.

3 detain
(dĭ-tān′)
-verb

- Paul's history teacher **detained** him after class to speak privately about his surprisingly low grade on the test.
- **Detained** at home by a friend in urgent need of advice, Gloria was late for work.

___ *Detain* means   A. to delay.   B. to leave.   C. to avoid.

4 diminish
(dĭ-mĭn′ĭsh)
-verb

- After Mother yelled, "Turn that thing down!" the sound from the stereo **diminished** from a roar to a soft hum.
- I waited for my anger to **diminish** before discussing the problem with my boss.

___ *Diminish* means   A. to grow.   B. to remain.   C. to become less.

5 procrastinate
(prō-krăs′tə-nāt′)
-verb

- Morgan **procrastinated** so long that when she finally returned the dress to the store, it was too late for a refund.
- I can't **procrastinate** any longer. I must study tonight because the final exam is tomorrow morning.

___ *Procrastinate* means   A. to do something efficiently.   B. to remember something.   C. to put off doing something.

6 simultaneous
(sī′məl-tā′nē-əs)
-adjective

- In a fair race, all starts must be **simultaneous**.
- Lightning and thunder don't seem to be **simultaneous**—we see the lightning before we hear the thunder.

___ *Simultaneous* means   A. similar.   B. happening at the same time.   C. delayed.

7 strategy
(străt'ə-jē)
-noun

● The best **strategy** for teaching children manners is for adults to use good manners themselves.
● The general's **strategy** was to surround the enemy troops during the night.

__ *Strategy* means   A. a reason.   B. a place.   C. a plan.

8 tedious
(tē'dē-əs)
-adjective

● **Tedious** chores, like washing dishes, are less boring if you do them while listening to music or talking with a friend.
● John found the homework assignment very **tedious**; the questions were dull and repetitious.

__ *Tedious* means   A. uninteresting.   B. serious.   C. unnecessary.

9 transaction
(trăn-săk'shən)
-noun

● **Transactions** at flea markets often involve bargaining.
● Among some business people, a **transaction** is concluded with a handshake. These business deals are never put in writing.

__ *Transaction* means   A. a mood.   B. a business interaction.   C. an instruction.

10 vital
(vīt'l)
-adjective

● Water is **vital** to the survival of all living things. For example, people who stop drinking liquids will die in just a few days.
● For Teresa to pass her math course, it is **vital** that she pass the final exam.

__ *Vital* means   A. unimportant.   B. essential.   C. not harmful.

Matching Words with Definitions

Following are definitions of the ten words. Clearly write or print each word next to its definition. The sentences above and on the previous page will help you decide on the meaning of each word.

1. _____   Happening or done at the same time

2. _____   To lessen; decrease

3. _____   A method; overall plan

4. _____   A result

5. _____   A business deal or action; exchange of money, goods, or services

6. _____   Necessary; extremely important

7. _____   Boring; uninteresting because of great length, slowness, or repetition

8. _____   To delay; keep from continuing

9. _____   To put off doing something until later

10. _____   Something bound to happen to someone; fate

CAUTION: Do not go any further until you are sure the above answers are correct. Then you can use the definitions to help you in the following practices. Your goal is eventually to know the words well enough so that you don't need to check the definitions at all.

Sentence Check 1

Using the answer line provided, complete each item below with the correct word from the box. Use each word once.

A. consequence	B. destiny	C. detain	D. diminish	E. procrastinate
F. simultaneous	G. strategy	H. tedious	I. transaction	J. vital

_____   1. The ___ at the checkout counter was delayed by an incorrect price label.

_____   2. The afternoon sunshine caused the snowman's height to ___ from six feet to three.

_____   3. To ___ is to follow the old saying "Never do today what you can put off until tomorrow."

_____   4. As a ___ of his staying out too late, Wilson wasn't allowed out for a week.

_____   5. The dancers' movements were meant to be ___. But when the ballerina leaped, her partner failed to move in time to catch her.

_____   6. Nikki's chess ___ is to make her moves so quickly that her opponent believes she's an expert.

_____   7. Ryan felt it was his wife's ___ to die in the fire. He refused to believe her death was meaningless.

_____   8. The secret agent paid for information he thought was ___ to our national safety, but he had been tricked into buying useless knowledge.

_____   9. "If my science teacher didn't ___ us every day, I wouldn't be late for my next class," explained George.

_____   10. To make raking autumn leaves less ___, my sister and I took turns jumping into the newly created piles.

NOTE: Now check your answers to these items by turning to page 179. Going over the answers carefully will help you prepare for the next two practices, for which answers are not given.

Sentence Check 2

Using the answer lines provided, complete each item below with **two** words from the box. Use each word once.

_____
_____   1–2. Before the tug-of-war started, the blue team decided on a ___: each time the captain shouted "Go!" all team members would give hard ___ pulls.

_____
_____   3–4. "I'm sorry to ___ you," the salesman said, "but a ___ involving payment with a personal check takes longer than a cash purchase."

_____
_____   5–6. The ___ of poor nutrition is illness. In addition to enough exercise and ample° sleep, a balanced diet is ___ for health.

_____   7–8. Unfortunately, it doesn't help to ___ in paying your bills—putting them off
_____   doesn't make them ___ or disappear. In fact, chronic° late payers not only
                                     impair° their credit ratings; they end up paying more because of late charges
                                     and interest payments.

_____   9–10. "This job is so ___ that I'm afraid I'll die of boredom," said the file clerk. "Is
_____   it my ___ to put things in alphabetical order for the rest of my life?"

Final Check: *Procrastinator*

Here is a final opportunity for you to strengthen your knowledge of the ten words. First read the following
selection carefully. Then fill in each blank with a word from the box at the top of the previous page.
(Context clues will help you figure out which word goes in which blank.) Use each word once.

One of these days there is going to be a "new me": I will no

longer (1)_____. I'm making this my New Year's

resolution. Well, yes, I concede° that it's March and I still haven't

acted. I was going to make this resolution in January, but all that

Christmas shopping and cookie baking (2)_____(e)d

me. In February I figured out a (3)_____ to help me

stop putting things off, and I'll get around to it soon because I know

it's (4)_____ for me to change my ways. My

problem is that some jobs are so (5)_____

that just thinking of them makes me want to yawn. But I know that the (6)_____

of putting things off is that nothing actually gets done. And once I get started on my New Year's

resolution, a new me will emerge°. As I adapt° to a different lifestyle, my tendency to delay will surely

gradually (7)_____. I'll finish every household project and financial

(8)_____ that I start. A good tactic° would be to make a list of activities that can

be done (9)_____ly, such as sewing while watching TV, or cleaning my junk drawer

and talking to my mother on the phone at the same time. I'd make a list now if I could just find a pen. I was

going to buy pens yesterday, but I figured I'd be at the mall on Friday, so why make a special trip? I'll make

the list later. Oh well, maybe it's just my (10)_____ to put things off. If it's inevitable°,

why fight it?

| Scores | Sentence Check 2 _____% | Final Check _____% |

-able	man
cent-, centi-	mem
in-	mono-, mon-
-logy, -ology	port
mal-	therm-, thermo-

Ten Word Parts in Context

Figure out the meanings of the following ten word parts by looking *closely* and *carefully* at the context in which they appear. Then, in the space provided, write the letter of the meaning closest to that of each word part.

1 -able

- The couch was too hard to be a **comfortable** bed.
- Come on, now. Can you really say a movie like *Slaughter in the Subway* is **enjoyable**?

___ The word part *-able* means
    A. hand.   B. able to.   C. theory.

2 cent-, centi-

- Contrary to popular belief, the 21st **century** didn't start in 2000. It actually started in 2001 and will end in 2100.
- The **centipede** doesn't really have a hundred feet; it just has so many that it seems there are a hundred of them.

___ The word part *cent-* or *centi-* means
    A. two.   B. hundred.   C. remember.

3 in-

- The glass on the door was so clean that it was **invisible**, which explains why I walked into the door instead of opening it.
- "Only an **inexperienced** burglar leaves fingerprints," said the detective.

___ The word part *in-* means
    A. not.   B. science.   C. heat.

4 -logy, -ology

- "I'd probably major in **biology**," Suki explained, "if I didn't have to kill those little frogs."
- To help them find petroleum, oil companies hire people who have studied **geology**.

___ The word part *-logy* or *-ology* means
    A. good.   B. carry.   C. study of.

5 mal-

- What should we do about the many children suffering from neglect and **maltreatment**?
- When the doctor gave his patient a medicine with harmful side effects, the patient sued for **malpractice**.

___ The word part *mal-* means
    A. in.   B. bad.   C. carry.

6 man

- Mark Twain may have been the first author ever to give a publisher an entire **manuscript** that was typed, rather than handwritten.
- The worker's rough hands show he's done much **manual** labor.

___ The word part *man* means
    A. against.   B. badly.   C. hand.

7 mem

- I wrote a **memo** to remind me what to do today, but I forgot where I put it.
- In the small cemetery, every flower left in **memory** of a loved one shows up brightly.

___ The word part *mem* means   A. carry.   B. heat.   C. remember.

8 mono-, mon-

- When Pastor Brook preached in a **monotone**, he found his congregation snoring in stereo.
- **Monogamy** is not the only type of marriage relationship. In many societies, a person may have more than one mate at the same time.

___ The word part *mono-* or *mon-* means   A. one.   B. theory.   C. heat.

9 port

- We had so many suitcases that we had a **porter** take them from the airport to our car.
- "My daughter is truly generous," said Salvador. "She volunteers, donates clothing to shelters, and **supports** efforts to help the homeless."

___ The word part *port* means   A. write.   B. badly.   C. carry.

10 therm-, thermo-

- In the fall, a **thermos** full of hot soup is a great addition to any hiking gear.
- A digital **thermometer** beeps when a person's body heat has been fully measured.

___ The word part *therm-* or *thermo-* means   A. new.   B. science.   C. heat.

Matching Word Parts with Definitions

Following are definitions of the ten word parts. Clearly write or print each word part next to its definition. The sentences above and on the previous page will help you decide on the meaning of each word part.

1. _____ Not, lack of

2. _____ Study of, science of

3. _____ Hundred

4. _____ Heat

5. _____ Hand

6. _____ One

7. _____ Bad, badly

8. _____ Carry

9. _____ Remember

10. _____ Able to, able to be

CAUTION: Do not go any further until you are sure the above answers are correct. Then you can use the definitions to help you in the following practices. Your goal is eventually to know the word parts well enough so that you don't need to check the definitions at all.

Sentence Check 1

Using the answer line provided, complete each *italicized* word below with the correct word part from the box. Use each word part once.

A. -able	B. cent-, centi-	C. in-	D. -logy, -ology	E. mal-
F. man	G. mem	H. mono-, mon-	I. port	J. therm-, thermo-

_____ 1. The dogs had been fed so poorly that they suffered from (. . . *nutrition*) ___.

_____ 2. Five (. . . *meters*) ___ means 5/100 of a meter—the length of an eyebrow.

_____ 3. (*Crimin* . . .) ___ now includes the study of computer crime.

_____ 4. I always feel unsafe on a(n) (. . . *rail*) ___. I think a train is more safe running on two rails than on one.

_____ 5. To (. . . *orize*) the names of the five Great Lakes, remember "HOMES," which is made up of the lakes' initials: Huron, Ontario, Michigan, Erie, and Superior.

_____ 6. Before there were machines and robots, everything had to be (. . . *ufactured*) ___ by hand.

_____ 7. Young children can take only small doses of (. . . *activity*) ___, and then they need to move around.

_____ 8. The union representative objected, saying, "Asking the workers to take a 20 percent pay cut would be (*laugh* . . .) ___ if it weren't so awful."

_____ 9. When I visit my relatives in Alaska during the winter, I pack several pairs of (. . . *al*) ___ underwear.

_____ 10. In 1856, the U.S. Cavalry (*im* . . . *ed*) thirty-three camels from Egypt to use as mounts for its soldiers.

NOTE: Now check your answers to these items by turning to page 179. Going over the answers carefully will help you prepare for the next two practices, for which answers are not given.

Sentence Check 2

Using the answer line provided, complete each *italicized* word in the sentences below with the correct word part from the box. Use each word part once.

_____
_____ 1–2. "There is room for only one (. . . *arch*) ___ in this country," announced the king. "Anyone who disagrees with me will get free sea (*trans* . . . *ation*) ___—without a boat."

_____
_____ 3–4. In 1963, during the (. . . *ennial*) ___ of the Civil War (1861–1865), we visited a (. . . *orial*) ___ to some of the soldiers who had died. It's hard to conceive° of the extreme loss of life in that war—at least half a million died in battle!

_____   5–6. While others study (*climat . . .*) ___, I ignore the weather and simply leave
_____   my (. . . *ostat*) ___ set at a constant, comfortable sixty-eight degrees.

_____   7–8. I (. . . *icure*) ___ my nails the (. . . *expensive*) ___ way—by biting them.
_____

_____   9–10. It was (*debat . . .*) ___ whether the cake looked so weird because the oven
_____   (. . . *functioned*) ___ or because I forgot an ingredient. To be candid°, I think
                                  it's my fault.

Final Check: *King of Cats*

Here is a final opportunity for you to strengthen your knowledge of the ten word parts. First read the
following selection carefully. Then complete each *italicized* word in the parentheses below with a word
part from the box at the top of the previous page. (Context clues will help you figure out which word part
goes in which blank.) Use each word part once.

They called him King of Cats. He was young, impulsive°, and so
hotheaded that he had an (. . . *ability*) (1)_____
to keep his temper. He lived in an Italian city baked by (. . . *al*)
(2)_____ winds in the summer. Life in that
hot city was never (. . . *tonous*) (3)_____,
especially when his street gang encountered° a rival gang. (*Re . . . s*)
(4)_____ of bloodshed often followed such meetings.
He was raised to fight for his family, including his beautiful cousin. He
was willing to do anything to keep her safe from insult or (. . . *treatment*) (5)_____.

This girl fell in love with the leader of a rival gang. Perhaps today's (*psych . . .*) (6)_____
could explain why. At the time, it seemed she was simply (. . . *ipulated*) (7)_____
by fate to fall in love with someone who would be (*unaccept . . .*) (8)_____ to
her relatives. One (. . . *orable*) (9)_____ afternoon of that sad year in the sixteenth
(. . . *ury*) (10)_____, blades flashed. The King of Cats lethally° stabbed a member of
that rival gang. His cousin's lover reciprocated° by stabbing him back—to his death, an action that led to
the lover's exile° . . . and even more tragic consequences°.

The King of Cats' name was Tybalt Capulet. His cousin was called Juliet; her lover was Romeo.

Scores   Sentence Check 2 _____%   Final Check _____%

The box at the right lists twenty-five words from Unit Four. Using the clues at the bottom of the page, fill in these words to complete the puzzle that follows.

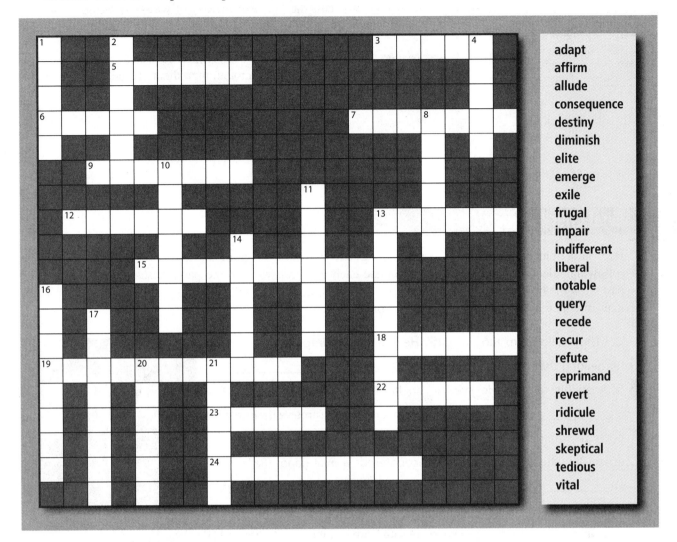

adapt
affirm
allude
consequence
destiny
diminish
elite
emerge
exile
frugal
impair
indifferent
liberal
notable
query
recede
recur
refute
reprimand
revert
ridicule
shrewd
skeptical
tedious
vital

ACROSS

3. Being or intended for the best or most privileged; superior

5. To rise up or come forth

6. To occur again; happen repeatedly

7. Famous; widely known

9. Something bound to happen to someone; fate

12. To refer indirectly

13. Clever; tricky

15. A result

18. To damage; weaken

19. Having no real interest; unconcerned

22. To adjust to a situation

23. Necessary; extremely important

24. A formal criticism; a harsh scolding

DOWN

1. To question; ask

2. To prove wrong or false

4. Separation from one's native country through force or choice

8. To indicate to be true; state with certainty

10. Boring; uninteresting because of great length, slowness, or repetition

11. Large in amount or quantity; generous

13. Doubting; questioning

14. To move back or away from a particular point or limit

16. To lessen; decrease

17. To make fun of; mock

20. Thrifty; avoiding unnecessary expenses

21. To return to a previous habit or condition

PART A

Choose the word that best completes each item and write it in the space provided.

_____ 1. It may not seem ___, but it's true—some people need only fifteen minutes of sleep a day.

    A. frugal   B. tedious   C. elaborate   D. plausible

_____ 2. In ___ translation, words are translated as they are spoken. The translator has to be able to listen and talk at the same time.

    A. simultaneous   B. liberal   C. mediocre   D. frugal

_____ 3. A bee will usually not sting unless you first ___ it—for example, by swatting at it.

    A. adapt   B. retain   C. provoke   D. allude

_____ 4. Many ___ shoppers buy soy-based foods because these foods are inexpensive sources of protein.

    A. tedious   B. impulsive   C. frugal   D. sadistic

_____ 5. The singer's voice is only ___, but he's very popular because his personality is so appealing.

    A. notable   B. mediocre   C. vital   D. elite

_____ 6. Although the police report mentioned a(n) ___ "break-in," the gold theft may actually have been an "inside" job.

    A. tedious   B. indulgent   C. alleged   D. indifferent

_____ 7. Tokyo, Japan, has a simple ___ for fitting as many people as possible into rush-hour trains: workers are hired to push people onto the trains.

    A. exile   B. stereotype   C. strategy   D. immunity

_____ 8. My teacher meant to ___, "Why did you miss the history lecture?" Instead he asked, "Why did you hiss the mystery lecture?"

    A. detain   B. recede   C. query   D. allude

_____ 9. The most important ___ in my parents' lives was the purchase of their house.

    A. stereotype   B. essence   C. query   D. transaction

_____ 10. Experts have ___ the idea that giant redwood trees are the oldest living things on Earth. Certain pine trees that are about 4,600 years of age are now known to be older.

    A. refuted   B. coerced   C. emerged   D. provoked

(Continues on next page)

PART B

On the answer line, write the letter of the choice that best completes each item.

_____ 11. Diners **emerge** from a restaurant
    A. to look for something to eat.
    B. after they have finished their meals.
    C. only if they have liked the food.
    D. according to its price, selection, and quality.

_____ 12. One **gesture** of friendship is
    A. offering to treat your friend to a meal.
    B. two people having many things in common.
    C. screening incoming phone calls.
    D. not having time to spend with friends.

_____ 13. **Sadistic** people are often the main characters in
    A. picture books.
    B. horror movies.
    C. TV sitcoms.
    D. romantic comedies.

_____ 14. "It is my **destiny** to be a star," Melanie insisted. She obviously
    A. feared she'd never be a star.
    B. was interested in astronomy.
    C. believed in fate.
    D. has no talent.

_____ 15. During the **tedious** TV movie, I
    A. laughed until I actually fell off my chair.
    B. covered my face in horror.
    C. cried until I used up all my tissues.
    D. made a grocery list, just to pass the time.

_____ 16. When he was told that the pay for his summer job would be **liberal**, Sammy said,
    A. "I can't afford to work for so little. I'll have to find another job."
    B. "It's not much, but I guess it will be OK."
    C. "Why are you paying me only once a month?"
    D. "Wonderful! I didn't expect to earn that much."

_____ 17. Naturally, the child received a **reprimand** when she
    A. purposely smashed her grandmother's favorite vase.
    B. rescued her little brother from the swimming pool.
    C. asked if she could have a puppy for her birthday.
    D. hugged her father when he lost his job, telling him, "Your boss is a naughty man."

_____ 18. The new beauty salon, Scissors Palace, is so **elite** that
    A. neighborhood kids go there for haircuts.
    B. people can get their hair done there without an appointment.
    C. most of its clients are celebrities.
    D. nobody goes there more than once—its stylists are terrible.

_____ 19. My dog's interest in the kitchen **diminished** when
    A. he realized the can I was opening was not for him.
    B. it was his usual lunchtime.
    C. someone in the kitchen called his name.
    D. he heard the sound of his dish being put on the floor.

_____ 20. LaTanya **alluded** to the size of the rich woman's five-carat diamond ring by
    A. saying, "Is it hailing tonight? Someone seems to have a big chunk of ice stuck to her hand."
    B. exclaiming in a loud voice, "Good grief, look at the size of that diamond!"
    C. asking the woman if she had had the ring for a long time.
    D. ignoring the woman and her ring completely.

Score   (Number correct) _____   x 5 = _____%

Enter your scores above and in the **Vocabulary Performance Chart** on the inside back cover of the book.

PART A

Complete each item with a word from the box. Use each word once.

A. **adapt**	B. **coerce**	C. **elaborate**	D. **essence**	E. **exile**
F. **indulgent**	G. **procrastinate**	H. **reciprocate**	I. **recur**	J. **retain**
K. **revert**	L. **stereotype**	M. **tactic**		

_____ 1. After my brother gave me the measles, I ___(e)d by giving him the mumps.

_____ 2. The ___ dollhouse included many realistic details, such as tiny lamps, clocks, and flowers in vases.

_____ 3. The ___ of a thunderstorm is energy—energy sometimes equal to that of a dozen atomic bombs.

_____ 4. To make sure a hamstring injury does not ___, always stretch your leg muscles before working out.

_____ 5. There's a club for people who like to ___. They haven't met yet because they keep postponing their first meeting.

_____ 6. The ___ of the cowboy is that of a rough and romantic loner, but most cowboys actually spent their days doing routine chores.

_____ 7. A well-known Chinese author had to leave his homeland to avoid being imprisoned. He was forced into ___ for attacking the Chinese government in his writings.

_____ 8. On New Year's Eve I decided to stop eating chocolate, but on January 4th I ___(e)d to my old ways—stocking up on on Mars bars and M&M's.

_____ 9. Deaf people have ___(e)d to today's technology in clever ways. For example, they use vibrating wireless pagers as their cell phones.

_____ 10. Many students have used the ___ of blaming the computer for their missed deadlines. They say, for example, "When I tried to print, it erased my whole paper."

_____ 11. In ancient Rome, some of the wealthiest and most self-___ people powdered their hair every day with pure gold dust.

_____ 12. Built of white marble and decorated with gems, the famous Taj Mahal of India has ___(e)d its beauty for more than three hundred years.

_____ 13. Because a thief might ___ you into handing over a wallet, carry an extra one with little money, an old ID card, and out-of-date credit cards.

(Continues on next page)

PART B

Write **C** if the italicized word is used **correctly**. Write **I** if the word is used **incorrectly**.

_____ 14. Judging by the smile of relief on his face, the x-ray *dismayed* Dr. Ali.

_____ 15. Iris is so *impulsive* that she won't even take a step outside without first listening to a weather report.

_____ 16. If you're entering a movie theater with a crowd, it's *shrewd* to go left. Since most people head right, you'll get a better choice of seats that way.

_____ 17. The construction company had its license *revoked* when its materials were found to be dangerously weak.

_____ 18. My brother used to *ridicule* me for talking on the phone so much. He would holler, "Get a doctor! A phone is growing out of Stacy's head."

_____ 19. Today, those who walk or drive in the city are *detained* by stoplights and traffic. In the future, however, moving sidewalks may make city travel faster by doing away with the need for vehicles and stoplights.

PART C

On the answer line, write the letter of the word that is the **synonym** of the boldfaced word.

Example: __A__ **plausible**   A. believable   B. doubtful   C. soft

_____ 20. **impair**   A. weaken   B. call   C. strengthen

_____ 21. **notable**   A. clumsy   B. unknown   C. famous

_____ 22. **exotic**   A. ordinary   B. unusual   C. fragrant

PART D

On the answer line, write the letter of the word that is the **antonym** of the boldfaced word.

Example: __B__ **plausible**   A. believable   B. doubtful   C. soft

_____ 23. **recede**   A. move   B. retreat   C. advance

_____ 24. **affirm**   A. deny   B. injure   C. state

_____ 25. **consequence**   A. pattern   B. result   C. cause

Score   (Number correct) _____ x 4 = _____ %

Each item below starts with a pair of words in CAPITAL LETTERS. For each item, figure out the relationship between these two words. Then decide which of the choices (A, B, C, or D) expresses a similar relationship. Write the letter of your choice on the answer line.

_____ 1. ADAPT : CLIMATE ::
    A. lose : discovery
    B. admire : criminal
    C. adjust : new job
    D. admit : denial

_____ 2. EXILE : HOMELAND ::
    A. engagement : wedding
    B. health : recovery
    C. divorce : spouse
    D. employment : career

_____ 3. RECEDE : MOVE BACK ::
    A. sit : move around
    B. climb : move sideways
    C. descend : move up
    D. advance : move forward

_____ 4. RITUAL : BAPTISM ::
    A. appliance : dishwasher
    B. tradition : cloning
    C. dinner : birthday cake
    D. superstition : voting

_____ 5. EXOTIC : LOCAL ::
    A. handmade : designed
    B. foreign : automobiles
    C. homegrown : planted
    D. fake : real

_____ 6. IMPULSIVE : UNPREDICTABLE ::
    A. first : last
    B. fearful : frightened
    C. well-organized : wealthy
    D. private : well-known

_____ 7. INDIFFERENT : CONCERNED ::
    A. calm : anxious
    B. confident : certain
    C. worried : nervous
    D. uninterested : bored

_____ 8. MEDIOCRE : AVERAGE ::
    A. good : best
    B. poor : below average
    C. bad : worst
    D. average : worse

_____ 9. AFFIRM : DENY ::
    A. state : swear
    B. gather : scatter
    C. promise : keep
    D. disagree : disprove

_____ 10. IMMUNITY : VACCINATION ::
    A. work : vacation
    B. relief : disappointment
    C. knowledge : education
    D. tiredness : rest

(Continues on next page)

____ 11. IMPAIR : DESTROY ::
    A. improve : make perfect   C. strengthen : weaken
    B. want : dislike   D. damage : build

____ 12. QUERY : ANSWER ::
    A. wed : career   C. speak : sentence
    B. sleep : dinner   D. invite : response

____ 13. PROVOKE : CALM ::
    A. delay : postpone   C. recognize : friendship
    B. discourage : stop   D. forbid : allow

____ 14. REPRIMAND : LAZY WORKER ::
    A. praise : noisy neighbor   C. thanks : rude store clerk
    B. compliment : mugger   D. scolding : disobedient child

____ 15. SKEPTICAL : LIAR ::
    A. admiring : cheater   C. fearful : killer
    B. pleased : driver   D. confused : comedian

____ 16. STEREOTYPE : IMAGE ::
    A. fact : falsehood   C. reality : dream
    B. opinion : view   D. wish : fear

____ 17. CONSEQUENCE : ACTION ::
    A. prediction : past   C. effect : cause
    B. odor : sight   D. absence : wish

____ 18. DETAIN : DELAY ::
    A. hurry : slow down   C. combine : separate
    B. dismiss : leave   D. chat : talk

____ 19. DIMINISH : INCREASE ::
    A. grow : mature   C. fall : rise
    B. weaken : die   D. spread : expand

____ 20. VITAL : NECESSARY ::
    A. interesting : boring   C. chosen : rejected
    B. useful : advice   D. outstanding : superior

Score   (Number correct) _____ x 5 = _____%

Enter your scores above and in the **Vocabulary Performance Chart** on the inside back cover of the book.

PART A

Listed in the left-hand column below are ten common word parts, followed by words in which the parts are used. In each blank, write in the letter of the correct definition on the right.

Word Parts	Examples	Definitions
____ 1. **-able**	comfortable, enjoyable	A. Carry
____ 2. **cent-, centi-**	century, centipede	B. By hand
____ 3. **in-**	invisible, inexperienced	C. Able to, able to be
____ 4. **-ology, -logy**	biology, geology	D. Hundred
____ 5. **mal-**	maltreatment, malpractice	E. Not, lack of
____ 6. **man**	manuscript, manual	F. Heat
____ 7. **mem**	memo, memorial	G. Study of, science of
____ 8. **mono-, mon-**	monotone, monogamy	H. One
____ 9. **port**	porter, support	I. Bad, badly
____ 10. **therm-, thermo-**	thermos, thermometer	J. Remember

PART B

Using the answer line provided, complete each *italicized* word in the sentences below with the correct word part from the box. Not every word part will be used.

A. **-able**	B. **cent-**	C. **in-**	D. **-ology**	E. **mal-**
F. **man**	G. **mem**	H. **mono-**	I. **port**	J. **therm-**

_____ 11. Someone who knows we all make mistakes invented an (*eras . . .*) ___ ink.

_____ 12. (*Soci . . .*) ___ is the study of the origins, development, and institutions of human society.

_____ 13. One mental patient has such a damaged (*. . . ory*) ___ that he can't remember what happened only a few minutes before.

_____ 14. After working so hard on my flower garden, I wish it were (*. . . able*) ___. Then I could take it with me next month when I move to a new house.

_____ 15. The lawyer claimed his client was (*. . . sane*) ___ when she killed her husband with a steam iron.

(Continues on next page)

PART C

Use your knowledge of word parts to determine the meaning of the **boldfaced** words. On the answer line, write the letter of each meaning.

_____ 16. My grandmother will be a **centenarian** next month, so we're having a huge party.

    A. student   B. hundred-year-old   C. great-great-grandmother

_____ 17. The first clay pot I ever made was very **malformed**.

    A. formed too small   B. poorly formed   C. formed by hand

_____ 18. Tarzan's vocabulary included many **monosyllabic** words: "Jane. Come. We find Boy."

    A. one-syllable   B. few-syllable   C. many-syllable

_____ 19. The sheriff reached for **manacles** to put on the violent drunk driver.

    A. ropes   B. chains   C. handcuffs

_____ 20. For silly fun, my family used to go on picnics in the winter. Mother would pack steaming thick soup in a **thermos** jug.

    A. a jug made by hand   B. a jug that can be carried   C. a jug that keeps things warm

Score   (Number correct) _____ x 5 = _____%

Enter your scores above and in the **Vocabulary Performance Chart** on the inside back cover of the book.

Unit Five

Chapter 25

discriminate	site
dismal	subside
dispense	summon
profound	theoretical
severity	vocation

Chapter 26

ascend	initiate
finite	literally
infinite	lure
inflict	mania
ingenious	nostalgia

Chapter 27

data	morbid
inept	obstinate
innate	parallel
intervene	perceptive
lament	sedate

Chapter 28

controversy	dominant
deduction	sequence
dimensions	sophisticated
disperse	treacherous
distort	trivial

Chapter 29

confirm	submit
deceptive	susceptible
defy	transmit
restrain	valid
seclusion	vigorous

Chapter 30

accelerate	comparable
adverse	competent
advocate	consecutive
audible	conspicuous
coherent	deteriorate

discriminate	site
dismal	subside
dispense	summon
profound	theoretical
severity	vocation

Ten Words in Context

In the space provided, write the letter of the meaning closest to that of each **boldfaced** word. Use the context of the sentences to help you figure out each word's meaning.

1 discriminate
(dĭ-skrĭm′ə-nāt′)
-verb

- It's easy to **discriminate** between canned and fresh vegetables—fresh vegetables taste much better.
- Tests show that women tend to **discriminate** among colors better than men. Cherry red, cranberry red, and purplish red are all simply dark red to many men.

___ *Discriminate* means   A. to tell the difference.   B. to become confused.   C. to make an error.

2 dismal
(dĭz′məl)
-adjective

- Tyrell was disappointed by the **dismal** news that his knee injury would keep him off the football team for a whole semester.
- "It is a **dismal**, rainy day," Mona told her disappointed children. "But we don't have to cancel the picnic—we can have it on the kitchen floor."

___ *Dismal* means   A. welcome.   B. lengthy.   C. gloomy.

3 dispense
(dĭ-spĕns′)
-verb

- The broken soda machine **dispensed** either a cup or soda, but not both together.
- Restroom soap holders that are supposed to **dispense** liquid soap at each push seem to be empty most of the time.

___ *Dispense* means   A. to pay.   B. to give out.   C. to do without.

4 profound
(prə-found′)
-adjective

- The death of a spouse can cause **profound** depression that, in some cases, can even lead to the death of the partner.
- Ever since her stepfather insulted her mother, Serena has had a **profound** hatred of him.

___ *Profound* means   A. deep.   B. mild.   C. accidental.

5 severity
(sə-vĕr′ə-tē)
-noun

- The **severity** of the fire could be seen in the burned, smoking ruins of the once beautiful building.
- Mark believes the **severity** of his punishment was too great. A hundred hours of weekend trash cleanup seemed too harsh a penalty for throwing two soft-drink cans onto the highway.

___ *Severity* means   A. gentleness.   B. intensity.   C. a cause.

6 site
(sīt)
-noun

- The oldest private home in the New England town was named a historical **site**.
- Wounded Knee, South Dakota, is the **site** of a conflict between the federal government and the Sioux Indians in 1973.

___ *Site* means   A. a state.   B. a fact.   C. a place.

7 subside
(səb-sīd′)
-verb

- When I'm really furious, a walk around the block makes my anger **subside**.
- Connie sat in her car until the storm **subsided**. Then she dashed up the sidewalk and into the school building.

___ *Subside* means   A. to begin.   B. to lessen.   C. to increase.

8 summon
(sŭm′ən)
-verb

- When the king couldn't sleep, he would **summon** the court clown to come and entertain him.
- The principal liked to **summon** troublesome students to his office by announcing their names over the loudspeaker.

___ *Summon* means   A. to send for.   B. to see.   C. to allow.

9 theoretical
(thē′ə-rĕt′ĭ-kəl)
-adjective

- At first, Phan enjoyed simply looking through his telescope. However, when questions occurred to him, he began to read **theoretical** explanations of what he was seeing.
- The teacher explained the **theoretical** basis for the chemistry experiment so the class would understand why it worked as it did.

___ *Theoretical* means   A. about action.   B. scientifically possible.   C. only imagined.

10 vocation
(vō-kā′shən)
-noun

- Raising collies was just a hobby for Louise. Her **vocation** was library science.
- If you can't decide on a career, you might wish to take a test that reveals which **vocations** you're suited for.

___ *Vocation* means   A. recreation.   B. an activity.   C. an occupation.

Matching Words with Definitions

Following are definitions of the ten words. Clearly write or print each word next to its definition. The sentences above and on the previous page will help you decide on the meaning of each word.

1. _____ Deeply felt

2. _____ To see differences; distinguish

3. _____ The past, present, or future location of a building or buildings or an event

4. _____ A profession or occupation

5. _____ About or based on theory (as opposed to practice or practical use); based on a possible explanation; hypothetical

6. _____ Gloomy; cheerless; depressing

7. _____ To send for; order to appear

8. _____ To give out in portions or amounts

9. _____ The condition or quality of being severe; harshness; intensity; seriousness

10. _____ To become less active; calm down; decrease

CAUTION: Do not go any further until you are sure the above answers are correct. Then you can use the definitions to help you in the following practices. Your goal is eventually to know the words well enough so that you don't need to check the definitions at all.

Sentence Check 1

Using the answer line provided, complete each item below with the correct word from the box. Use each word once.

A. **discriminate**	B. **dismal**	C. **dispense**	D. **profound**	E. **severity**
F. **site**	G. **subside**	H. **summon**	I. **theoretical**	J. **vocation**

_____ 1. Since the alligator and the crocodile look a lot alike, most people cannot ___ between them.

_____ 2. Growing up with poverty gave Juanita a ___ desire to help others in need.

_____ 3. Near the shore, the waves were enormous, but as we rowed out into open water, they began to ___.

_____ 4. I thought I was in trouble when my boss ___(e)d me to her office—until she told me I was getting a raise.

_____ 5. Among the most dangerous ___s are deep-sea diving, mining, and construction.

_____ 6. This room is too ___. It needs a party to brighten it up.

_____ 7. Do you think food machines at public schools should ___ only nutritious foods, such as fruit and juices?

_____ 8. Medication should match the ___ of a problem. A powerful painkiller isn't needed for a hangnail.

_____ 9. I can use the math formulas, but I don't understand the ___ basis for them.

_____ 10. Although the ___ where the hiker claimed a spaceship had landed was burned, no one believed his story.

NOTE: Now check your answers to these items by turning to page 179. Going over the answers carefully will help you prepare for the next two practices, for which answers are not given.

Sentence Check 2

Using the answer lines provided, complete each item below with **two** words from the box. Use each word once.

_____
_____ 1–2. My visit to the school for learning-disabled children had a ___ effect on me—it altered° my career plans. I was going to be a nurse, but that day I decided my ___ would be in special education.

_____
_____ 3–4. It is hard to convey° the terror one feels in seeing someone get hit by a car. It was not until I was ten miles away from the ___ of the accident that my shaking began to ___.

_____
_____ 5–6. The movie was meant to be a dark comedy, but I found it to be ___. I often couldn't ___ between lines in the dialog° that were meant to be funny and lines that were just depressing.

_____ 7–8. If you have a question about the principles of this music, we will have to
_____   ___ Mr. Burns from his office. A notable° author of music textbooks, he has
                              studied music for years. I can play the music, but I have no ___ knowledge.

_____ 9–10. Some hospitals now allow patients to judge the ___ of their own pain and to
_____   ___ small amounts of medication to themselves as necessary until the pain
                               diminishes°.

Final Check: *A Change in View*

Here is a final opportunity for you to strengthen your knowledge of the ten words. First read the following
selection carefully. Then fill in each blank with a word from the box at the top of the previous page.
(Context clues will help you figure out which word goes in which blank.) Use each word once.

What an education I got yesterday! I am studying to be a
nurse. Part of my preparation for this (1)_____
is (2)_____, and part is practical experience.
Yesterday, after weeks of studying about mental illness in textbooks,
I began my training in a mental hospital. Influenced by the movie
stereotype° of such hospitals as being full of zombies and wild
people, I was scared. I imagined dark, (3)_____
rooms where people sat staring and drooling. I pictured screaming,
sadistic° patients trying to hurt me so badly that I would have to
(4)_____ the guards. I wondered how I would
survive this ordeal°.

But yesterday my view of mental hospitals and their patients
went through a (5)_____ change. First of all, the (6)_____ of the
hospital is at the edge of a lovely small town, and its grounds are green and neat. When I arrived there, I
was brought to a big, cheerful room, decorated in vivid° colors, and filled with patients whose morale° was
high. They were talking, doing craft projects, or playing Ping-Pong or cards.

I spoke to one patient. She seemed like a nice, normal person who happened to have problems. She
reminisced° about the time she first came to the hospital, when the (7)_____ of her illness
had been much greater. At that time, she could not always (8)_____ between reality and
her delusions°. Like many patients, she was often upset and confused. But the doctors put her on medicine,
which the nurses still (9)_____ three times a day. The medicine, as well as talks with the
doctors, nurses, and other patients, has helped make her symptoms (10)_____. Perhaps
our conversation was helpful to her; I know it helped me. Now I'm thinking about working in the mental
health field after I get my nursing degree.

| Scores | Sentence Check 2 _____% | Final Check _____% |

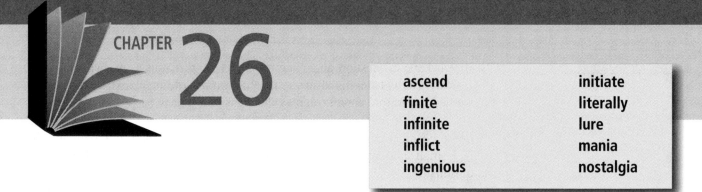

ascend	initiate
finite	literally
infinite	lure
inflict	mania
ingenious	nostalgia

Ten Words in Context

In the space provided, write the letter of the meaning closest to that of each **boldfaced** word. Use the context of the sentences to help you figure out each word's meaning.

1 ascend
(ə-sĕnd′)
-verb

- The express elevator **ascends** directly from the hotel lobby to the restaurant on the twentieth floor.
- Edgar is the boss's son, so he expects to **ascend** to the presidency of the company after his father retires.

___ *Ascend* means   A. to go slowly.   B. to go down.   C. to move upward.

2 finite
(fī′nīt′)
-adjective

- The earth's supply of natural resources is **finite**. If we are not careful, we will use it up.
- Judging by their endless requests for money, most children don't seem to realize that their parents' income is **finite**.

___ *Finite* means   A. limited.   B. endless.   C. fine.

3 infinite
(ĭn′fə-nĭt)
-adjective

- Some scientists do not believe the universe is **infinite**; they think it actually has limits.
- Dealing with my baby brother, who cries a lot, requires an **infinite** amount of patience.

___ *Infinite* means   A. endless.   B. known.   C. small.

4 inflict
(ĭn-flĭkt′)
-verb

- When Marge is angry, she tries to **inflict** pain with a cutting remark—a habit that does not make her popular with her classmates.
- Loud music can eventually **inflict** permanent damage on your hearing.

___ *Inflict* means   A. to prevent.   B. to cause.   C. to recognize.

5 ingenious
(ĭn-gēn′yəs)
-adjective

- Fran thought she had an **ingenious** plan to sneak out of the house, but it wasn't clever enough to fool her grandmother.
- Few people have been as **ingenious** as Thomas Edison, inventor of the electric light, the phonograph, and the movie camera.

___ *Ingenious* means   A. average.   B. unimaginative.   C. clever.

6 initiate
(ĭ-nĭsh′ē-āt′)
-verb

- Eric **initiated** a change in his company's hiring policy by suggesting that all job openings be advertised.
- True leaders **initiate** new practices, rather than simply following other people's programs.

___ *Initiate* means   A. to remember.   B. to begin.   C. to oppose.

7 literally
(lĭt′ər-ə-lē)
-adverb

● As a child, Jan took the term "man in the moon" **literally**. She was sure she saw his eyes, nose, and mouth up there.

● When I told my nephew to "go fly a kite," I was speaking **literally**—I gave him a kite for his birthday.

__ *Literally* means   A. exactly.   B. angrily.   C. fearfully.

8 lure
(lo͞or)
-verb

● The bakery **lured** customers by displaying richly decorated cakes and cookies in its windows.

● The loud music and flashing lights **lured** many teens to the carnival.

__ *Lure* means   A. to force.   B. to discourage.   C. to tempt.

9 mania
(mā′nē-ə)
-noun

● My sister has such a **mania** for birdwatching that she once climbed a tree to get a better view of a woodpecker.

● Because he's so thin, you'd never guess Ken has a **mania** for chocolate, which he eats daily.

__ *Mania* means   A. a memory.   B. an intense enthusiasm.   C. respect.

10 nostalgia
(nŏ-stăl′jə)
-noun

● Music from the 1940s fills my grandparents with **nostalgia** because it reminds them of their carefree youth.

● When he came across an old photo of his Little League team, Jerry was overcome with **nostalgia**. He wished he could be ten years old again.

__ *Nostalgia* means   A. a sense of freedom.   B. thoughts of the future.   C. a longing for the past.

Matching Words with Definitions

Following are definitions of the ten words. Clearly write or print each word next to its definition. The sentences above and on the previous page will help you decide on the meaning of each word.

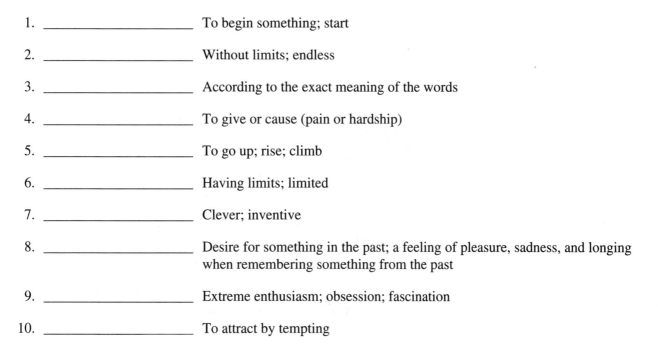

1. _____ To begin something; start

2. _____ Without limits; endless

3. _____ According to the exact meaning of the words

4. _____ To give or cause (pain or hardship)

5. _____ To go up; rise; climb

6. _____ Having limits; limited

7. _____ Clever; inventive

8. _____ Desire for something in the past; a feeling of pleasure, sadness, and longing when remembering something from the past

9. _____ Extreme enthusiasm; obsession; fascination

10. _____ To attract by tempting

CAUTION: Do not go any further until you are sure the above answers are correct. Then you can use the definitions to help you in the following practices. Your goal is eventually to know the words well enough so that you don't need to check the definitions at all.

Sentence Check 1

Using the answer line provided, complete each item below with the correct word from the box. Use each word once.

A. **ascend**	B. **finite**	C. **infinite**	D. **inflict**	E. **ingenious**
F. **initiate**	G. **literally**	H. **lure**	I. **mania**	J. **nostalgia**

_____ 1. We often ___ conversations with routine questions or comments, such as "How are you today?" or "Hello there."

_____ 2. Although the English alphabet is ____, the possible combinations of its letters are almost endless.

_____ 3. Many people think of dentists as people who actually like to ___ pain.

_____ 4. Sue feels a wave of ___ when she thinks about the happy days of her childhood on the farm.

_____ 5. The opportunity to be helpful ___s people to such fields as nursing and teaching.

_____ 6. Because of a(n) ___ for the latest computer game, stores couldn't keep enough in stock.

_____ 7. By working hard, Layla quickly ___(e)d the ladder of success, from secretary to office manager.

_____ 8. There are so many stars in the sky that their number seems ___.

_____ 9. When temperatures are in the nineties, I'm grateful to the ___ person who invented the air conditioner.

_____ 10. Felipe kicked the bucket—___. In other words, he only stubbed his toe; he didn't die.

NOTE: Now check your answers to these items by turning to page 179. Going over the answers carefully will help you prepare for the next two practices, for which answers are not given.

Sentence Check 2

Using the answer lines provided, complete each item below with **two** words from the box. Use each word once.

_____
_____ 1–2. Some say it is good that our lifetimes are ___, that a(n) ___ number of years would make life less meaningful. However, everyone agrees we should still try to find ways to fight illness and prolong° life.

_____
_____ 3–4. The West continues to ___ my grandfather, who was raised there. Because of his ___ for his youth, he drives from Florida to Colorado every summer.

_____
_____ 5–6. As the documentary film *Trekkies* shows, some fans of the TV series *Star Trek* have such a ___ for their favorite characters that they even ___ plastic surgery on themselves in an effort to resemble those characters.

_____   7–8. A red-tailed hawk can ___ hundreds of feet into the air by locking its wings
_____   open and riding an upward wind. Then it merely folds its wings and aims at
                                   the ground to ___ a dive.

_____   9–10. One of the world's most ___ scientists, Albert Einstein, ___ gave his brain to
_____   science. As one final gesture° of his love for science, he ordered in his will
                                   that his brain be given for study to a laboratory in Wichita, Kansas.

Final Check: *Balloon Flight*

Here is a final opportunity for you to strengthen your knowledge of the ten words. First read the following selection carefully. Then fill in each blank with a word from the box at the top of the previous page. (Context clues will help you figure out which word goes in which blank.) Use each word once.

Human flight was (1)_____(e)d by a rooster, a duck, and a sheep. A(n) (2)_____ inventor got them to try out the first flying machine. Of course, skeptical° people ridiculed° the idea that a machine could fly. But they were forced to defer° to the clever inventor when the animals left the (3)_____ world of the ground to fly into the endless sky for eight minutes. The year was 1783, the place was France, and the aircraft was a hot-air balloon. (Because hot air rises, heating the air in the balloon causes it to (4)_____.)

Since the experience didn't (5)_____ any serious injury on the animals, three months later the idea of flying (6)_____(e)d a man named de Rozier, who became the first human to look down on the rooftops of Paris from a hot-air balloon.

In the early 1900s, after 125 years had elapsed°, ballooning was at its peak. In 1910, one retail company described ballooning in its catalog with these words, "The whole world is before us in the (7)_____ loveliness of dawn!" (Daybreak, with its calm air, is the best time as well as one of the most beautiful times to fly.)

Although flight has certainly evolved° since the eighteenth century, hot-air balloon rides are still available in some places. For people with (8)_____ for the olden days, before the (9)_____ for faster and faster travel, a balloon flight is a wonderful way to spend some delightful time (10)_____ floating on air.

Scores   Sentence Check 2 _____%   Final Check _____%

data	morbid
inept	obstinate
innate	parallel
intervene	parallel
lament	perceptive
	sedate

Ten Words in Context

In the space provided, write the letter of the meaning closest to that of each **boldfaced** word. Use the context of the sentences to help you figure out each word's meaning.

1 data
(dā′tə)
-*noun*

● Marva considers the available **data** on a car—including its fuel economy, safety, and repair record—before deciding whether to buy it.

● Jane Goodall collected important **data** on chimpanzees by observing them in the wild.

___ *Data* means   A. dates.   B. information.   C. goals.

2 inept
(ĭn-ĕpt′)
-*adjective*

● I am so **inept** at carpentry that in my hand, a hammer is a dangerous weapon.

● Since the actress was **inept** at playing comic characters, she decided to try out only for dramatic roles.

___ *Inept* means   A. effective.   B. unskilled.   C. calm.

3 innate
(ĭ-nāt′)
-*adjective*

● Rick's musical ability must be **innate**. Even as a young child, he could play the piano by ear and make up his own songs.

● Psychologists try to learn which of our abilities and interests are **innate** and which of them we gain through experience.

___ *Innate* means   A. present from birth.   B. worthwhile.   C. learned through experience.

4 intervene
(ĭn′tər-vēn′)
-*verb*

● The two boxers would have killed each other if the referee hadn't finally **intervened**.

● When my brothers argue, I get out of the way rather than trying to **intervene**.

___ *Intervene* means   A. to leave.   B. to pass through.   C. to come between.

5 lament
(lə-mĕnt′)
-*verb*

● When her mother died, Evelyn **lamented** her passing for weeks, crying every day.

● Blues songs **lament** loneliness, sadness, and the hardships of life, rather than celebrating happy situations.

___ *Lament* means   A. to mourn.   B. to doubt.   C. to disturb.

6 morbid
(môr′bĭd)
-*adjective*

● Great comedians can turn a topic as **morbid** as murder into a source of laughter.

● On Halloween, sweet little Nickie chose a **morbid** costume—a disgusting-looking monster with a "bloody" hand and hatchet.

___ *Morbid* means   A. horrible.   B. convenient.   C. boring.

7 obstinate
(ŏb′stə-nĭt)
-adjective

- No matter how much I urged him, Andrew remained **obstinate**—he refused to make up with Lonnell, who was once his best friend.
- My father is usually very **obstinate**, but not with his sister, who is even more stubborn than he is.

___ *Obstinate* means   A. lazy.   B. dishonest.   C. stubborn.

8 parallel
(păr′ə-lĕl′)
-adjective

- To make the stripes he was painting **parallel**, Alexei measured to be sure there were exactly three inches between them at the top, middle, and bottom.
- **Parallel** lines run alongside each other but never meet.

___ *Parallel* means   A. clear.   B. apart an equal distance at every point.   C. going up and down.

9 perceptive
(pər-sĕp′tĭv)
-adjective

- Children are more **perceptive** than many people think. They can usually sense their parents' moods and know whether or not it is a good time to ask for something.
- Professor Banks is very **perceptive**. She always seems to know which of her students are under unusual stress.

___ *Perceptive* means   A. detached.   B. aware.   C. selfish.

10 sedate
(sĭ-dāt′)
-adjective

- While the officer wrote out the ticket, Beverly remained **sedate**, and then she even wished him a pleasant day. But after he left, she pounded the steering wheel and screamed, "Why me!?"
- An experienced surgeon, Dr. Greenbaum remains **sedate** even in an emergency, performing the most complicated operations with complete self-control.

___ *Sedate* means   A. angry.   B. doubtful.   C. calm.

Matching Words with Definitions

Following are definitions of the ten words. Clearly write or print each word next to its definition. The sentences above and on the previous page will help you decide on the meaning of each word.

1. _____ To come between in order to influence an action, an argument, etc.

2. _____ Calm and dignified; serious and unemotional

3. _____ The same distance apart at every point

4. _____ Understanding and insightful; observant; aware

5. _____ Information gathered for a study or a decision

6. _____ Possessed at birth; inborn

7. _____ To express sorrow for or about; mourn for

8. _____ Shocking and disgusting; horrible; gruesome

9. _____ Clumsy; unskillful

10. _____ Stubborn

CAUTION: Do not go any further until you are sure the above answers are correct. Then you can use the definitions to help you in the following practices. Your goal is eventually to know the words well enough so that you don't need to check the definitions at all.

Sentence Check 1

Using the answer line provided, complete each item below with the correct word from the box. Use each word once.

A. data	B. inept	C. innate	D. intervene	E. lament
F. morbid	G. obstate	H. parallel	I. perceptive	J. sedate

_____ 1. For his psychology experiment, Rudy is gathering ___ to show which memory aids work best for students.

_____ 2. I'm so ___ at bowling that I usually roll the ball straight into the gutter.

_____ 3. The child had nightmares after he listened to a(n) ___ story about Dracula that was full of attacks by vampires.

_____ 4. While my dog gets excited easily, my cat remains ___ even when everyone around her is in a whirl of activity.

_____ 5. When you frame a picture, the picture's edges should be ___ to those of the frame, not dipping down or slanting up.

_____ 6. Kwan is so ___ that she often correctly judges a person's character after a brief conversation.

_____ 7. When children get into a fight, it is sometimes best not to ___, but to let them work it out themselves.

_____ 8. Shawna tried to persuade her son to join the family for dinner, but he was ___, refusing to leave his room no matter what she said.

_____ 9. People all over the United States ___(e)d the death of Martin Luther King, Jr., who is now honored with a national holiday on his birthday.

_____ 10. Richard's gift for fixing machines seems ___. Even as a child, he could take one look at a broken machine and know what was wrong with it.

NOTE: Now check your answers to these items by turning to page 179. Going over the answers carefully will help you prepare for the next two practices, for which answers are not given.

Sentence Check 2

Using the answer lines provided, complete each item below with **two** words from the box. Use each word once.

_____
_____ 1–2. As a child, Calvin was ___, rarely excited or upset. As a teenager, however, he is often angry and ___—so stubborn that he hates to change his mind. We hope that after adolescence, he'll revert° to being calm again.

_____
_____ 3–4. Angie loves shocking films. She has seen every ___ horror movie ever made and even collects ___ about the films—dates, actors, directors, etc.

_____   5–6. Jason's math ability must be ___. By age 2 he could add and subtract, and by
_____   7 he understood the concept that two ___ lines can't meet no matter how long
                                          they are.

_____   7–8. "I ___ the passing of the days when employees did their jobs right," the shop
_____   owner complained. "Today, workers not only are ___ but also do nothing to
                                          improve their skills."

_____   9–10. A good marriage counselor is ___ enough to understand both the husband's
_____   and the wife's points of view. And rather than ___ in the couple's arguments,
                                          the counselor helps them learn strategies° for solving their problems
                                          themselves.

Final Check: *Family Differences*

Here is a final opportunity for you to strengthen your knowledge of the ten words. First read the following
selection carefully. Then fill in each blank with a word from the box at the top of the previous page.
(Context clues will help you figure out which word goes in which blank.) Use each word once.

I am always amazed at how different all of my brothers and sisters are.
Sheila, who succeeds at everything she tries, simply has no patience with
the rest of us. She thinks we are (1)_____ at everything
and that it's up to her to (2)_____ in what we do so
that things will be done the right way—her way. Jack, on the other hand,
is very (3)_____. He doesn't let anything bother him,
and so he rarely loses his temper and is quite indulgent° of the desires of
others. Chris is the one who never gives in. As a baby, he was already so
(4)_____ that he would spit food he didn't like right at
my mother. Daisy, the most social, likes people and seems to have a(n)
(5)_____ ability to make them feel good. She has always
been very (6)_____, knowing just what mood others
were in and what kind of advice to dispense°. Frank is the weird one. He has always been attracted by
unusual activities. While the rest of us kids would be riding bikes or jumping ropes, he would be doing
something (7)_____, like holding a funeral for a dead frog or bird or snake. He got
mad at us whenever we failed to (8)_____ a death as much as he did. Betty has the
quickest mind of us all. When she was just four years old, she told my dad, "Those two shelves aren't
(9)_____—they are farther apart on the left than on the right." By age 6, she was
collecting (10)_____ for a book she was writing on insects. Also ingenious°, Betty has
devised° various gadgets around our house, including a doorbell for our dog. Yes, my brothers and sisters
are all different. They may be strange at times, but they're never boring.

| Scores | Sentence Check 2 _____% | Final Check _____% |

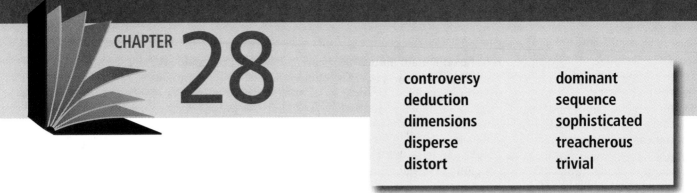

controversy	dominant
deduction	sequence
dimensions	sophisticated
disperse	treacherous
distort	trivial

Ten Words in Context

In the space provided, write the letter of the meaning closest to that of each **boldfaced** word. Use the context of the sentences to help you figure out each word's meaning.

1 controversy
(kŏn′trə-vûr′sē)
-noun

- There was no longer any **controversy**—everyone agreed that the all-male dining club should now accept female members.
- Our class is studying the **controversy** over whether or not the death penalty should exist.

___ *Controversy* means   A. an agreement.   B. an argument.   C. an order.

2 deduction
(dĭ-dŭk′shən)
-noun

- When the dog barked, I figured he had to go out again. But my **deduction** was incorrect—he was barking at a raccoon in our trash can.
- The great fictional detective Sherlock Holmes was a master at making **deductions**, reasoning out solutions to puzzling crimes.

___ *Deduction* means   A. a mistake.   B. a conclusion.   C. a question.

3 dimensions
(dĭ-mĕn′shəns)
-noun

- The pool's **dimensions** were odd—its length and width were huge, yet it wasn't very deep.
- Let's write down the **dimensions** of the kitchen walls so we can buy the right amount of wallpaper.

___ *Dimensions* means   A. measurements.   B. colors.   C. wallpaper.

4 disperse
(dĭ-spûrs′)
-verb

- The basketball landed in the midst of some pigeons, causing them to **disperse** in all directions.
- The police made the large crowd **disperse** because people are easier to manage in small groups.

___ *Disperse* means   A. to stay.   B. to call out.   C. to scatter.

5 distort
(dĭ-stôrt′)
-verb

- To sell more papers, some newspapers **distort** the news by reporting rumors as if they were true.
- Don't believe everything you hear—people often **distort** facts when they gossip.

___ *Distort* means   A. to tell accurately.   B. to blame.   C. to twist.

6 dominant
(dŏm′ə-nənt)
-adjective

- The **dominant** baboons of a troop are the biggest, most aggressive males. Fearful of these males, the other baboons yield to them.
- Mr. Rodriguez may be quiet, but he's the **dominant** person in this office. No one questions his authority.

___ *Dominant* means   A. most helpful.   B. youngest.   C. most powerful.

7 sequence
(sē′kwĕns)
-noun

● The code's **sequence** was essential: 342 would turn off the alarm, but 432 or 234 would not.

● The lawyer established the **sequence** of events: The robber first climbed onto the roof and then entered the house through the attic. Then he went to the bedroom and stole the jewelry.

___ *Sequence* means   A. an order.   B. a purpose.   C. a value.

8 sophisticated
(sə-fĭs′tĭ-kā′tĭd)
-adjective

● Having already worked for four years, sixteen-year-old Eddie is more **sophisticated** about the world of work than any of his friends.

● Don't let the professor's simple clothes and manner fool you. When it comes to teaching and science, he's very **sophisticated**.

___ *Sophisticated* means   A. honest.   B. lacking in confidence.   C. well-informed.

9 treacherous
(trĕch′ər-əs)
-adjective

● During the American Revolution, the **treacherous** American soldier Benedict Arnold tried to aid the British.

● I felt it was **treacherous** of my friend Juan to go out with my old girlfriend the day after she and I broke up.

___ *Treacherous* means   A. disloyal.   B. surprising.   C. influential.

10 trivial
(trĭv′ē-əl)
-adjective

● The vice-principal had a reputation for suspending students for **trivial** offenses, such as talking too loudly in the hallways.

● When I'm nervous, it helps me to concentrate on some **trivial** activity, such as washing dishes or watching a game show.

___ *Trivial* means   A. unusual.   B. serious.   C. unimportant.

Matching Words with Definitions

Following are definitions of the ten words. Clearly write or print each word next to its definition. The sentences above and on the previous page will help you decide on the meaning of each word.

1. _____   To break up and spread out; scatter

2. _____   Disloyal; traitorous

3. _____   A conclusion reached through reasoning

4. _____   Unimportant; not significant

5. _____   A debate; an argument; discussion of an important issue with opposing views

6. _____   Having or using the most control or influence

7. _____   Wise about the ways of the world; knowledgeable; experienced

8. _____   Measurements in width, length, and sometimes depth

9. _____   To misrepresent; tell in an untrue or misleading way

10. _____   The order in which one thing follows another

CAUTION: Do not go any further until you are sure the above answers are correct. Then you can use the definitions to help you in the following practices. Your goal is eventually to know the words well enough so that you don't need to check the definitions at all.

Sentence Check 1

Using the answer line provided, complete each item below with the correct word from the box. Use each word once.

A. controversy	B. deduction	C. dimensions	D. disperse	E. distort
F. dominant	G. sequence	H. sophisticated	I. treacherous	J. trivial

_____   1. When I flipped on the kitchen light, roaches quickly ___(e)d in all directions.

_____   2. Scientists observe facts and then make ___s based on those facts.

_____   3. There's a ___ in this country over global warming—is it actually happening?

_____   4. Flora was the ___ person in the business. Her partner, Inez, wasn't the type to take charge of things.

_____   5. With each retelling of the story, Wes ___(e)d the facts even more. Before long, the fish had become a giant tuna, and the battle had lasted for hours.

_____   6. Children often argue about things that seem ___ to adults, such as who gets to sit in the front seat of the car and whose turn it is to feed the cats.

_____   7. In Tokyo, space is so limited that most apartments and homes are very small. The ___ of some bedrooms are barely larger than a closet's.

_____   8. After my family moved and I joined the baseball team at a new school, I felt ___ when I had to pitch against the team from my old school.

_____   9. If Art were a more ___ dresser, he might be promoted. But if he continues to wear jeans and dirty running shoes to work, he'll be in the mailroom forever.

_____   10. The ___ of moves for a basketball layup is simple: first leap toward the hoop, and then release the ball with one hand so that it gently hits the backboard and drops into the net.

NOTE: Now check your answers to these items by turning to page 179. Going over the answers carefully will help you prepare for the next two practices, for which answers are not given.

Sentence Check 2

Using the answer lines provided, complete each item below with **two** words from the box. Use each word once.

_____
_____   1–2. "Check the ___ of your bookcase very carefully to be sure it is standing straight and the shelves are parallel°," said the carpentry teacher. "Even a mistake of a quarter of an inch is not ___."

_____
_____   3–4. After learning that a ___ member of their unit had told the enemy their location, the sergeant ordered his men to ___ throughout the forest.

_____
_____   5–6. My boss often ___s the truth by suggesting he's the ___ person in the shoe store. In reality, the store owner makes all the important decisions.

_____   7–8. On the basis of my experience, I have made this ___: managers are often
_____   ___ about financial transactions° but not so knowledgeable when it comes to
                                  handling people.

_____   9–10. The ___ on the movie set was about the ___ of scenes. Some actors thought
_____   the love scene should come before the chase scene, but the director wanted
                                   the opposite.

Final Check: *Murder Mystery*

Here is a final opportunity for you to strengthen your knowledge of the ten words. First read the following selection carefully. Then fill in each blank with a word from the box at the top of the previous page. (Context clues will help you figure out which word goes in which blank.) Use each word once.

There was a great deal of (1)_____ among the London police over who could have killed the city's richest citizen and how to find the killer. They finally agreed to summon° the world-famous detective Ernest G. Mann. Mr. Mann was a shrewd° and (2)_____ gentleman— he knew the world and understood people. And when it came to murder, he spoke with such authority that no one doubted who was the (3)_____ person in the room.

Mr. Mann immediately ordered the crowd of policemen to (4)_____ throughout the house so he could examine the site° where the murder had occurred, the dining room. One quick glance told him the room's (5)_____ to the nearest inch. He circled the room, eyeing every item in it, looking closely at the overturned chair, the blood-soaked carpet where the body had fallen, and the stains on the tablecloth. "Nothing can be considered (6)_____ when murder is concerned," he said. "All evidence is important. It is vital° that I see everything! *Everything!*"

After studying the morbid° scene, he read the data° in the police report. This information gave him the (7)_____ of events—the words, the angry toss, the punch, the fatal shot—in chronological° order.

Finally, he queried° the cook. "Ah, Mr. Cook," he finally said, "what you have just told me is *not* what you told the police. Are you trying to (8)_____ the truth?"

At that, the red-faced cook jumped up and headed for the door. "Stop him!" shouted Mr. Mann to the police in the hallway. "Arrest that man! The mystery is solved." Then he said to the police, "That cook is a (9)_____ man. Anyone who would kill his employer over a reprimand° about lumpy gravy is too dangerous to walk the streets."

"But . . . but . . . how did you know?" cried the cook.

"It was a simple (10)_____, sir. The facts were all here. They just needed a logical mind to put them together correctly." And with that, Ernest G. Mann turned and left.

Scores   Sentence Check 2 _____%   Final Check _____%

confirm	submit
deceptive	susceptible
defy	transmit
restrain	valid
seclusion	vigorous

Ten Words in Context

In the space provided, write the letter of the meaning closest to that of each **boldfaced** word. Use the context of the sentences to help you figure out each word's meaning.

1 confirm
(kən-fûrm′)
-verb

● Mr. Smith was released by the police when someone **confirmed** his statement that he had been out of town the day of the murder.

● "Yes, it's true," the manager said, **confirming** the report that his star player had asked to be traded to another team.

__ *Confirm* means   A. to deny.   B. to back up.   C. to ignore.

2 deceptive
(dĭ-sĕp′tĭv)
-adjective

● The seeming ease with which Naomi plays the piano is **deceptive**. Actually, she practices four hours each day.

● After stealing the MP3 player, Meg remained silent while another student was wrongly accused. Her silence was as **deceptive** as an outright lie.

__ *Deceptive* means   A. modest.   B. flexible.   C. misleading.

3 defy
(dĭ-fī′)
-verb

● The automotive plant workers voted to **defy** the company and go on strike.

● After being forbidden to go out three evenings in a row, Ted **defied** his parents by walking right out the front door.

__ *Defy* means   A. to oppose.   B. to support.   C. to learn from.

4 restrain
(rĭ-strān′)
-verb

● I **restrained** myself from laughing when my brother made a funny face while Uncle William told us—yet again—the story of his operation. I certainly did not want to hurt Uncle Will's feelings.

● Deion was so angry that we had to **restrain** him by force from punching Neal.

__ *Restrain* means   A. to forgive.   B. to control.   C. to train.

5 seclusion
(sĭ-klo͞o′zhən)
-noun

● The **seclusion** of the mountain cabin started to bother Veronica. She missed the city and being with other people.

● I work best in **seclusion**, where no one can interrupt the flow of my thoughts.

__ *Seclusion* means   A. being alone.   B. being in a crowd.   C. being relaxed.

6 submit
(səb-mĭt′)
-verb

● After bucking wildly for several minutes, the horse calmed down and **submitted** to the rider.

● For reasons of security, travelers must **submit** to having their luggage inspected at airports.

__ *Submit* means   A. to object.   B. to admit.   C. to give in.

7 susceptible
(sə-sĕp′tə-bəl)
-adjective

● Lina is so **susceptible** to blushing that she turns away whenever she is embarrassed so that no one will see her face change color.

● People who smoke are more **susceptible** to colds than others.

__ *Susceptible* means   A. happy about.   B. likely to be affected with.   C. attracted by.

8 transmit
(trăns-mĭt′)
-verb

● Emergency messages were **transmitted** over all the city's radio stations.

● Before the microscope was invented, no one knew that a person could **transmit** a disease to someone else through "invisible" germs.

__ *Transmit* means   A. to pass along.   B. to check.   C. to lose.

9 valid
(văl′ĭd)
-adjective

● The research study was not **valid** because much of the "evidence" had been made up by the researcher.

● "Your accusation that I'm not responsible isn't **valid**," Myra told her father. "I've done all my homework already and even cleaned the living room."

__ *Valid* means   A. obvious.   B. well-supported.   C. wrong.

10 vigorous
(vĭg′ər-əs)
-adjective

● My eighty-year-old grandmother is still **vigorous** enough to walk five miles every day.

● The best instructors have **vigorous** teaching styles, lively enough to make any lesson interesting.

__ *Vigorous* means   A. strict.   B. quiet.   C. energetic.

Matching Words with Definitions

Following are definitions of the ten words. Clearly write or print each word next to its definition. The sentences above and on the previous page will help you decide on the meaning of each word.

1. _____ The condition of being apart or far from others; isolation

2. _____ Likely to be affected with or influenced; likely to be infected

3. _____ Misleading; intended or intending to deceive

4. _____ To boldly oppose; openly resist; stand up to

5. _____ To support; show the truth of; verify°

6. _____ Firmly based on facts or logic; logical; based on good reasons

7. _____ Lively; energetic; strong

8. _____ To give in to another's authority or will; yield

9. _____ To communicate; pass or spread (information, an illness, etc.)

10. _____ To hold back from action

CAUTION: Do not go any further until you are sure the above answers are correct. Then you can use the definitions to help you in the following practices. Your goal is eventually to know the words well enough so that you don't need to check the definitions at all.

Sentence Check 1

Using the answer line provided, complete each item below with the correct word from the box. Use each word once.

A. confirm	B. deceptive	C. defy	D. restrain	E. seclusion
F. submit	G. susceptible	H. transmit	I. valid	J. vigorous

_____ 1. I gave the bottle such a ___ shake that it leaked Russian dressing all over my hands.

_____ 2. The dinosaur theory seemed ___ because all the available evidence supported it.

_____ 3. I don't go to the beach because I'm so ___ to sunburn.

_____ 4. At the party, Marco ___(e)d the rumor that he was engaged when he introduced his date as his fiancée.

_____ 5. In prison, the criminal had to ___ to more rules than he had ever thought possible.

_____ 6. The widow stayed in ___ for a period of mourning, not seeing visitors or going to any social events.

_____ 7. The little boy tried to ___ his big dog from chasing a car, but he could not hold the dog back.

_____ 8. "Looks can be ___," Ray's big brother warned. "Wendy may have a cute, childish face, but she's far from sweet."

_____ 9. To save on long-distance telephone charges, Tia decided to ___ the news about the baby's birth by e-mail.

_____ 10. The daring thief liked to openly ___ the police by leaving this note at the scene of the crime: "Love and kisses from 'The Uncatchable One.'"

NOTE: Now check your answers to these items by turning to page 179. Going over the answers carefully will help you prepare for the next two practices, for which answers are not given.

Sentence Check 2

Using the answer lines provided, complete each item below with **two** words from the box. Use each word once.

_____
_____ 1–2. The police made a ___ effort to ___ the angry mob from pushing through the gates. However, the mob prevailed° and pushed the gates open wide.

_____
_____ 3–4. Children who must ___ to overly strict rules often openly ___ their parents when they get older.

_____
_____ 5–6. Buddy is so ___ to ear infections that he is never surprised to hear the doctor ___ his suspicion that he has yet another one.

_____   7–8. The prisoners of war were kept in ___ for three months except for Christmas
_____   Day, when they were permitted to see others and to ___ messages to their
                                  families over a radio.

_____   9–10. The title of the magazine article—"Miracle Weight Loss"—was ___. It
_____   suggested that there is a magical way to lose weight, but such a claim isn't
                                  ___—the facts show otherwise.

Final Check: *Chicken Pox*

Here is a final opportunity for you to strengthen your knowledge of the ten words. First read the following
selection carefully. Then fill in each blank with a word from the box at the top of the previous page.
(Context clues will help you figure out which word goes in which blank.) Use each word once.

    I remember the day my brother Danny dragged himself home
from third grade and complained, "Mommy, I don't feel too good."
My mother took one look at my usually (1)_____
brother, yelled "Aargh!" and flew up the stairs with him. The other
four of us ran after them, demanding to know what deadly disease
he had. "Get away!" my mother cried. "It's chicken pox. He has to
stay in (2)_____ until all his spots are gone."

    Poor Danny had to (3)_____ to having
his spots checked by all the other mothers in the neighborhood.
"Spots can be (4)_____," one woman explained. "They might have been measles, but I
have to (5)_____ your mother's conclusion. These are definitely chicken pox." Another
mother brought a photo from a medical book that verified° the diagnosis of chicken pox.

    After the women left, my mother said firmly, "None of you is to set foot in Danny's room for at least
seven days, until his spots subside°. I don't want him to (6)_____ this disease to you. I don't
think I could survive having the other four of you sick all at once."

    Then I made an interesting deduction°: if my mother's claim that Danny's spots would last at least
a week was (7)_____, that meant he would get out of school for a week. I was filled with
jealousy. Still, I didn't want to openly (8)_____ my mother, so I didn't go to Danny's
room during the daylight hours. However, unable to (9)_____ myself, I crawled into bed
with him each night, lured° by the promise of a one-week vacation.

    Although my mother says I purposely set out to destroy her sanity, the situation wasn't all that drastic°.
The four of us didn't get sick simultaneously°. Instead, my sisters got sick two weeks after I did. Today, we
are no longer (10)_____ to chicken pox—we all have immunity°. Now, if we want to
stay home from school, we'll have to catch something else.

Scores   Sentence Check 2 _____%   Final Check _____%

accelerate	comparable
accelerate	comparable
adverse	competent
advocate	consecutive
audible	conspicuous
coherent	deteriorate

Ten Words in Context

In the space provided, write the letter of the meaning closest to that of each **boldfaced** word. Use the context of the sentences to help you figure out each word's meaning.

1 accelerate
(ăk-sĕl′ə-rāt′)
-*verb*

● The sleds began sliding down the hill slowly and then **accelerated** to top speed.
● Brendan's car **accelerated** rapidly, allowing him to catch up with the slowly moving ice-cream truck.

__ *Accelerate* means   A. to go down.   B. to go faster.   C. to hesitate.

2 adverse
(ăd-vûrs′)
-*adjective*

● Mozart created musical masterpieces in spite of his **adverse** circumstances—illness and debt.
● **Adverse** newspaper reviews persuaded many people not to see the violent new movie.

__ *Adverse* means   A. unknown.   B. unfavorable.   C. unnecessary.

3 advocate
(ăd′və-kĭt)
-*noun*

● My physician is an **advocate** of using nicotine gum to quit smoking. She says the gum helps people resist cigarettes.
● Our mayor is a strong **advocate** of a drug-free America. He often mentions it in his talks to different civic groups.

__ *Advocate* means   A. a critic.   B. an example.   C. a supporter.

4 audible
(ô′də-bəl)
-*adjective*

● Dogs, bats, and other animals can hear high-pitched sounds that are not **audible** to humans.
● The argument next door was barely **audible**. So I put a plastic cup on the wall and put my ear to the cup so I could hear better.

__ *Audible* means   A. useful.   B. logical.   C. hearable.

5 coherent
(kō-hîr′ənt)
-*adjective*

● To be sure that your essay has a **coherent** organization, write an outline first.
● The article about the robbery was not **coherent**. The events were not presented in logical order.

__ *Coherent* means   A. clear.   B. complicated.   C. long.

6 comparable
(kŏm′pər-ə-bəl)
-*adjective*

● Since the quality of low-mileage used cars is often **comparable** to that of brand-new ones, my parents never buy new cars.
● Because the two jobs were **comparable** in challenge, interest, and salary, Santos had trouble deciding which to take.

__ *Comparable* means   A. helpful.   B. nearly alike.   C. different.

7 competent
(kŏm′pĭ-tənt)
-adjective

- Some secretaries are more **competent** than their bosses. They know more about the business, are better organized, and work much harder.
- To be a **competent** juggler takes a lot of practice.

__ *Competent* means   A. honest.   B. friendly.   C. skilled.

8 consecutive
(kən-sĕk′yə-tĭv)
-adjective

- The reporters would work nights for two **consecutive** weeks, and then they'd work days for a month straight.
- First Reiko had the flu. That was immediately followed by strep throat, which was followed by pneumonia. These **consecutive** illnesses kept her out of work for two months.

__ *Consecutive* means   A. minor.   B. obvious.   C. happening in a row.

9 conspicuous
(kən-spĭk′yoo-əs)
-adjective

- Nina's wide-brimmed red hat is so **conspicuous** that it's impossible not to catch sight of her in a crowd.
- The new skyscraper stands fifty stories high, making it the tallest and thus the most **conspicuous** building in the city's skyline.

__ *Conspicuous* means   A. noticeable.   B. poor in quality or condition.   C. serious.

10 deteriorate
(dĭ-tîr′ē-ə-rāt′)
-verb

- Over many years, the abandoned house had **deteriorated** until its walls crumbled and its floorboards rotted.
- Tonya's health continued to **deteriorate** until her classmates started to visit her regularly. Then she began to improve.

__ *Deteriorate* means   A. to stay the same.   B. to improve.   C. to decay.

Matching Words with Definitions

Following are definitions of the ten words. Clearly write or print each word next to its definition. The sentences above and on the previous page will help you decide on the meaning of each word.

1. _____ Able to be heard

2. _____ Following one after another without interruption

3. _____ Similar; able to be compared

4. _____ Harmful; unfavorable

5. _____ To speed up

6. _____ Obvious; easily noticed

7. _____ Organized in a logical and orderly way

8. _____ A supporter; someone who argues for a cause

9. _____ To become worse; become weaker or damaged

10. _____ Capable; well qualified; skilled

CAUTION: Do not go any further until you are sure the above answers are correct. Then you can use the definitions to help you in the following practices. Your goal is eventually to know the words well enough so that you don't need to check the definitions at all.

Sentence Check 1

Using the answer line provided, complete each item below with the correct word from the box. Use each word once.

A. accelerate	B. adverse	C. advocate	D. audible	E. coherent
F. comparable	G. competent	H. consecutive	I. conspicuous	J. deteriorate

_____ 1. Dee doesn't like to be ___, so she sits in the back of the classroom, where few people can see her.

_____ 2. Anyone can become a(n) ___ cook, but few people develop into great chefs.

_____ 3. The weather was bad, and two of the astronauts were sick. Because of these ___ conditions, the shuttle flight was canceled.

_____ 4. Since I care about the environment, I'm a(n) ___ of passing laws that limit the amount of pollution in the air.

_____ 5. When the comedian sensed his audience was becoming bored, he ___d his pace to more jokes per minute.

_____ 6. At the movies, Tina put her arm around Ben and said in a barely ___ whisper, "I love you. Pass the popcorn."

_____ 7. Ben and Tina's relationship began to ___ after they had a big fight over money.

_____ 8. People often bring up their own children in a manner that is ___ to the way they were raised. Thus abused children may become abusing parents.

_____ 9. During her high fever, Celia loudly called out broken words and phrases. She seemed unable to speak in full, ___ sentences.

_____ 10. There was no break in the summer's heat. Records were set nationwide for the number of ___ days above ninety degrees.

NOTE: Now check your answers to these items by turning to page 179. Going over the answers carefully will help you prepare for the next two practices, for which answers are not given.

Sentence Check 2

Using the answer lines provided, complete each item below with **two** words from the box. Use each word once.

_____
_____ 1–2. "Has your marriage started to ___ because of recurring° conflicts?" asked the radio announcer. "If so, you may benefit from the services of Dr. Louis Frank, one of the city's most ___ and perceptive° marriage counselors."

_____
_____ 3–4. Our neighbors have had parties this week on three ___ nights—Friday, Saturday, and Sunday. And they played their sound system so loudly that it was ___ in our bedrooms.

_____   5–6. The sun has a(n) ___ effect on the skin. It ___s the aging of the skin, resulting

_____   in more wrinkles at a younger age. It also makes people susceptible° to skin cancer, which can be lethal°.

_____   7–8. Since the assembly instructions were not ___, we had to figure out ourselves

_____   how to put the bike together. Including such poorly written instructions is ___ to including none at all.

_____   9–10. After driving around a neighborhood for twenty minutes before finding the

_____   address we were looking for, we became ___s of ___ house numbers—not ones hidden by shrubs.

Final Check: *Walking*

Here is a final opportunity for you to strengthen your knowledge of the ten words. First read the following selection carefully. Then fill in each blank with a word from the box at the top of the previous page. (Context clues will help you figure out which word goes in which blank.) Use each word once.

I am a strong (1)_____ of walking rather than jogging. The two activities are in no way (2)_____. Walking is deceptive°; while it seems very relaxing, it nevertheless is vigorous° enough exercise to stimulate° the heart and other muscles. Walking can also be done during all but the most (3)_____ conditions, such as icy sidewalks or a thunderstorm. Walking is also rather easy to learn; most people, in fact, are quite (4)_____ at it by their teens (but then they learn to drive, and the ability starts to (5)_____). Moreover, walking is so harmless that one can walk on as many (6)_____ days as one wishes. By contrast, jogging is treacherous°. It jolts the body so much that one cannot do it even two days in a row without inflicting° damage on his or her internal organs. In addition, the heavy impact° of joggers' steps makes their fronts and rears shake in such a (7)_____ manner that passersby can't help staring. Walkers, on the other hand, keep their pride. Unlike a runner, a walker needs to (8)_____ only if a growling dog appears nearby. Also, walkers can hold a conversation while walking that is (9)_____ enough to make sense. In contrast, the jogger's brain is too shaken to produce orderly sentences, and the voice is reduced to a barely (10)_____ gasp. All this data° confirms° that walking is in every way superior to jogging. In walking, you just pass by. In jogging, you also pass out.

Scores	Sentence Check 2 _____%	Final Check _____%

The box at the right lists twenty-five words from Unit Five. Using the clues at the bottom of the page, fill in these words to complete the puzzle that follows.

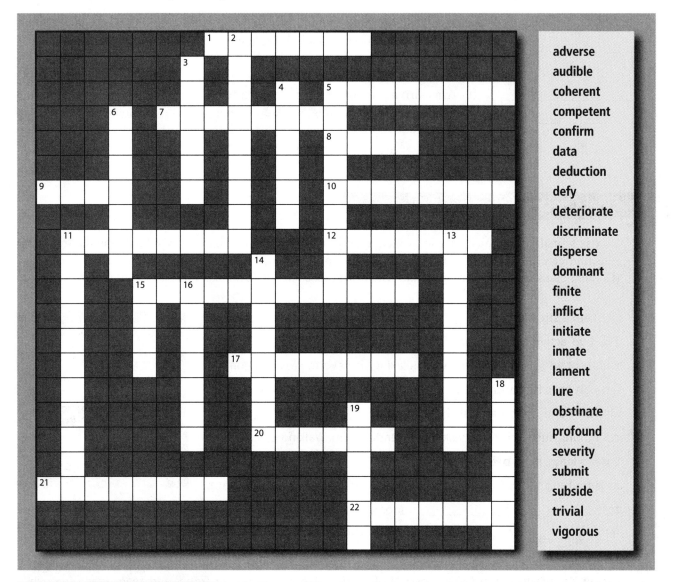

adverse
audible
coherent
competent
confirm
data
deduction
defy
deteriorate
discriminate
disperse
dominant
finite
inflict
initiate
innate
lament
lure
obstinate
profound
severity
submit
subside
trivial
vigorous

ACROSS

1. To support; show the truth of
5. Having or using the most control or influence
7. To begin something; start
8. Information gathered for a study or decision
9. To attract by tempting
10. Organized in a logical, orderly way
11. To break up and spread out; scatter
12. To give or cause (pain or hardship)
15. To see differences; distinguish
17. Deeply felt
20. To give in to another's power or authority; yield
21. The condition or quality of being severe; harshness; intensity; seriousness
22. Unimportant; not significant

DOWN

2. Stubborn
3. Possessed at birth; inborn
4. To express sorrow; mourn for
5. A conclusion reached through reasoning
6. Harmful; unfavorable
11. To become worse; become weaker or damaged
13. Capable; well qualified; skilled
14. Lively; energetic; strong
15. To boldly oppose; openly resist; stand up to
16. To become less active; calm down; decrease
18. Able to be heard
19. Having limits; limited

PART A

Choose the word that best completes each item and write it in the space provided.

_____ 1. Bernard is ___ to headaches. Whenever he has to study, his head starts to pound.

    A. perceptive   B. susceptible   C. profound   D. infinite

_____ 2. A huge mall now stands on the ___ where the racetrack had burned down.

    A. site   B. vocation   C. sequence   D. seclusion

_____ 3. As his attacker was about to ___ serious injury, Robert broke free and ran away.

    A. disperse   B. inflict   C. subside   D. restrain

_____ 4. After doing a great deal of research, Sharon feels she now has enough ___ to begin writing her report on eating disorders.

    A. data   B. severity   C. nostalgia   D. mania

_____ 5. While Melba was pregnant, one of her students ___ German measles to her.

    A. confirmed   B. transmitted   C. distorted   D. deteriorated

_____ 6. To devote herself so fully to the poor, Mother Teresa must have had a(n) ___ amount of love for them.

    A. morbid   B. susceptible   C. adverse   D. infinite

_____ 7. Instead of choosing a ___ typist, the supervisor hired someone who types with one finger and usually hits the wrong key.

    A. competent   B. theoretical   C. deceptive   D. conspicuous

_____ 8. My English instructor has such high standards that a B from her is ___ to an A from most other teachers.

    A. susceptible   B. adverse   C. comparable   D. finite

_____ 9. Pablo bought orange socks instead of red because the store was poorly lit, and he couldn't ___ between the two colors.

    A. deteriorate   B. initiate   C. dispense   D. discriminate

_____ 10. Because of her world travels, Jessie is more ___ than her cousin Leona, who has never left their small hometown.

    A. sophisticated   B. inept   C. dismal   D. susceptible

(Continues on next page)

PART B

On the answer line, write the letter of the choice that best completes each item.

_____ 11. The frightened kitten puffed up its fur until it was **literally** the size of a
  A. basketball.   C. garbage can.
  B. Volkswagen Beetle.   D. small school district.

_____ 12. Three **consecutive** months are
  A. January, March, May.   C. July, June, April.
  B. August, September, October.   D. January, June, July.

_____ 13. In order to **accelerate** a car, you must
  A. clean it thoroughly, inside and out.   C. step on the gas pedal.
  B. take it to a service station.   D. hit the brakes.

_____ 14. In a **controversy**, people express their
  A. opposing views.   C. confidence in one another.
  B. affection for one another.   D. feelings of grief.

_____ 15. "Enrique has **innate** talent for baseball," his coach said. "He
  A. is naturally clumsy."   C. has never played the game."
  B. pitched well even in elementary school." D. has had to work harder than other players."

_____ 16. One product that is intended to **restrain** a person is
  A. handcuffs.   C. a pair of sunglasses.
  B. an umbrella.   D. a bicycle.

_____ 17. The two boys punched each other wildly, and then one **submitted** to the other, saying,
  A. "I'll beat you to a pulp!"   C. "I give up."
  B. "Let's move this fight outside."   D. "You're a yellow-bellied chicken!"

_____ 18. Megan **lamented** her grade on the exam, saying,
  A. "I can't believe I did so well—I didn't even study!"
  B. "Naturally I got a good grade. I'm brilliant."
  C. "It's not great, but it's not awful either. It's what I deserved."
  D. "This is terrible! What am I going to do? Oh, I wish I had studied more."

_____ 19. When it saw the much larger dog, the little dog demonstrated its **dominant** nature by
  A. rushing bravely up to the larger dog and scaring it away.
  B. turning around and racing for home.
  C. rolling over on its back in a helpless posture.
  D. wagging its tail.

_____ 20. After the little girl loudly announced, "I'm going to Japan tomorrow!" her mother **confirmed**
  her statement by saying to her,
  A. "You're _not_ going to Japan. Where do you get these ideas?"
  B. "It's possible that we'll go to Japan next year, but nothing is certain."
  C. "No, honey. We're going to Jackson, not Japan."
  D. "That's right. Daddy is in the military there, and we're going to join him."

Score   (Number correct) _____ x 5 = _____%

PART A

Complete each item with a word from the box. Use each word once.

A. **audible**	B. **deceptive**	C. **deduction**	D. **deteriorate**	E. **dimensions**
F. **dispense**	G. **disperse**	H. **intervene**	I. **mania**	J. **nostalgia**
K. **parallel**	L. **perceptive**	M. **vocation**		

_____ 1. As the sprinkle turned into a downpour, the crowd at the baseball game began to ___.

_____ 2. Certain servers at the school cafeteria ___ larger portions than others, so we try to get into their lines.

_____ 3. My aunt has trouble parking ___ to the curb. Her car is always farther out in back than in front.

_____ 4. My grandparents rarely ___ in family fights. They believe their children and grandchildren should work things out for themselves.

_____ 5. On Career Day, professionals came to the high school to tell students about their ___s.

_____ 6. No one responded when the speaker asked, "Can you hear me?" because his words were too soft to be ___.

_____ 7. I was shocked to see how my old school has ___(e)d since I moved away. It's in great need of repairs.

_____ 8. The picture in the magazine ad is ___. It makes the doll look much larger than it really is.

_____ 9. My counselor is very ___. The other day she knew something was bothering me even though I said, "I'm fine."

_____ 10. Looking over his high-school yearbook and remembering all the fun he had made Corey feel great ___ for his school days.

_____ 11. Since I didn't know the exact ___ of my bedroom windows, I had to guess which size curtains to buy.

_____ 12. The inspector concluded that the thief was a woman. His ___ was based on the scent of lilac perfume inside the house and the imprint of high heels outside a window.

_____ 13. Henry Ford had a(n) ___ for using soybeans. He once came to a meeting wearing clothing that, except for his shoes, was made of soybean products.

(Continues on next page)

PART B

Write **C** if the italicized word is used **correctly**. Write **I** if the word is used **incorrectly**.

_____ 14. When the intoxicated driver crashed into a tree, the dangers of drinking and driving became *theoretical*.

_____ 15. I didn't realize the *severity* of Bill's injuries until I heard he was still in the hospital three months after his accident.

_____ 16. Koko is certainly *morbid*. The only movies she ever wants to see are musicals and light comedies.

_____ 17. Before my TV broke down completely, it *distorted* the picture so that everything was stretched sideways.

_____ 18. Joyce's baby is more *sedate* than most. When he isn't climbing all over the furniture, he's screaming.

_____ 19. Since words and music can be combined in *finite* ways, there is no end to the number of songs that can be written.

PART C

On the answer line, write the letter of the word that is the **synonym** of the boldfaced word.

Example: __A__ **innate**   A. inborn   B. learned   C. important

_____ 20. **ascend**   A. rise   B. agree   C. fall

_____ 21. **sequence**   A. confusion   B. order   C. ending

_____ 22. **profound**   A. shallow   B. hidden   C. deep

PART D

On the answer line, write the letter of the word that is the **antonym** of the boldfaced word.

Example: __B__ **innate**   A. inborn   B. learned   C. important

_____ 23. **initiate**   A. raise   B. begin   C. end

_____ 24. **conspicuous**   A. obvious   B. hidden   C. greedy

_____ 25. **subside**   A. examine   B. lessen   C. increase

Score   (Number correct) _____ x 4 = _____%

Each item below starts with a pair of words in CAPITAL LETTERS. For each item, figure out the relationship between these two words. Then decide which of the choices (A, B, C, or D) expresses a similar relationship. Write the letter of your choice on the answer line.

_____ 1. DISMAL : CHEERFUL ::
    A. old : antique   C. wound : pain
    B. disappointing : satisfying   D. real : actual

_____ 2. SUBSIDE : DECREASE ::
    A. spend : pay out   C. look : avoid
    B. keep : discard   D. run : walk

_____ 3. SUMMON : DISMISS ::
    A. drive : steer   C. stay : remain
    B. try : struggle   D. throw : catch

_____ 4. VOCATION : TEACHING ::
    A. work : vacation   C. salary : bill
    B. hobby : gardening   D. strength : weakness

_____ 5. INGENIOUS : INVENTOR ::
    A. clumsy : gymnast   C. tall : jockey
    B. musical : singer   D. calm : comedian

_____ 6. LURE : TEMPTATION ::
    A. fear : height   C. warn : threat
    B. enter : leave   D. construct : destruction

_____ 7. NOSTALGIA : PAST ::
    A. hope : future   C. memory : present
    B. forgetting : tomorrow   D. darkness : night

_____ 8. INEPT : SKILLFUL ::
    A. cautious : careful   C. lovely : colorful
    B. glad : rewarding   D. sweet : sour

_____ 9. OBSTINATE : MULE ::
    A. vicious : lamb   C. tiny : whale
    B. loyal : dog   D. safe : wolf

_____ 10. PERCEPTIVE : OBSERVE ::
    A. happy : mourn   C. sad : rejoice
    B. emotional : feel   D. forgetful : remember

(Continues on next page)

_____ 11. DISPERSE : BRING TOGETHER ::
A. attract : hire   C. dismiss : send home
B. seek : lose   D. forgive : pardon

_____ 12. TREACHEROUS : LOYAL ::
A. spoken : said   C. quiet : silent
B. closed : shut   D. odd : even

_____ 13. TRIVIAL : MINOR ::
A. important : major   C. excellent : average
B. meaningful : nonsense   D. detailed : fact

_____ 14. DEFY : OBEY ::
A. fight : win   C. defend : fight
B. enlarge : shrink   D. insist : demand

_____ 15. SECLUSION : SOLITARY CONFINEMENT ::
A. school : library   C. cold : freezer
B. relaxation : court   D. light source : candle

_____ 16. VALID : UNTRUE ::
A. waterproofed : rainy   C. insulated : protected
B. proved : factual   D. confusing : clear

_____ 17. VIGOROUS : JOGGING ::
A. relaxed : boxing   C. unkind : praying
B. peaceful: meditating   D. ancient : jumping rope

_____ 18. ADVERSE : UNFAVORABLE ::
A. good : luck   C. bad : worse
B. average : ordinary   D. ugly : attractive

_____ 19. ADVOCATE : SUPPORTS ::
A. assistant : helps   C. manager : waits
B. enemy : loses   D. king : obeys

_____ 20. COHERENT : ILLOGICAL ::
A. organized : orderly   C. long : lengthy
B. forceful : weak   D. clear : reasoned

Score   (Number correct) _____ x 5 = _____%

Enter your scores above and in the **Vocabulary Performance Chart** on the inside back cover of the book.

Appendixes

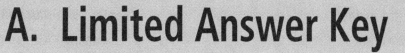

A. Limited Answer Key

IMPORTANT NOTE: Be sure to use this answer key as a learning tool only. You should not turn to this key until you have considered carefully the sentence in which a given word appears.

Used properly, the key will help you to learn words and to prepare for the activities and tests for which answers are not given. For ease of reference, the title of the "Final Check" passage in each chapter appears in parentheses.

Chapter 1 (Taking Exams)

Sentence Check 1

1. candid
2. anecdote
3. drastic
4. avert
5. concise
6. comply
7. compel
8. alternative
9. acknowledge
10. appropriate

Chapter 2 (Nate the Woodsman)

Sentence Check 1

1. erratic
2. refuge
3. fortify
4. forfeit
5. isolate
6. reminisce
7. illuminate
8. dialog
9. extensive
10. urban

Chapter 3 (Who's on Trial?)

Sentence Check 1

1. impartial
2. undermine
3. menace
4. morale
5. legitimate
6. naive
7. delete
8. overt
9. lenient
10. integrity

Chapter 4 (Students and Politics)

Sentence Check 1

1. ruthless
2. bland
3. relevant
4. reinforce
5. prospects
6. antidote
7. agenda
8. radical
9. apathy
10. propaganda

Chapter 5 (Night Nurse)

Sentence Check 1

1. gruesome
2. erode
3. imply
4. novice
5. idealistic
6. hypocrite
7. endorse
8. impact
9. obstacle
10. illusion

Chapter 6 (Theo's Perfect Car)

Sentence Check 1

1. rebuilt
2. visible
3. supermarkets
4. prejudge
5. restful
6. unicorn
7. extract
8. autobiography
9. multipurpose
10. unlucky

Chapter 7 (Relating to Parents)

Sentence Check 1

1. scapegoat
2. sustain
3. denounce
4. concede
5. deter
6. superficial
7. disclose
8. transition
9. contrary
10. conservative

Chapter 8 (Job Choices)

Sentence Check 1

1. derive
2. verify
3. moderate
4. tentative
5. surpass
6. supplement
7. inhibit
8. conceive
9. diversity
10. compensate

Chapter 9 (No Joking)

Sentence Check 1

1. refrain
2. optimist
3. alter
4. prolong
5. ample
6. remorse
7. blunt
8. chronological
9. chronic
10. pretense

Chapter 10 (Museum Pet)

Sentence Check 1

1. phobia
2. anonymous
3. acute
4. arrogant
5. recipient
6. bestow
7. prudent
8. apprehensive
9. donor
10. prominent

Chapter 11 (Unacceptable Boyfriends)

Sentence Check 1

1. assess
2. affluent
3. alienate
4. contempt
5. compile
6. doctrine
7. adhere
8. defect
9. dogmatic
10. absurd

Chapter 12 (Coping with Snow)

Sentence Check 1

1. spectacular
2. phonetics
3. interrupt
4. enclosing
5. autobiography
6. antisocial
7. binoculars
8. cordless
9. Postnatal
10. submerge

Chapter 13 (Our Headstrong Baby)

Sentence Check 1

1. prevail
2. propel
3. retrieve
4. exempt
5. accessible
6. awe
7. compatible
8. cite
9. rational
10. retort

Chapter 14 (Mr. Perfect?)

Sentence Check 1

1. miserly
2. liable
3. fictitious
4. dubious
5. encounter
6. ecstatic
7. pessimist
8. fallacy
9. gullible
10. evolve

Chapter 15 (A Narrow Escape)

Sentence Check 1

1. fluent
2. harass
3. obsession
4. evasive
5. elapse
6. lethal
7. ordeal
8. futile
9. persistent
10. infer

Chapter 16 (The Power of Advertising)

Sentence Check 1

1. devise
2. universal
3. savor
4. subtle
5. vivid
6. stimulate
7. convey
8. delusion
9. unique
10. versatile

Chapter 17 (Waiter)

Sentence Check 1

1. inevitable
2. option
3. equate
4. passive
5. patron
6. malicious
7. impose
8. indignant
9. defer
10. endeavor

Chapter 18 (Black Widow Spiders)

Sentence Check 1

1. predicted
2. pedals
3. tripod
4. transplant
5. partnership
6. conform
7. disagree
8. microfilm
9. Scriptures
10. televised

Chapter 19 (Adjusting to a New Culture)

Sentence Check 1

1. dismay
2. recede
3. refute
4. gesture
5. retain
6. revert
7. adapt
8. exile
9. reciprocate
10. ritual

Chapter 20 (A Dream about Wealth)

Sentence Check 1

1. mediocre
2. indulgent
3. emerge
4. notable
5. liberal
6. elaborate
7. indifferent
8. frugal
9. impulsive
10. exotic

Chapter 21 (Children and Drugs)

Sentence Check 1

1. coerce
2. sadistic
3. impair
4. essence
5. immunity
6. affirm
7. alleged
8. elite
9. query
10. allude

Chapter 22 (Party House)

Sentence Check 1

1. ridicule
2. stereotype
3. plausible
4. shrewd
5. recur
6. tactic
7. skeptical
8. reprimand
9. provoke
10. revoke

Chapter 23 (Procrastinator)

Sentence Check 1

1. transaction
2. diminish
3. procrastinate
4. consequence
5. simultaneous
6. strategy
7. destiny
8. vital
9. detain
10. tedious

Chapter 24 (King of Cats)

Sentence Check 1

1. malnutrition
2. centimeters
3. Criminology
4. monorail
5. memorize
6. manufactured
7. inactivity
8. laughable
9. thermal
10. imported

Chapter 25 (A Change in View)

Sentence Check 1

1. discriminate
2. profound
3. subside
4. summon
5. vocation
6. dismal
7. dispense
8. severity
9. theoretical
10. site

Chapter 26 (Balloon Flight)

Sentence Check 1

1. initiate
2. finite
3. inflict
4. nostalgia
5. lure
6. mania
7. ascend
8. infinite
9. ingenious
10. literally

Chapter 27 (Family Differences)

Sentence Check 1

1. data
2. inept
3. morbid
4. sedate
5. parallel
6. perceptive
7. intervene
8. obstinate
9. lament
10. innate

Chapter 28 (Murder Mystery)

Sentence Check 1

1. disperse
2. deduction
3. controversy
4. dominant
5. distort
6. trivial
7. dimensions
8. treacherous
9. sophisticated
10. sequence

Chapter 29 (Chicken Pox)

Sentence Check 1

1. vigorous
2. valid
3. susceptible
4. confirm
5. submit
6. seclusion
7. restrain
8. deceptive
9. transmit
10. defy

Chapter 30 (Walking)

Sentence Check 1

1. conspicuous
2. competent
3. adverse
4. advocate
5. accelerate
6. audible
7. deteriorate
8. comparable
9. coherent
10. consecutive

B. Dictionary Use

It isn't always possible to figure out the meaning of a word from its context, and that's where a dictionary comes in. Following is some basic information to help you use a dictionary.

How to Find a Word

A dictionary contains so many words that it can take a while to find the one you're looking for. But if you know how to use guidewords, you can find a word rather quickly. *Guidewords* are the two words at the top of each dictionary page. The first guideword tells what the first word is on the page. The second guideword tells what the last word is on that page. The other words on a page fall alphabetically between the two guidewords. So when you look up a word, find the two guidewords that alphabetically surround the word you're looking for.

● Which of the following pairs of guidewords would be on the page with the word *skirmish*?

    skimp / skyscraper   **skyward / slave**   **sixty / skimming**

The answer to this question and the questions that follow are given on the next page.

How to Use a Dictionary Listing

A dictionary listing includes many pieces of information. For example, here is a typical listing. Note that it includes much more than just a definition.

> **driz•zle** (drĭz′əl) *v.* **-zled, -zling.** To rain gently and steadily in fine drops.
> — *n.* A very light rain. —**driz′zly,** *adj.*

Key parts of a dictionary entry are listed and explained below.

Syllables. Dots separate dictionary entry words into syllables. Note that *drizzle* has one dot, which breaks the word into two syllables.

● To practice seeing the syllable breakdown in a dictionary entry, write the number of syllables in each word below.

    glam•our _____   **mi•cro•wave** _____   **in•de•scrib•a•ble** _____

Pronunciation guide. The information within parentheses after the entry word shows how to pronounce the entry word. This pronunciation guide includes two types of symbols: pronunciation symbols and accent marks.

Pronunciation symbols represent the consonant and vowel sounds in a word. The consonant sounds are probably very familiar to you, but you may find it helpful to review some of the sounds of the vowels—*a, e, i, o,* and *u.* Every dictionary has a key explaining the sounds of its pronunciation symbols, including the long and short sounds of vowels.

    Long vowels have the sound of their own names. For example, the *a* in *pay* and the *o* in *no* both have long vowel sounds. Long vowel sounds are shown by a straight line above the vowel.

    In many dictionaries, the *short vowels* are shown by a curved line above the vowel. Thus the *i* in the first syllable of *drizzle* is a short *i.* The pronunciation chart on the inside front cover of this book indicates that the short *i* has the sound of *i* in *ill.* It also indicates that the short *a* has the sound of *a* in *apple,* that the short *e* has the sound of *e* in *end,* and so on.

● Which of the words below have a short vowel sound? Which has a long vowel sound?

    drug _____   **night** _____   **sand** _____

Another pronunciation symbol is the *schwa* (ə), which looks like an upside-down *e*. It stands for certain rapidly spoken, unaccented vowel sounds, such as the *a* in *above*, the *e* in *item*, the *i* in *easily*, the *o* in *gallop*, and the *u* in *circus*. More generally, it has an "uh" sound, like the "uh" a speaker makes when hesitating. Here are three words that include the schwa sound:

    in•fant (ĭn′fənt)   **bum•ble** (bŭm′bəl)   **de•liv•er** (dĭ-lĭv′ər)

● Which syllable in *drizzle* contains the schwa sound, the first or the second? _____

Accent marks are small black marks that tell you which syllable to emphasize, or stress, as you say a word. An accent mark follows *driz* in the pronunciation guide for *drizzle,* which tells you to stress the first syllable of *drizzle*. Syllables with no accent mark are not stressed. Some syllables are in between, and they are marked with a lighter accent mark.

● Which syllable has the stronger accent in *sentimental*? _____

    sen•ti•men•tal (sĕn′tə-mĕn′tl)

Parts of speech. After the pronunciation key and before each set of definitions, the entry word's parts of speech are given. The parts of speech are abbreviated as follows:

    noun—*n.*   pronoun—*pron.*   adjective—*adj.*   adverb—*adv.*   verb—*v.*

● The listing for *drizzle* shows that it can be two parts of speech. Write them below:

    _____   _____

Definitions. Words often have more than one meaning. When they do, each meaning is usually numbered in the dictionary. You can tell which definition of a word fits a given sentence by the meaning of the sentence. For example, the word *charge* has several definitions, including these two: **1.** To ask as a price. **2.** To accuse or blame.

● Show with a check ( ) which definition (1 or 2) applies in each sentence below:

The store charged me less for the blouse because it was missing a button.   1 ___   2 ___

My neighbor has been charged with shoplifting.   1 ___   2 ___

Other information. After the definitions in a listing in a hardbound dictionary, you may get information about the *origin* of a word. Such information about origins, also known as *etymology,* is usually given in brackets. And you may sometimes be given one or more synonyms or antonyms for the entry word. *Synonyms* are words that are similar in meaning to the entry word; *antonyms* are words that are opposite in meaning.

Which Dictionaries to Own

You will find it useful to own two recent dictionaries: a small paperback dictionary to carry to class and a hardbound dictionary, which contains more information than a small paperback version. Among the good dictionaries strongly recommended are both the paperback and the hardcover editions of the following:

    The American Heritage Dictionary
    The Random House College Dictionary
    Webster's New World Dictionary

Answers to the Dictionary Questions

Guidewords: *skimp/skyscraper*
Number of syllables: 2, 3, 5
Vowels: *drug, sand* (short); *night* (long)
Schwa: second syllable of *drizzle*

Accent: stronger accent on third syllable *(men)*
Parts of speech: noun and verb
Definitions: 1; 2

C. Topics for Discussion and Writing

NOTE: The first three items for each chapter are intended for discussion; the last three, for writing. Feel free, however, to either talk or write about any of the items.

Chapter 1 (Taking Exams)

1. Just about everyone catches a cold or the flu from time to time, but there are ways to lessen one's chances of infection. What are some methods you would recommend to **avert** sickness?

2. What is considered **appropriate** dress at your school or workplace? Do you think people in a school or an office should be **compelled** to dress a certain way? Why or why not?

3. When someone says, "Tell me the truth," should you always **comply**? Is there such a thing as being too **candid**?

4. Imagine that your class has been asked to produce a collection of short, true stories. Write out a favorite family **anecdote** that would be suitable to include in such a collection.

5. What are you hoping to do after you complete your education? Write about several **alternatives** you might pursue.

6. Think of someone you know who has made a truly **drastic** change in his or her life. Write a paper about that person's life change and its results.

Chapter 2 (Nate the Woodsman)

1. Where would you prefer to live: in the country, or in a more **urban** setting? Why? If you had to forever **forfeit** any chance of living in the other setting, is there anything you would miss?

2. Think of someone who has an **extensive** collection—for example, of baseball cards, Barbie dolls, or travel souvenirs. Why might this person enjoy collecting? If you're a collector yourself, tell about your own reasons for choosing this hobby.

3. When you know you have a demanding day ahead, what do you do to **fortify** yourself?

4. Do you know someone—a grandparent, perhaps, or an older friend—who likes to **reminisce** about his or her younger days? Write a paper describing some of this person's memories. You might begin with a main idea such as this: *When my grandmother lived with my family, she told me many rich stories about her childhood.*

5. Almost everyone has times that he or she wants to be alone. When you want to **isolate** yourself, where do you go? Describe this special place in writing. When you take **refuge** in this place, what do you like to do or think about?

6. Have you ever had a teacher, employer, or acquaintance whose **erratic** behavior made him or her hard to deal with? Write a paper in which you describe the person's actions and your response to them.

Chapter 3 (Who's on Trial?)

1. What do you think are the worst **menaces** threatening the environment? Explain what you feel the dangers are and suggest any ideas you have on how to deal with them.

2. Would you say your parents were **lenient** with you—or were they strict? Were they **impartial** with their children, or did they seem to prefer one child or another? Give examples.

3. If you were a teacher, what would you consider **legitimate** excuses for students' not having homework done? What excuses, if any, would you *not* accept?

4. Write a paper about someone in public life or someone you know who has **integrity**. What has this person done or said to make you think he or she is especially moral?

5. If you could undo the past, what is one experience in your life you would **delete**? Write a paper in which you tell about this occurrence and why you'd like to erase it from your life.

6. Have you ever been the victim of **overt** prejudice because of your race, gender, religion, or another characteristic? Describe the incident. How did it leave you feeling? Did it **undermine** your **morale**, or did it have another effect? If you prefer, write about another person's experience with prejudice.

Chapter 4 (Students and Politics)

1. With your classmates, brainstorm some causes of student **apathy**. Are teachers too **bland**? Do students feel classes are not **relevant** to their lives? Can you come up with **antidotes** to student boredom and lack of involvement in the classroom?

2. People who will stop at nothing to get what they want are often the subjects of books, movies, and TV shows. Think of such a **ruthless** fictional character and give at least one specific example of the character's ruthlessness.

3. What's an example of **propaganda** that you have come in contact with lately? What ideas did it promote?

4. Write a paper about a time when you had a strong first impression of someone—perhaps you liked this person very much or thought he or she was rude. Did getting to know the person **reinforce** your impression? Or did you discover that your first opinion was incorrect?

5. Whom do you know whose **prospects** to become rich and/or famous are better than average? Write a paper describing that person and explaining why you think he or she might achieve wealth or fame.

6. If you wrote a to-do list of things to change at your school, what item would be first on the **agenda**? Write about the first thing you would change, and why. Also describe and explain the most **radical** change you would recommend.

Chapter 5 (Night Nurse)

1. With your classmates, brainstorm a list of celebrities you've seen **endorse** products on television. Does a celebrity's support make you think a product is a good one? Why or why not?

2. What are some of the most **gruesome** movies you've ever seen? What made them gruesome? How do you respond to such films?

3. Think of something that you would like very much to have or to achieve. What is the biggest **obstacle** that stands between you and this goal? How might you remove this obstacle?

4. Which word better describes you: *idealistic* or *practical*? Write a paper in which you explain why you chose the word you did, giving examples to prove your point.

5. Write a paper in which you describe a time that a person you know was a **hypocrite**. In your opinion, what did the person's actions **imply** about his or her character? Here's a sample main idea for this paper: *When I learned that an "old friend" of mine was a hypocrite, I realized his/her character was very different from what I had supposed.*

6. Probably everyone has believed something was true, but later realized it was just an **illusion**. For instance, you might have felt someone was angry at you, and later discovered he or she was angry about something else. Write a paper about a time you were mistaken about something. Did discovering you were wrong **erode** your self-confidence, or did you feel it had been an understandable mistake?

Chapter 7 (Relating to Parents)

1. Suppose you've been told an important secret. Under what circumstances might it be better to **disclose** this information? Why?

2. Do you believe that capital punishment **deters** people from committing murder? If not, do you think execution serves any purpose?

3. In your opinion, which television programs present more than a **superficial** view of their subject? What important themes do these programs deal with? Give examples.

4. Have you ever felt that you've been unfairly used as a **scapegoat** in some situation? How did you respond? Did you **denounce** the person who tried to blame you? Write about the situation and its outcome.

5. Think of two people you know with **contrary** personalities: one quite **conservative**, resisting change and liking to do things the tried-and-true way, and the other more adventurous, always wanting to try something new. Write a paper that contrasts these two people and their very different approaches to life.

6. Life is typically full of changes—from being a high-school student to being a college student, from being single to being part of a couple (or vice versa), and so on. Write a paper describing a **transition** in your own life that was difficult. How did you **sustain** your good humor and belief in yourself during this time of change?

Chapter 8 (Job Choices)

1. Many people have hobbies from which they **derive** enjoyment and satisfaction. Do you have a hobby? What is it? How much **diversity** in hobbies is there among your classmates?

2. Do you know someone who "moonlights" at a second job in order to **supplement** his or her income? What sacrifices has the person made in order to hold two jobs at once? In your opinion, do the benefits of the second job outweigh the drawbacks? Why or why not?

3. What do you expect to do next summer? Are your plans **tentative**, or are they definite?

4. Suppose you were in charge of coming up with ideas to **inhibit** people from drinking and driving in your community. What can you **conceive** of that might be effective? Write a paper explaining your ideas.

5. Think of something you've tried to accomplish recently, but with which you have had only **moderate** success. Maybe you've tried to eat healthier foods, improve your grades, or get along better with someone. Write a paper about what you tried to do, how well or poorly it worked, and if you plan to **surpass** these efforts in the future.

6. People choose careers for different reasons, such as personal satisfaction, how the job **compensates** them financially, and the ability to use their talents. Write a paper about your career plans and why a certain career appeals to you.

Chapter 9 (No Joking)

1. Have you ever pretended to feel sorry about something, but in your heart you weren't sorry at all? When have you made such a **pretense** of **remorse**? What happened as a result?

2. Do you know someone you would describe as a **chronic optimist**? Give an example of this person's upbeat attitude. Would you want to be like this person? Why or why not?

3. We've all been in classes where a student or two can't **refrain** from blurting out responses to questions without thinking. Teachers often find it difficult to be **blunt** with students who do this. How might teachers handle students who continue this type of behavior?

4. Write a paper describing a day in your life that was either especially pleasant or especially unpleasant. Your account of the day should be in **chronological** order. Include **ample** details to make it clear why the day was so nice or so nasty.

5. If you could change one thing about yourself (not your appearance, but your internal self), what would it be? Would you become more patient? Better organized? Less hot-tempered? Write a paper describing how you would **alter** yourself and why.

6. If someone decides to end a friendship or romance, what's the best way to do it? Should the breakup be quick and definite, or is a breakup less painful if it's **prolonged**? Write a paper stating your opinion and why you feel as you do.

Chapter 10 (Museum Pet)

1. Certain situations make almost everyone **apprehensive**. For example, many people get nervous about taking tests, speaking in public, and going on job interviews. What are a few situations that make you apprehensive? A **phobia**, on the other hand, is far more extreme than a normal feeling of apprehension. Does anyone you know suffer from a phobia? What is the person so afraid of? What does the phobia keep him or her from doing?

2. Some newspapers will publish **anonymous** letters to the editor. Others refuse to print letters unless the writer's name is signed. Which policy do you think is better? Why? Are there good reasons that a writer might not want his or her name attached to a letter?

3. Every neighborhood has some features—maybe a particular store, tree, or house—that stand out for some reason. What are some **prominent** sights in your neighborhood? What makes them prominent?

4. A person who applies for a driver's license may sign a card stating that upon death, he or she will allow his or her organs—such as the heart, lungs, or kidneys—to be given to a **recipient** who needs them. Would you be an organ **donor**? Write a paper in which you explain why or why not.

5. Imagine that you have a child. (If you do have a child, think of him or her.) If you were able to **bestow** one quality upon that child, what would it be? Courage? The ability to love others? Kindness? Intelligence? Good business sense? Write a paper explaining which single quality you would give the child and why.

6. Write a paper describing a time when you acted in a way that was not **prudent**. What did you do? What happened as a result? Did you learn anything useful from the experience?

Chapter 11 (Unacceptable Boyfriends)

1. Do you know someone who is **dogmatic**? Does this person's tendency to be very opinionated **alienate** people around him or her, or do they like the person anyway? Explain.

2. Think of a person whom you admire very much. From what you observe of this person, what **doctrines** would you say guide his or her life?

3. What are some **absurd** situations that you have enjoyed in comedy movies? What about them was so ridiculous?

4. "Money can't buy happiness," we're told. Do you agree? Write a paper about how you think being **affluent** would or would not bring you happiness.

5. **Compile** a list of things you like and a list of things you don't like about where you are living now. Use those lists to write a paper explaining that your home has more good qualities than **defects**—or the other way around. Your main idea might look like this: *Despite some glaring defects, my apartment serves my purposes very well.*

6. Some individuals tend to see only the good in people, while others seem to view most humans with **contempt**. Write a paper about someone you know who falls into the second category. Give examples of how that person expresses his or her lack of respect for others.

Chapter 13 (Our Headstrong Baby)

1. Who is a person—living or dead—for whom you would feel real **awe** if the two of you could meet? Why do you regard this person with such great respect?

2. What are two foods you like to eat together, or two articles of clothing you like to wear together, that most people would not think are **compatible**? What do you like about this combination?

3. Do you think that people who object to serving in the military for religious reasons should be **exempt** from military service? Why or why not?

4. Some people get married after giving the decision a lot of **rational** thought. Others plunge into marriage largely on the basis of their emotions. Write about which style of decision-making you think leads to better marriages. **Cite** examples to back up your opinion.

5. Write a paper about a recent argument you've had with someone close to you. What was the argument about? In the end, whose opinion do you think **prevailed**?

6. How do you deal with unwanted telephone sales calls? Do you talk to the caller politely? Hang up? Make a rude **retort**? Write about how you respond to such calls—and why.

Chapter 14 (Mr. Perfect?)

1. What should you do when you see a friend feeling **ecstatic** about a situation that you are **dubious** about? For example, you may have a friend who is very happy about a new boyfriend or girlfriend, while you are not at all sure the person is good for your friend. In such situations, is it best to speak up, or to keep your mouth shut? Why?

2. Who is your favorite **fictitious** character? The character might come from a book, television show, or movie. What do you like about this character?

3. If you inherited a lot of money, how do you think you would deal with it? Would you be **liable** to spend it all quickly? Would you become **miserly**, refusing to part with any of it? Would you invest it? Explain.

4. Write a paper about the first time you **encountered** someone who later became important in your life. Describe that first meeting; then tell how your relationship with this person has **evolved**.

5. Have you been **gullible** and been taken advantage of, for example, in a personal relationship or a school or job situation? Write a paper about the time you were fooled and what happened as a result.

6. Write a paper on whether you think of yourself as an optimist or a **pessimist**. Provide some examples to show your usual attitude.

Chapter 15 (A Narrow Escape)

1. Many people feel that **lethal** weapons are too easily available in our society. Do you agree? What controls, if any, do you think there should be on gun sales and ownership?

2. What examples have you heard of that show a fan's unhealthy **obsession** with a celebrity? In your opinion, would the rewards of being famous make up for the possibility of going through such an **ordeal**?

3. Take a survey in your class: How many students are **fluent** in two languages? Three? More than three? How many have relatives who are fluent in two or more languages? Has the knowledge of additional languages affected people's lives in any way?

4. Sometimes when a guy or girl asks someone out, the other person gives an **evasive** answer such as "Not this weekend" or "I'll think about it." Write a paper about the effect of such an answer. Does it make the one who asks more **persistent**, thinking he or she will hear "yes" another time? Or would he or she conclude it's **futile** to ask again?

5. In most schools there are bullies and people they make a habit of picking on. Write a paper about a bully you've observed and the person (or people) the bully **harassed**. What can you **infer** about why the bully acted the way he or she did?

6. What do you do in the time that **elapses** between the minute you get home after school or work and the time you go to bed? Write a paper that describes a typical evening for you.

Chapter 16 (The Power of Advertising)

1. If you were in charge of decorating a restaurant, what colors would you use? Do you think that **vivid** colors **stimulate** the appetite, or do soft, pastel colors make people hungrier? In other words, what kind of surroundings make you really **savor** your food?

2. As you were growing up, did your parents have certain "looks" or signals that **conveyed** unspoken messages to you—such as "Stop that!" or "We're leaving now"? What were some of your family's **unique** messages that were communicated without words?

3. Little children often develop some innocent **delusions**: for instance, some assume that their teachers live at their school. Can you remember having any such mistaken beliefs? Or does a child you know have such a belief?

4. If you saw a picture of yourself taken a few years ago next to a picture of yourself taken today, what differences would you notice? Write a paper describing those differences, indicating whether they are **subtle** or dramatic.

5. Some countries have a policy of **universal** military service: Every person, male and female, spends several years in the country's army. Would you support such a policy in this country? Write a paper explaining why or why not.

6. Imagine that you are a very creative inventor—maybe even a bit of a mad scientist. Write a humorous paper describing "The Household Friend," a marvelous machine that you have **devised**. This **versatile** machine can do a number of helpful tasks around the house. A reading machine, for instance, might provide light for reading, play soft background music, and turn a page at your command. Include details of your machine's appearance and functions.

Chapter 17 (Waiter)

1. How do people in your family behave during an argument? Are any of them **passive** people who sit back, say little, and let others do the talking? Do any tend to be **malicious**, making hurtful remarks? And what is *your* argument style? Give examples.

2. Describe a store or restaurant where you are a regular **patron**. Do you visit that place often because you have no other **option**, or is there something about it that you particularly like? If so, what is it?

3. People become **indignant** when they or someone else is **imposed** upon or otherwise treated unfairly. Describe an occasion when you were angry because a person was unfair to you or someone else. What did you do or say in response?

4. Have you **endeavored** to warn a friend that something he or she was doing would get him or her in trouble, but the friend ignored your warning? How did you feel when the **inevitable** result occurred, and the friend *did* get in trouble? How did the friend respond? Write a paper describing what happened.

5. An old line from the cartoon "Peanuts" is "Happiness is a warm puppy." What quality or thing do you **equate** with happiness? Write a paper in which you complete and explain this sentence: "For me, happiness is _____."

6. Have you ever **deferred** to someone in an argument, even though you really believed that you were right? Why did you give in? Do you think now that giving in was the best thing to do? Write a paper describing the argument, what you did, and how you now feel about it.

Chapter 19 (Adjusting to a New Culture)

1. Athletes are well-known for having certain **rituals**. For instance, a baseball pitcher may go through a series of "good-luck" motions before he throws the ball. Share with your classmates any good-luck ritual you may have for a specific situation, such as playing a sport or taking a test. When did you begin using this ritual, and why?

2. Think of a time when you began something new, such as going to a new school, starting a new job, or moving to a new home or city. What were some of the things that **dismayed** you at first about the new experience? Did you eventually **adapt** to those things, or do they still bother you?

3. When someone gives you a compliment or does you a favor, do you always feel you must **reciprocate**? What **gestures** have you used to show how you feel about someone in one of those situations?

4. When something bad happens to you, what helps you to **retain** your good spirits and a positive attitude? Talking with friends? Applying your sense of humor? Exercising? Explain in writing how you try to overcome the effects of an unhappy circumstance.

5. Have you ever stopped a bad habit and then **reverted** to it? Write a paper explaining what the habit was, how long you were able to avoid it, and why you began it again.

6. Do you think this country should have the death penalty? Do you think cigarette smoking should be outlawed? Write a paper explaining your reasoning on *one* of those two questions. Also **refute** some of the reasons someone arguing on the other side might offer.

Chapter 20 (A Dream about Wealth)

1. What is one exotic place you've never been to, but would like to visit? Why would you like to go there? For example, does it have gorgeous scenery, interesting tourist attractions, or notable people associated with it? Share with your classmates what you know about this place and why it appeals to you.

2. You'd love to go out and have some fun this weekend, but your supply of money has nearly run out. Brainstorm with your class ways to amuse yourself while still being frugal.

3. What are some problems facing your school that you think people are indifferent to? Examine ways each problem might be solved. Perhaps some practical solutions will emerge from your discussion.

4. Think of an activity that requires elaborate preparation—otherwise the results will be, at best, mediocre. Possibilities include a surprise party, a school paper, or a satisfying meal. Make a list of everything you need to do ahead of time. Then write a paper of advice on how to make the project a success.

5. Write a paper about someone you know who is impulsive. In your paper, include an interesting example of a time that this person acted without thinking ahead.

6. What do you think of indulgent parents who give liberal presents and privileges to their children, no matter how the children behave? Write a paper explaining why that style of parenting has either good or bad results. Include specific examples, such as what happens when parents do children's chores for them or when children are allowed to come home as late as they wish.

Chapter 21 (Children and Drugs)

1. Sadly, there are incidents involving children who are alleged to have committed serious offenses, such as the six-year-old boy who picked up a loaded gun and shot his sister. In your opinion, should young children be tried in court for these offenses, or should their age give them immunity from criminal charges?

2. Suppose you have been admitted to an elite group: those reporters whose job it is to question the President of the United States. At the next press conference, you will be permitted to query the President on any topic you wish. What question would you ask, and why?

3. Some people think products that impair our health, such as cigarettes and alcoholic beverages, should be made illegal. Do you agree? Or do you feel that it's wrong to pass laws that coerce people to do what's good for them?

4. Imagine that you'd like to make a friend aware of a bad habit and how much it annoys others, but you don't want to say anything too obvious. How might you allude to the habit and how to deal with it? Write a paper in which you describe your friend's habit and explain how and what you would hint to him or her about it.

5. We may not always affirm our feelings for others in words, but we can show our feelings in other ways. We might, for instance, do a chore for a grandparent or help a friend paint a bedroom. Write about how your family and/or friends have affirmed feelings for one another through both speech and actions.

6. We all have different heroes, but our heroes probably have a good deal in common. What would you say is the essence of heroism? Write a paper beginning with the main idea *The essence of heroism is _____*. Then develop your paper with at least one example of someone whose character or actions demonstrate this quality.

Chapter 22 (Party House)

1. You were supposed to give an oral report in class today, but you forgot to prepare it. You don't want to make up a report because you think you'd look like a fool and your classmates might **ridicule** you. What **plausible** excuse—one that would convince a **skeptical** teacher—could you give for your lack of preparation? Brainstorm a list of such excuses with your classmates.

2. In your opinion, what are some of the best **tactics** for doing well on a test? See how long a list of suggestions you and your classmates can create.

3. What are some of the ways that young children **provoke** their older brothers and sisters or their parents? Why is this behavior so annoying? What can older children or parents do to make sure that it will not **recur** in the future?

4. Have you or has someone you know ever had a privilege **revoked**? In a paper, describe the situation that resulted in losing the privilege. How long did it take to earn it back again?

5. Write about an incident that taught you how wrong a **stereotype** can be. For example, you might have met an older person with very "young" ideas or behavior. Begin with a main idea like this: *Before I met _____, I believed the stereotype that all _____s were _____, but I know better now.*

6. You are the manager of a store in which a new employee has made a habit of leaving twenty minutes early, with excuses such as needing to take a relative to the doctor or to meet a friend for dinner. The store owner asks you to write a **reprimand** to this employee, telling him what he has done wrong and making suggestions for future behavior. What would you say? Write the full reprimand you would give the employee.

Chapter 23 (Procrastinator)

1. Do you believe your future is largely determined by **destiny,** by pure luck, or by your own actions? Explain your point of view.

2. What might your closest friend be worried about right now? Rather than simply saying, "Forget about it," what could you do to **diminish** his or her anxiety?

3. Imagine that you have made **simultaneous** commitments to meet two different people. One is an older relative who is depending on your help. The other is someone your own age who would be a great deal more fun to spend time with. Which commitment do you honor? Why?

4. When was the last time you **procrastinated**? What did you delay doing, and what were the **consequences**? Describe the situation in a paper, using either a humorous or a serious approach.

5. Think of an activity you regard as **tedious**—for example, waiting in line at a supermarket or doing a really boring household chore. What **strategy** do you use to make the activity more bearable? Write a paper of advice on how to pass the time during boring activities.

6. Most of us have things we think we cannot do without—in addition to the obvious ones: food, water, clothing, shelter. Besides these, what things—either major or minor—would you say are **vital** to you at this point in your life? Describe at least three of them in a paper and explain why they are so important to you.

Chapter 25 (A Change in View)

1. Suppose two young men are found guilty of robbing a convenience store. The first is a well-to-do college student who committed the robbery on a dare. The second man is out of work and needed money to buy food and medicine for a sick child. Should the two men receive different sentences? Or should the **severity** of the punishment be the same for both?

2. Think of the last time you were really angry with someone. What did you do to make your anger **subside**?

3. Many people read and write to newspaper advice columns for help with serious questions, such as what to do about a disturbed child or how to handle a **profound** loss. In your opinion, should advice columnists have to take courses in psychology and human relations—even pass exams and obtain degrees—before they are permitted to **dispense** advice on such matters? Why or why not?

4. If you were about to complete your education and go to work, what would your dream career be like? Write a paper about your ideal **vocation**.

5. Make a list of several **sites** in your community that are **dismal**. Use this list to write a paper on how to make your community more cheerful and inviting by improving those places.

6. Imagine this problem: The same required course is taught by two different teachers. Students may sign up for whichever teacher they prefer. How could a student **discriminate** between the two teachers? Offer some suggestions in a paper.

Chapter 26 (Balloon Flight)

1. Advertisers use all sorts of tricks to **lure** us into buying their products. What are some of the most **ingenious** ads you've seen on television or in print? Describe them. Have any of these ads actually gotten you to buy the products?

2. Imagine there's a large unused plot of land on your school's grounds. You feel neighborhood families could benefit from using the land for a vegetable garden. How would you go about **initiating** such a garden project?

3. Would you say there's an **infinite** number of possible partners for anyone looking for romance? Or do you think each of us has only a small, **finite** number of possible boyfriends or girlfriends or spouses? Explain.

4. Have you ever felt **nostalgia** for a time in your life when things seemed, for example, less complicated? Think of such a pleasant time, and describe it in a paper. You might begin with a main idea similar to this: *Whenever December approaches, I become nostalgic for the years when I didn't have to spend all my free time buying holiday gifts for family, friends, and coworkers.*

5. Do you know someone who could be described as having a **mania** for something, such as chocolate, a certain singer, or a hobby? Write a paper about this person, explaining and giving examples of his or her extreme involvement.

6. You've probably heard the saying "Sticks and stones will break my bones, but names will never hurt me." It means that sticks and stones will injure us (though usually they don't **literally** break bones), but calling us names will not **inflict** pain. Do you agree? Write about a time when name-calling was (or was not) hurtful to you.

Chapter 27 (Family Differences)

1. A common belief is that men are **inept** when it comes to observing others' feelings and expressing their own, while women are emotionally **perceptive** and communicative. Do you agree? Use examples from your own experience to either support or attack these views.

2. Do you feel it is harmful for young children to play **morbid** video games, where they see brutal attacks and murders? If you've known children who have played these games, how do you think the experiences affected them?

3. Older people sometimes **lament** the loss of a simpler society, saying sadly that life is more complicated or dangerous now than it was years ago. What recent changes in society do you think are for the worse? Which do you think are valuable? Consider, for example, the influence of computers, sport utility vehicles, or cell phones.

4. Which of your abilities would you identify as purely **innate**? Write a paper describing one or more talents of yours and how you have or have not developed them.

5. How do you usually respond to a crisis? Do you remain **sedate**, or do you become so disturbed that someone must **intervene** to calm you down? Write a paper about your response to crises. Provide one or two examples.

6. Imagine you've decided it's time to move somewhere completely new, but you're unsure about where. What kinds of **data** would you need to help you make the decision about where to go? Which specific qualities of a city would you be **obstinate** about? Which would you be more flexible about?

Chapter 28 (Murder Mystery)

1. What do you consider to be **treacherous** conduct in a good friend? Is it disloyal for a friend to tell a parent or teacher about some self-destructive actions of yours, such as taking drugs? How about if the friend goes out with an old boyfriend or girlfriend of yours?

2. When you meet someone new, what is the **dominant** impression that you hope you leave on that person? How does the impression you want to make differ depending on whom you are meeting?

3. There's a **controversy** in your hometown concerning school uniforms. What reasons might those who support uniforms have? What reasons might the opponents have? What's your opinion?

4. When you were younger, what goals did you set for yourself, and what was the **sequence** in which you expected to reach them? Have your expectations changed since then? Write about your original goals and how they have or have not changed.

5. What is something you once worried a great deal about but now realize was **trivial**? Your wardrobe? A few pounds? What has changed to allow your attitude to shift—have you become more **sophisticated**, or have outside circumstances changed? In a paper, describe your change of attitude and explain how and why it changed.

6. Consider the proverb, "Don't judge a book by its cover." Think of a time when you made an incorrect **deduction** about someone based on a first impression. In a paper, describe your first impression, and then tell how you came to change your mind.

Chapter 29 (Chicken Pox)

1. As you must know, being a student can be stressful. Brainstorm with classmates and develop some steps students can take to make themselves less **susceptible** to school-related stress.

2. Many people criticize TV and magazine advertisements for being **deceptive**. Describe and discuss some examples of ads you feel are misleading. What is misleading about them?

3. Share with classmates your ideal vacation. Do you seek relaxation and **seclusion**—or **vigorous** sports and excitement? What are some places you think would fit your vacation ideal? Do your classmates have similar or very different visions of the ideal vacation?

4. We have all been in situations where we tried to **restrain** ourselves from doing something that was not appropriate. Maybe we had to hold back giggles in class or found ourselves staring impolitely at someone. Write a paper describing in detail a time you had difficulty keeping yourself from acting improperly.

5. Have you ever discovered that a juicy rumor about someone (even yourself) was not **valid** and people were **transmitting** this rumor to others without **confirming** it? Write a paper telling what the rumor was, how it spread, and what you think the truth of the matter was.

6. Describe a time when you **defied** a rule that you now feel you should have **submitted** to. For instance, you might have skipped many days of school when you were younger and now realize you harmed your education. Write about one or more such times, explaining why you regret not following the rule(s).

Chapter 30 (Walking)

1. What are some **adverse** conditions in your school? Overcrowded classes? A building that's beginning to **deteriorate**? A lack of school spirit? Brainstorm with classmates a list of school problems as well as some ways that they might be overcome.

2. Tell about someone you know who is especially **competent** at what he or she does. After classmates have described their choices, try to identify together the qualities and habits that are shared by all these skillful people.

3. How are playing the piano and riding a bike similar? The answer is that you may become rusty, but you never forget how to do them. Name two other activities that, on the surface, are very dissimilar but on closer examination are actually **comparable** in some way. For instance, how are cooking and eating alike?

4. Two keys to a successful classroom presentation are being **audible** and being **coherent**. What are some others? Prepare a short list of ingredients for a successful speech. Then use the list to write a paper in which you explain how to go about "wowing" your classmates and instructor with a presentation.

5. An old saying goes, "When it rains, it pours." Think of a time in your life when two or more **consecutive** bad events—or good events—happened. Write a paper describing the negative or positive occurrences, their effects on you, and your reactions.

6. Think of a position of which you are a firm **advocate**. Are you a strong supporter of recycling? Of teaching a second language to elementary-school students? Write a paper in which you try to persuade the reader of the correctness of your position. Begin by stating your position in your main idea: *Every elementary-school student should be taught a second language.* Then go on to present and explain one or more reasons—for example: *First of all, contact with people in other countries, either in person or on the Internet, is becoming more common. . . .*

D. List of Words and Word Parts

-able, 130
absurd, 58
accelerate, 164
accessible, 76
acknowledge, 8
acute, 54
adapt, 110
adhere, 58
adverse, 164
advocate, 164
affirm, 118
affluent, 58
agenda, 20
alienate, 58
alleged, 118
allude, 118
alter, 50
alternative, 8
ample, 50
anecdote, 8
anonymous, 54
anti-, 62
antidote, 20
apathy, 20
apprehensive, 54
appropriate, 8
arrogant, 54
ascend, 148
assess, 58
audible, 164
auto-, 28
avert, 8
awe, 76
bestow, 54
bi-, 62
bland, 20
blunt, 50
candid, 8
cent-, centi-, 130
chronic, 50
chronological, 50
cite, 76
coerce, 118
coherent, 164

comparable, 164
compatible, 76
compel, 9
compensate, 46
competent, 165
compile, 58
comply, 9
con-, 96
concede, 42
conceive, 46
concise, 9
confirm, 160
consecutive, 165
consequence, 126
conservative, 42
conspicuous, 165
contempt, 59
contrary, 42
controversy, 156
convey, 88
data, 152
deceptive, 160
deduction, 156
defect, 59
defer, 92
defy, 160
delete, 16
delusion, 88
denounce, 42
derive, 46
destiny, 126
detain, 126
deter, 42
deteriorate, 165
devise, 88
dialog, 12
dict, 96
dimensions, 156
diminish, 126
dis-, 96
disclose, 42
discriminate, 144
dismal, 144
dismay, 110

dispense, 144
disperse, 156
distort, 156
diversity, 46
doctrine, 59
dogmatic, 59
dominant, 156
donor, 54
drastic, 9
dubious, 80
ecstatic, 80
elaborate, 114
elapse, 84
elite, 118
emerge, 114
en-, em-, 62
encounter, 80
endeavor, 92
endorse, 24
equate, 92
erode, 24
erratic, 12
essence, 118
evasive, 84
evolve, 80
ex-, 28
exempt, 76
exile, 110
exotic, 114
extensive, 12
fallacy, 80
fictitious, 80
finite, 148
fluent, 84
forfeit, 12
fortify, 12
frugal, 114
-ful, 28
futile, 84
gesture, 110
graph, gram, 62
gruesome, 24
gullible, 81
harass, 84